böhlau

Reihe Jüdische Moderne

Herausgegeben von
Alfred Bodenheimer, Jacques Picard,
Monica Rüthers und Daniel Wildmann

Band 22

Hélène Oberlé

It's All About Emotions

Narratives of highly skilled migrants: A study
of Swiss in Israel and Israelis in Switzerland

BÖHLAU VERLAG WIEN KÖLN

Die Druckvorstufe dieser Publikation wurde vom Schweizerischen Nationalfonds zur Förderung der wissenschaftlichen Forschung, der Graduate School of Social Sciences (Universität Basel), dem Reisefonds für den akademischen Nachwuchs der Universität Basel und der Freiwilligen Akademischen Gesellschaft Basel unterstützt.

Bibliographic information published by the Deutsche Nationalbibliothek:
The Deutsche Nationalbibliothek lists this publication in the Deutsche Nationalbibliografie; detailed bibliographic data available online: https://dnb.de.

© 2023 by Böhlau, Lindenstraße 14, D-50674 Köln, an imprint of the Brill-Group (Koninklijke Brill NV, Leiden, Niederlande; Brill USA Inc., Boston MA, USA; Brill Asia Pte Ltd, Singapore; Brill Deutschland GmbH, Paderborn, Germany; Brill Österreich GmbH, Vienna, Austria)
Koninklijke Brill NV incorporates the Imprints Brill, Brill Nijhoff, Brill Schöningh, Brill Fink, Brill mentis, Brill Wageningen Academic, Vandenhoeck & Ruprecht, Böhlau, and V&R unipress.

This publication is licensed under a Creative Commons Attribution – Non Commercial – No Derivatives 4.0 International license, at https://doi.org/10.13109/9783412529048. For a copy of this license go to https://creativecommons.org/licenses/by-nc-nd/4.0/. Any use in cases other than those permitted by this license requires the prior written permission from the publisher.

Cover image: Oskar Koller, 1997, aquarelle, 12 × 12 cm

Cover design: Michael Haderer, Vienna
Proofreading: Katherine Bird, Berlin
Typesetting: le-tex publishing services, Leipzig
Printed and bound: ⊕ Hubert & Co, Göttingen
Printed in the EU

Vandenhoeck & Ruprecht Verlage | www.vandenhoeck-ruprecht-verlage.com

ISBN (print): 978-3-412-52903-1
ISBN (digital): 978-3-412-52904-8

Abstract

This study focuses on highly skilled migrants, specifically, Swiss in Israel and Israelis in Switzerland. Considering as a broader context the empirical reality of globalization, processes of transnationalism, as well as the national frameworks of Israel and Switzerland, the focus of the study lies on the significance of migration within (multi-sited) biographies and the meaning and use of emotions in migration narratives. Twelve main protagonists are presented, and their migration stories, perceptions, interpretations, and construals, are discussed in detail. The emphasis on emotions leads to the uncovering of various tensions or dichotomies within narratives of high skilled migration. Within their stories and biographies, feelings of (non-)belonging to places and specific groups are discussed as the first of three main emotional themes. The second theme is the discussion of past, present, and future in the form of nostalgia, irritation, and expectation. Finally, notions of "going abroad" as a feeling of accomplishment emerging within the narratives are presented. Overall, the protagonists construct a self which is flexibly adapted to the empirical reality of globalization, experiences struggles and tensions yet creates meaningful connections to specific places and times through the use of various emotions and retrospectively presents migration as a successful, if not always planned or strategic event, within their biography.

Acknowledgements

This book is based on my thesis, which would not have been achievable without the assistance and support of my doctoral advisor, Professor Dr. Jacques Picard. I would like to express my deepest gratitude for the trust he had in me and for his unwavering belief in my abilities. Without his guidance, encouragement, wisdom, patience, and kindness this project would not have been realized.

My sincere thanks to my second advisor, Professor Dr. Dan Rabinowitz, for his wonderfully worthwhile suggestions and ideas.

I am particularly grateful to the individuals who were willing to be interviewed and who shared their life stories, experiences, thoughts, and emotions with me and to all the people I met during field research who were open and generous enough to offer me some of their valuable time. This thesis would not have been conceivable without them.

Through my work on this thesis I met my PhD colleague and project partner, Dr. phil. des. Khadeeja Haddy Sarr. I am extremely grateful for her helpful advice, her pushing me when necessary and most importantly for our friendship.

Many thanks to the *Swiss National Science Foundation* for rendering this research project possible through a research grant. I also generously received a start-up scholarship from the *University of Basel* through the *Graduate School of Social Sciences*, support from the *Reisefonds für den akademischen Nachwuchs der Universität Basel*, and a finalization scholarship from the *Freiwillige Akademische Gesellschaft Basel*.

For her help with reading over these chapters and sharpening the language great thanks to my editor, Dr. Carolyn Groff. Thank you as well to Dr. Kristine Jones, for her suggestions on the methodology section of this thesis. For her invaluable advice on how to write better to-do lists and many other practical suggestions, great thanks to Mag. Alexandra Deubner, MSc. Thank you too to the colleagues and staff I met at the *Seminar für Kulturwissenschaft und Europäische Ethnologie der Universität Basel* for their help, their insightful input, and the scientific and non-scientific conversations in seminars, at conferences, and around the coffee machine.

Finally and essentially: I wish to acknowledge the love of my friends and family, especially my mother.

Table of Contents

Abstract 5

Acknowledgements 7

"IT'S ALL ABOUT EMOTIONS". A study of Swiss in Israel and
Israelis in Switzerland 13

1.   Highly Skilled Migrants: Swiss in Israel and Israelis in Switzerland...   15

2.   Context and Surroundings 23
2.1   Global Context: Globalization and Transnationalism 23
2.1.1 Understanding globalization 24
2.1.2 Understanding transnationalism 25
2.1.3 Methodological nationalism 27
2.2   Local Context: Two Small Exceptional States 29
2.2.1 Israel and Switzerland: historical and contemporary connections 31
2.2.2 Migration in Israel 34
2.2.3 Migration in Switzerland 36
2.3   Defining the Main Terms through Research and Literature 37
2.3.1 Who are skilled and highly skilled migrants? 37
2.3.2 What are emotions? 41
2.4   Approach and Methods 46
2.4.1 Fieldwork and data collection 47
2.4.2 Data analysis 51
2.4.3 The researcher's position in the field 52
2.5   Conclusion and Outlook: Swiss in Israel and Israelis in Switzerland 54

3.   Ethnographic Portraits 57
3.1   Swiss in Israel 57
3.2   Israelis in Switzerland 61
3.3   Conclusion and Outlook: Twelve Protagonists in two Places 65

4.   Narratives of Belonging in Multi-Sited Biographies 67
4.1   Putting the Self in Place 68
4.1.1 National identities and flexible citizenship 71
4.1.2 Brain drain and brain gain 73

	4.1.3	Self-descriptions and distinctions	76
4.2		Bubbles, Cheese Domes, and Ghettos	79
	4.2.1	Reflections on home and homesickness	82
	4.2.2	Tradition and religion	88
	4.2.3	Language as a strategy of (non-)belonging	93
4.3		Conclusion and Outlook: Narratives of Belonging in Multi-Sited Biographies	98
5.		Past, Present, and Future, or Nostalgia, Irritation, and Expectation	99
5.1		A Place of Yearning and a Place to Savor	100
	5.1.1	Memories and hopes	100
	5.1.2	Imaginaries and realities	110
5.2		The Daily Struggle	114
	5.2.1	Taking a break and gaining through distance	115
	5.2.2	Contested frameworks and political activities	123
5.3		Conclusion and Outlook: Nostalgia, Irritation, and Expectation	126
6.		Going Abroad and Staying on the Move	129
6.1		Not a Migrant	130
	6.1.1	Occurrences and circumstances	131
	6.1.2	Reasons for migration: love, cosmopolitan imaginaries, transnational ideals	135
6.2		Feelings of Accomplishment	138
	6.2.1	Gendered experiences	139
	6.2.2	Reflections on happiness	144
6.3		Conclusion and Outlook: Going Abroad and Staying on the Move	147
7.		Conclusion: Migration and Emotion	149
7.1		Emotional Dimensions in Migration Narratives	152
7.2		Comments on Frameworks and Surroundings	153
7.3		Outlook and Future Research	154

References 157

Sources 173
List of Main Protagonists 173
Additional Sources 173
Newspaper Articles 175

Appendices 177
Appendix A: Information on Broader Research Project............................. 177
Summary Case Study B/Senegambia and Switzerland 178
Appendix B: Call for Participants 180
Appendix C: Qualitative Interview Guide... 181
Appendix D: Informed Consent Form 183
Appendix E: Basic Questionnaire 185

"IT'S ALL ABOUT EMOTIONS"

A study of Swiss in Israel and Israelis in Switzerland

> *And I really find that every migration contains a certain fracture, even when it is voluntary and positive and actually boosts your life or something, but you always have to think about what am I ready to relinquish and then, yeah, you suddenly become scared, that you kind of have to deny your past in order to reinvent yourself and I had to find a balance in order to be able to say: "I'm willing to adapt and want to be a part of here, but I'm also someone else and have a different background and I also want to keep that".*[1]
> (Transcript Isabella, pp. 12–13)[2]

Story telling is part and parcel of the human condition and helps migrants and non-migrants alike to make sense of their (sometimes ruptured) lives.
(Svašek, 2013, p. 72)

---

[1] Translated from Swiss German: *"I find würklich, dass jedi Migration so en gwüsse Bruch mit beinhaltet, au wäns freiwillig isch und, und s positiv isch und eigentlich wie so dis Läbe steigeret oder so, ab du musch dir immer überlege, uf was bin ich bereits z verzichte und, und dann, ja und plötzlich chunsch au Angst über, dass wie so dimi Vergangenheit musch verlügne zum dis neue Ich erfinde, und ich han da wie so chli s Mittelmäss müesse finde zum au chöne säge, ich pass mich scho a, und wot scho au en Teil vo da si, aber ich bin au no öper andersch und no, no en andere Background, won ich doch au wett bewahre, oder."*

[2] About interview quotations: Translations of quotations throughout the text are my own. Interview quotations in this text have been edited to make them more coherent in written form when necessary. All interviews were originally transcribed including pauses, interruptions, and utterances, as well as mistakes made due to talking in a foreign language. Explanatory comments and anonymizing redactions are marked with square brackets, omissions with parentheses.

1. Highly Skilled Migrants: Swiss in Israel and Israelis in Switzerland

The title of this thesis, "It's all about emotions", is a quotation from an expert interview I conducted with Prof. Dr. David Horn.[3] The summary of the experiences and decision-makings of highly skilled migrants as being "all about emotions" is the central theme and one of the main narratives[4] emerging in the stories analyzed in the course of this study.

This study focuses on skilled migrants from Israel in Switzerland and skilled migrants from Switzerland in Israel and the significance migration has within their life stories. Skilled and highly skilled migrants are part of the contemporary streams of migrants in a globalized and interconnected world.[5] Highly skilled and qualified migrants from Western[6] countries are privileged and often can choose where they would like to live while looking for the best professional opportunities in a global job market. This often makes it appear as if national borders and citizenship, as well as questions of belonging to or integration into specific places, do not play a role in their individual biographies. Research on skilled migration tends to focus on general social, cultural, political, and economic dimensions of knowledge-based societies within a globally multifaceted context. When talking about migration, the focus often lies on economic aspects and decisions, or questions of integration and borders, and, in the case of skilled migrants on professional profiles. However, individual migration experiences also provide an extensive field for in-depth analyses of narratives of identity and constructions of the self or subjectivities, especially when taking into account the connection between emotions and migration. While long overlooked, there now exists a field of interdisciplinary research looking at

---

3 Prof. Dr. David Horn is an expert on international research infrastructures and highly skilled migration in the field of academia. For more information about Prof. Horn see p. 53 of this dissertation and his website for information about projects on research infrastructures: http://horn.tau.ac.il, accessed: August, 8, 2023.

4 In this study "narrative" describes not only text (e. g., interview transcripts and stories) but also construals of meaning and the self, such as narratives of identity, of specific emotions, or of positions within society.

5 I am writing this in March 2020, while in "Corona-Lockdown". The world today seems quite different from the one we lived in when I started this research, and crossing borders, while still possible, has become more complicated.

6 For simplicity's sake I talk about Switzerland and Israel as "Western countries" even though I realize it is a problematic term. I include Israel as a "Western" country even if it is geographically in the Middle East due to its close (historic) ties with Europe and the fact that it is understood as being part of the Global North.

the relationship between emotional processes and human mobility (Skrbiš, 2008; Svašek, 2010, p. 865). This intersection between migration and emotion is important enough to warrant more research (Boccagni & Baldassar, 2015).

The transnational context within which skilled migrants move and live produces complex narratives, which could be called "multi-sited biographies", and experiences that are connected to various times and places, and reflected upon in migration stories. Therefore, the guiding question here is:

What role do emotions play in these migration stories?

In this study, examining the aspect of emotions in the migration narratives of highly skilled migrants serves as a way to understand the significance of migration within singular multi-sited biographies in the specific localities of Israel and Switzerland. In these stories, migration and connected activities are based on decisions justified by various motivations and framed emotionally as unique narratives of belonging, nostalgia, irritation, expectation, and notions of going abroad as an accomplishment. Through the use of emotions in their singular migration stories, highly skilled migrants are able to construct an independent and successful self, and give meaning to migration within their biography.

While the stories told by the study's protagonists provide a "mélange" of themes and views, specific emotions are presented to illustrate how highly skilled migrants construct an independent and successful self. These are, as just mentioned, feelings of belonging, nostalgia, irritation, expectation, as well as the desire to go abroad and "staying on the move". The narratives show how emotions are not only a reaction to something; they are simultaneously produced by surroundings, or cultures, states, and the constraints put on one's subjective position within society. Highly skilled migrants position themselves in various ways through transnational or multi-sited ties, the use of memories and hopes, and overall present the significance of their migration experiences as something that leads to feelings of accomplishment in the form of a successful, independent, or free self on the way to, or currently being, happy and leading a "good life", even if this is not always specifically the stated aim at the beginning of the migration stories.

Migration: As the *International Organization for Migration* (IOM) recognizes the term, "migration" itself is not as clear cut as one might think at first, and it is important to differentiate between "migrant" and "migration". "Migration" is the process, while "migrant" is the individual being mobile (International Organization for Migration, IOM, 2019a, p. 29). While migration processes are touched upon as part of contextualization, the focus of the study lies on individual migrants and their stories. One of the groups of people on the move are (highly) skilled and qualified migrants,[7] whose definition is an ongoing discourse in literature. In this study (highly) skilled migrants are individuals with at least a bachelor's degree working successfully in various fields (ranging from international organizations to the arts) and who moved from Israel to Switzerland or vice versa voluntarily and due to mainly professional reasons.

Beyond political or social discussions, from an anthropological perspective, migration is simply one event in someone's life story; there are many other major or minor events in one's biography. In order to give meaning to events and make sense of life stories, emotions are used to construct a distinct self, or as a "tool" of subjectivity within narratives, which is why they provide an interesting lens through which to look at migration or migration experiences.

Migration is a reality of past as well as today's societies. While modern forms of migration might be new, mobility has always been part of humanity. Moving from one place to another – which is what migration is, in the strict sense of the term (IOM, 2019b), even if it is politically and socially loaded, and occasionally associated with negative connotations of transgression or positive connotations of success – has been part and parcel of human history since its beginnings, as biological anthropology and archeology can demonstrate (Brettell, 2013; Brettell & Hollifield, 2015).

Worldwide a vast number of people are "on the move": 272 million in 2019. It has to be acknowledged that academic and policy discourses sometimes make it seem like whole populations are constantly on the move when in fact these are only 3.5% of the world's population (IOM, 2019a, p. 3). People migrate due to various reasons: some owing to displacement, others voluntarily. In OECD countries[8] there are generally more tertiary-educated immigrants than low educated ones, a trend that is likely to continue over the next ten years (Organisation for Economic Co-operation and Development, OECD, 2017; 2019). Knowledge-based societies such as Israel and Switzerland are reliant on an economic system that needs transnational highly qualified and/or skilled migrants, and in consequence, directly or indirectly encourage them to come into the country through various policies and institutions.

Due to the structure of our world, people moving across state borders raises questions for nation-states, societies, and individuals. While migration is a popular theme within academia and the media, there is still more to learn about the

---

7 Though often used interchangeably, there is a difference between "highly skilled" (being about ability) and "highly qualified" (being about certification): a discussion of the term highly qualified/skilled can be found in section 2.3.1.
8 Switzerland is one of the founding members of the *Organisation for Economic Co-operation and Development/OECD*, thus a member since 1961, Israel joined in 2010 (http://www.oecd.org).

significance of individual migratory experiences and the role of emotions within migration stories of highly qualified migrants.

Numbers about migration processes are highly informative, however, they tell us nothing about the meaning of migration for the people who are actually on the move. "This is especially so in the case of studying a particular diaspora or a migrant culture. The fact that a migrant has moved or continues to move every now and then is of course obvious. But the significance of this movement in their lives is not clear" (Hage, 2005, p. 469).[9]

In light of this research, questions that should be asked here include: How do highly qualified migrants themselves experience their mobility? What does their daily life look like? How do they cross borders? Where do they emplace themselves within their multi-sited biographies or transnational trajectories? What role – if any – does migration play for their processes of identity and feelings of belonging? How important or unimportant is migration in their overall life stories? Is migration always narrated as "rupture" or can it be a story of achievement as well?

Additionally, we need to ask ourselves: Why should we research highly qualified and skilled migrants specifically? For a long time, migration research in anthropology and related disciplines focused on unqualified or labor migrants and refugees, often ignoring highly skilled and more privileged migrants. However, highly skilled migrants might have different experiences than the already extensively studied other groups of migrants. For example, highly skilled migrants usually cross borders easily and can be seen as relatively privileged migrants which might shape their migration experiences and the significance of migration in their biographies.

In the cases in which highly qualified migrants have been mentioned, it was usually in a general and broad manner, leaving out the context in which these migrants live and often not considering their experiences: for instance, assuming they are detached from the country in which they live or reducing the discussions to "expats" who do not need to integrate (as noted by Favell, 2003; Smith & Favell, 2006; Suter, 2017). This gap within migration research has been recognized in recent years (Hercog & Sandoz, 2018a), with a growing number of studies focusing on highly qualified migrants and their spouses, expatriates, lifestyle migration, cosmopolitanism, and related topics (e. g.: Benson & O'Reilly, 2009; Friedman, 2004, 2017; Hannerz, 2002; King, 2002), many of which can be seen as part of or overlapping with research on highly skilled migrants. The strong focus on migration in connection with purely economic factors and developments moreover led to a

---

9 Ghassan Hage (2005, p. 469) also notes that the actual act of migrating in the sense of moving from one place to another rarely takes up more than a few days of a migrant's life.

blind spot concerning emotional aspects of migration that is now being recognized (Boccagni & Baldassar, 2015).

Emotions: Based mainly on John Leavitt (1996, p. 515 f.) and Maruška Svašek (2013, p. 69 f.), I look at emotions as complex everyday concepts that involve cultural as well as bodily dimensions. Specifically, in this study, emotions are understood as a tool used for the construal of meaning and the self in relation to experiences, narratives, as well as frameworks and surroundings. Or, as Maruška Svašek (2010, p. 868) puts it in more detail: "I have argued that it is useful to regard emotions as dynamic processes through which individuals experience and interpret the changing world, position themselves *vis-à-vis* others, and shape their subjectivities." Highly skilled migrants use emotions in various ways in their stories in order to engage and position their selves with the past, present, and future (Svašek, 2010, p. 868; Walsh, 2011), and consequently to give meaning to and make sense of their migration experiences and their current self.

Researching emotions and their changing over time and place has a long tradition in anthropology; for example, in ethnographic travel reports from the 18th century, comparing European emotional expressions to the ones of other regions. In the 1980s, researching emotions was a way for anthropologists to question fixed notions about the world (Plamper, 2012). Emotion research also has a longstanding tradition in sociology: namely, with Arlie Hochschild (1979) in her research on emotion work amongst female flight attendants and, more recently, Eva Illouz (2007), who looks at the commercialization of feelings and the contradictions of love in a capitalist world. In recent years, there has been something of an "emotional turn" in various social sciences such as geography and political science (Davidson, Bondi & Smith, 2007; Gonzáles-Hidalgo & Zografos, 2019; Gonzáles, 2017; Simonova, 2019) and several studies on emotions and migration have been published in anthropology and related disciplines (e. g.: Boccagni & Baldassar, 2015; Pine, 2014; Skrbiš, 2008; Svašek, 2005, 2013; Walsh, 2009, 2012). The present study adds to the existing body of literature on migration and emotion.

While there has been a focus on emotions within anthropology and other social sciences in recent years, emotions in connection with migration are often looked at in terms of singular emotions such as "hope" and "belonging" (Ho, 2009; Pine, 2014). In this project, different emotional dimensions of migration narratives will be discussed. Emotions are a component of human life (Gray, 2008; Plamper, 2012) and abound with culture and society (Illouz, 2007), making them an interesting aspect to examine in connection with skilled migration in a globalized world.

"Indeed, the notion of the 'migrant condition' is a reference to the characteristic ambiguities and tensions around emotional connections to 'here' and 'there'" (Boccagni & Baldassar, 2015, p. 74). Emotions can be found within the language and narratives themselves, but manifest as experiences, feelings, and (inter-)actions (Barbalet, 1996; Connor, 2007; Walsh, 2012) in interviewees' recollections as well. Emotions thus become an important aspect in making sense of the self and in construals of meaning, or as one component of complex narratives, which can lead to dichotomies and contradictions. Specifically, questions of belonging in multi-sited biographies, feelings of nostalgia, irritation, and expectation as well as accomplishment related to the activity of going abroad and migration experiences are discussed.

"[N]arrative is integral to sociality. So too, of course, is emotion; and so is each to the other, since anger, hope, and regret are forms of explaining, predicting, and judging. Whether we think in pictures or stories, resist or relish mind-reading, speak as *we* or *I*, love or loathe anecdotes, we are all narrators because we all have emotions; and emotions tell their own story" (Beatty, 2014, p. 560). Biographies are culturally universal phenomena and are a way to make sense of, as well as emphasize uniqueness in life stories (Picard, 2014, p. 177). As anthropologists we can learn a lot from individual stories, which is why twelve main protagonists and their stories are at the heart of the following text and will be presented in chapter 3.

Through narration, life stories or biographies become "journeys" with different stations, where some parts are highlighted and other parts are censored (Picard, 2014). In a study on migration, the act of migration becomes or is made into a key event in people's lives. Or, at the very least, it is a major event in a biographical narrative jointly produced by the researcher and the researched subject. Within these narratives, emotions play a crucial role in various ways; for instance, directly in the language, in descriptions of experiences and interactions, or as new feelings emerging through the narration and reflection.

Approach: Results for this study[10] are based on qualitative research in two localities, Israel and Switzerland, that took place mainly from 2015 to 2019. Twelve exemplary protagonists with unique stories of migration are the foci and additional empirical data is used to paint a full picture of the experience of highly skilled migrants in their local and global contexts. While looking at the two small states of Israel and Switzerland in connection with each other might seem like a peculiar choice due to their distance and geo-political dissimilarities, the countries do share

---

10 This thesis was conceived as part of a broader qualitative research project on the migration of highly qualified people funded by the *Swiss National Science Foundation* and running from 2015–2018. The title of the project was: "Narratives of Identity, Multi-sited Biographies, and Transnational Life-Modes of Highly Qualified Migrants. Two Case Studies". Two dissertations emerged out of that project: the present one, and another written by Khadeeja Haddy Sarr, focusing on highly qualified Senegambia migrants in Switzerland and Swiss migrants in the Senegambia region and the notion of being a stranger. For more information on the research project see appendix A. Additionally, the project was part of a larger cluster of migration researchers focusing on highly qualified migrants and transnationalism at the *Institute for Cultural Anthropology and European Ethnology* at the *University of Basel*.

a strong historical bond and certain characteristics that make them interesting cases to compare, contrast, and connect. Focusing on small groups of migrants deserves attention because it has the potential to explain characteristics of other groups of skilled migrants within specific frameworks.

Israel and Switzerland as specific localities are significant due to their historical, sociocultural, political, and religious characteristics creating distinct frameworks (Kreutner, 2013), possibly influencing the emplacement, interactions, emotions, and experiences of highly skilled migrants and their perception of the world. The two groups and localities serve as examples for discussing and hopefully providing a better understanding of emotional dimensions in the narratives of highly skilled migrants. Before looking at the question of the role of emotions in migrants' narratives, it is crucial to discuss the topic of high skilled migration in the current global context.

Within this study, the aspect of emotions emerged naturally out of the empirical material and reflects the ambivalent and multifaceted themes touched upon by skilled and highly skilled migrants themselves when narrating their migration experiences. Still, one should ask: What does the inclusion of emotions add to migration research? And the other way around: What does a better understanding of migrant experiences add to social science debates on emotion (Boccagni & Baldassar, 2015, p. 74)?

To summarize, this project is focusing on highly skilled Swiss in Israel and highly skilled Israelis in Switzerland and is using these locales and samples as case studies on the contemporary migration of highly skilled people living transnationally in or between these two countries. It is additionally an attempt to fill a gap, as there has not been a qualitative study focusing on these two groups and places in this manner.

This introduction offered a short overview of the topic, the context, and the approach. The thesis is sectioned into seven chapters. In the next chapter (chapter 2) more information about the background and context of the study is presented: first the wider context of globalization and transnationalism, and second, the local contexts of Israel and Switzerland. In addition, the second chapter also provides a discussion of the main terms: "highly skilled migrants" and "emotions", and the relevant literature about these terms. Further, a report on the approach and methods specifies some information about the empirical data. The next section, starting with chapter 3 focuses on the main results. First, the twelve main protagonists of the study are presented. Next, three groups of emotions and related themes and narratives – belonging; nostalgia, irritation, expectation; the desire to go abroad and feelings of accomplishments – are explored (chapters 4, 5, 6). Finally, a concluding chapter (chapter 7) provides a summary of the main results and a section on outlooks and potential follow-up studies.

2. Context and Surroundings

As mentioned, the focus of this thesis lies on emotions and migration. More specifically, it focuses on the way emotions serve as "tools" to make sense of experiences and construct or present the self in migration narratives. Notably, the two different localities, surroundings, and frameworks can lead to varying experiences, emotions, and narratives, and are part of the highly skilled migrants' stories. Context about these localities and frameworks play a significant role for a better understanding of the results. For this reason, I will discuss historical, political, economic, and social conditions in Israel and Switzerland in the following section.

In this chapter I will provide a comprehensive contextualization of the research project on a global, local, theoretical, and methodological level. I discuss why globalization and transnationalism are central concepts for this research as well as provide short economic, political, and social descriptions of the two fields of Israel and Switzerland. In order to understand the realities of highly skilled and skilled migrants, and the meaning of emotions in their narratives, it is necessary to understand the context in which these subjects move. Following this, the main terms of the thesis – (highly) skilled migrant and emotion – are presented. Then, a concise description of the approach and methods used for this study follows.

2.1 Global Context: Globalization and Transnationalism

The terms globalization, transnationalism, and related terminologies such as mobility are sometimes contested and often used interchangeably, making them somewhat inconclusive. While they are closely related, it is important to be precise. In this thesis, globalization is seen as a current empirical reality and transnationalism serves as a useful description of the border-crossing activities of skilled and highly skilled migrants. In other words, globalization is seen as a process taking place in an interconnected world system that involves movement in population (such as the migration of highly qualified and skilled people), skills, capital, technology, knowledge, and ideas (Barnard, 2000, p. 168). Transnationalism – literally crossing national borders – on the other hand is understood as an activity that crosses or extends beyond national borders, and creates ongoing linkages and exchanges. Transnationalism can be seen as a manifestation of globalization (Vertovec, 2009).

2.1.1 Understanding globalization

Put simply, the world of globalization is a complex "intensely interconnected world", or a "world of motion". While capital and goods move almost freely, people move readily, but not always as freely. These processes make the world shrink; however, this is not true everywhere and for everyone (Inda & Rosaldo, 2008, p. 6). The aim of this section is not to provide a finalized and completed definition of globalization, but rather to bring attention to the complexity of the process, provide an insight into the context in which highly qualified migrants move around the world, and discuss globalization as empirical reality within which transnational activities such as migration take place.

Looking at the multifaceted topic of the migration of highly qualified and skilled people means one has to consider issues of globalization and transnationalism. Globalization could be seen as a dynamic and sometimes turbulent phenomenon with constructive as well as destructive effects that not only transcends, but likewise disregards boundaries, and involves an essential reconfiguration of localities (Sassen, 1996, 2010) and sometimes biographies. Such processes can create tensions and countercurrents, such as trends of renationalization (including changing migration policies and debates around national identities and integration) and extreme protectionist or conservative movements, observable across the globe. This could be seen as representing a societal antagonism between high mobility versus a desire for settlement and stability, and between policies on migration and national profiling versus the demands for trained experts. It is worth exploring how or to what extent these aspects of globalization are perceived by highly skilled migrants as shaping their life experiences and emotions. It is likewise worth examining how they position themselves within a globalized as well as localized setting, and how they discuss transnational activities.

One common denominator of various definitions of globalization is the idea that modern globalization in general means an increase of interconnectedness across boundaries. In other words, it is the compression of time and space (Harvey, 1989, 2005). From an anthropological perspective the complexity of the term means that single aspects of globalization have to be scrutinized in order to better understand the process as a whole. As various scholars agree, globalization cannot be described as a single concept, but has to be seen as consisting of various processes (Ong, 1996; Bekemans, 2002; Dee Haas & Czaika, 2013; Pries & Westerholt, 2013, pp. 51–52; Matei, 2014). One of these processes worth researching is the migration of highly qualified and skilled people. Others are, for example, the study of the implications of a borderless world on citizenship and belonging, as suggested by John Urry (1999a), or studies on cultural globalization and various "scapes", as suggested by Arjun Appadurai (1997).

Using specific cases in order to produce in-depth analyses of issues that can be contextualized within a broader context is one of the fundamental ideas of anthropology. Using case studies to understand more about globalization is, for instance, suggested by the anthropologist Gisela Welz. In her paper, "Sighting/Siting Globalization" (2009), she argues that in order to understand the consequences of globalization researchers have to use strategic and expedient case studies as an approach. She calls this "sighting globalization" and according to her, case studies are a good way of making globalization visible on the microlevel. At the same time, it is necessary to choose specific places where one can empirically observe globalization processes. Gisela Welz (2009) calls this "siting". Research on globalization always raises questions of space, as the idea of globalization *per se* does not happen in a specific space but rather in a global imaginary of space. Based on this argument, researching a specific population of highly qualified and skilled migrants in specific spaces in order to understand more about their life experiences, imaginaries, emotions, and mobilities within a globalized world is a sound process.

2.1.2 Understanding transnationalism

While "transnationalism" is not a perfect term and sometimes might be used to depoliticize or muddle activities and effects, it underlines that we have not outgrown the nation-state, ideas of citizenship, or notions of insiders and outsiders, natives and strangers. When using the term "transnationalism", "nation" plays a role, and we have a way of understanding political discourses around topics of migration (Mohanty, 2013).

Transnational practices or groups can be seen as ongoing linkages and exchanges among non-state actors across national borders. Transnationalism is the general process of such connections (Vertovec, 2009, p. 3). Transnationalism in the sense of linkages and exchanges predates today's nation-states. In its current form it "… describes a condition in which, despite great distances and notwithstanding the presence of international borders …, certain kinds of relationships have been globally intensified and now take place paradoxically in a planet-spanning yet common – however virtual – arena of activity" (Vertovec, 2009, p. 3).

In the presented research, the consideration of the condition of transnationalism ensures that cultural, political, spatial, and social dimensions are taken into account whilst examining the experiences of highly qualified migrants. Transnational activities should not only be characterized as exchange of ideas and thoughts, but also as a universal approach to communication, which allow migrants to connect across geographical and cultural borders (Jagannath, 2014; Nedelcu, 2012; Ong, 1999). Transnationalism is a "mental activity" too, meaning migrants can cross national borders without physically moving across space (Cappai, 2013), creating and maintaining links through social relations (Basch, Glick Schiller, Szanton

Blanc, 1994). In some respects this is easy thanks to modern technologies such as communication and social media applications, the availability of news from all over the world and "ethnic food markets" in all global cities. Additionally, migrants bring past experiences from other places to their host country (Levitt, 2003a) and can influence their new home through their activities, such as creating businesses and networks. Of course, things are not always as simple as performing a *Skype* call or investing in a business "back home", but even such small activities can play important roles for individuals. While not all migrants engage in transnationalism (Vertovec, 2009 p. 17), and not all people are able to move freely across the globe, highly qualified migrants, especially the ones who move from country to country for professional reasons, are part of a privileged class of migrants and can often engage in transnational activities without encountering many obstacles.

Some authors find it useful to talk about a "transnational habitus" or a "transnational capitalist class" (joined by economic interests and promotion of globalization) (Nedelcu, 2012; Sklair, 2002; Weiss, 2006). In the same vein as looking at specific aspects and/or localities, another approach to understanding more about transnationalism could be looking at how it is shaped by and affects the habitus. "By conceptualizing transnational experience through the idea of *habitus*, social scientists might better appreciate how dual orientations arise and are acted upon. The notion also shines light upon the ways in which transnational life experiences may give rise not only to dual orientations but also to a personal repertoire comprising varied values and potential action-sets drawn from diverse cultural configurations" (Vertovec, 2009, p. 69).

The physical and mental mobility of transnational lives can be turned into capital, an adaptability and flexibility reflecting the expectations of today's knowledge societies with soft skills such as "international experience", "cultural sensitivity" and comprehensive language skills. A repertoire of cultural competences and skills, or transnational habitus, is created that, in turn, leads to a "cosmopolitanization of attitudes and values" (Vertovec, 2009, p. 69 f.) that is also articulated by the migrants I interviewed for this study. This notion of mobility as capital is called "motility" by authors (Kaufmann, Bergman & Joye, 2004; Leivestad, 2016; Salazar & Jayaram, 2016) researching specifically this aspect of mobilities and transnationalism.

Transnationalism is relevant for this study when it is seen as a "social formation spanning borders" (Vertovec, 2009, p. 4). For the individuals participating in the study, the transnational context seems to produce what could be called "multi-sited biographies" that are justified in the narrative construction of the protagonists' self and various identities with the help of emotions. The interesting aspect of transnational identities and activities as they are reflected in the narratives of multi-sited biographies is that they can be numerous. From the perspective of transnationalism, several nations (Vertovec, 2009, p. 6) or multiple places can be linked simultaneously.

Topics of migration and transnationalism often raise questions of integration. If one assumes identities are tied to nations and their specific locality, the crossing of national borders by migrants leads to expectations of integration into the national identity of a new locality. It is a problematic concept (integration into which society exactly?), not used for this research but still relevant as it is a major component of the political and academic (Basch, Glick Schiller & Szanton Blanc, 1994)[11] discussion of migration. "In addition to realizing that the relationship between transnationalism and integration is not a zero-sum game, it is important to understand that neither concept is of a piece; that is, various modes of components can be selectively combined by migrants" (Vertovec, 2009, p. 80).

One formal aspect of this is multiple citizenship. For example, there are about 18,700 Swiss-Israeli dual citizens living in Israel (only about 10% of the 20,885 Swiss in Israel do not have dual citizenship) (Bundesamt für Statistik, BFS, 2019a). The existence of dual citizenship can be controversial, as, like transnationalism, it questions traditional models of membership to a state (Bloemraad, 2004).

Migration confronts identities, borders, orders, and a sense of boundedness of spaces in various ways (Vertovec, 2009, p. 87 f.) and through the use of the term "transnationalism", the political and national dimensions are inherent in the research. For instance, the results show that the emotion of belonging can be formulated as either national belonging to a specific space, or as more cosmopolitan belonging to an international class of highly skilled migrants. However, as the next section shows, thinking in nation-states can be limiting for migration research too.

2.1.3 Methodological nationalism

"Trans*national* semantically refers us to the non-trans*national* or simply to the national as the entity that is crossed or superseded" (Wimmer & Glick Schiller, 2002, p. 324). The approach of transnationalism goes hand in hand with a critique of so-called "methodological nationalism" and the need to think beyond nation-states as the only possible frameworks (Beck & Grande, 2010; Bommes, 2002; Das & Poole, 2004; Levitt, 2012; Wimmer & Glick Schiller, 2002). Concepts such as mobility, translocal, transcontinental, transmigrants, multilocal, transcultural, cosmopolitan, mobility, trans-statal, and others are various terms used in research on transnationalism and transnationalization, and are often used to look at specific activities or groups (e. g.: Appadurai, 1995, 1997; Basch, Glick Schiller & Szanton Blanc, 1994, 1995; Cattacin & Chimienti, 2009; Glick Schiller & Çağlar, 2009; Götz, Lehnert,

---

11 The often-cited book "Nations Unbound" by Linda Basch, Nina Glick Schiller and Cristina Szanton Blanc (1994) can be seen as an anthropological argument against still prevailing discourses of integration, as one of the main arguments is that people can be "integrated" multiple times or in multiple places at once.

Lemberger & Sondelmayer, 2010; Götzö & Sontag, 2015; Hannerz, 2002; Kearney, 1995; Helbling & Kriesi, 2014; Jagannath, 2014; Portes, Guarnizo & Landolt, 1999; Pries, 2008; Randeria & Eckert, 2009; Urry, 1999b, 2007). The discourse on methodological nationalism highlights that it is crucial to think beyond nation-states as the only "natural", possible division of the world, as doing so limits migration research and consequently reproduces "container-thinking". The way migration is perceived by states and also by social scientific research on the topic is strongly shaped by nation-state building processes (Wimmer & Glick Schiller, 2002, p. 301).

Furthermore, nation-states are still a political reality and migrants (highly qualified as well as lesser or unqualified, and refugees) have no choice but to deal with nation-states, their specificities, and their bureaucratic constraints due to the simple fact that they are migrants and move across state borders in a world that is organized in states and divides people into groups of nationals and foreigners. Nation-states play a practical as well as ideological role in daily life and disregarding the nation-state is not always useful from a theoretical level. Exceptional situations such as the European "refugee crisis" of 2015/16[12] and the recent Covid-19 pandemic starting in 2020 show that states quickly fall back on closing borders and emphasize their own nationhood despite international organizations, proclaimed solidarity, and freely moving capital and goods. "It has become increasingly apparent that the nation-state 'has been rather more successful in weathering the storms of post-socialism, post-colonialism, and globalization' than was the case in the early days of globalization research" (Wimmer & Glick Schiller, 2002, p. 323).

Due to our thinking and perceiving in terms of nation-states, migration and transnational lives are often seen as something that need to be justified – on an individual basis (for instance, during the interviews conducted for this study, as I framed the move to another country as a central theme to be discussed), at the political level, and even from a scientific point of view: the existence of migration research in itself is a sign that the scientific community perceives it as something that is worth studying as it is defying and questioning existing structures. And while thinking of nation-states as the only possible framework is rightfully questioned, an examination of nation and citizenship cannot completely be left out of a project on migration such as this one, as it is part of the political reality and thus context – even for highly qualified migrants and even when not looking at specific states, but when using a different containment such as qualification or profession.

---

12 During this time many refugees from countries in conflict and insecurity, mainly Syria, Afghanistan, and Iraq came to Europe across the Mediterranean Sea. This was and is not a new phenomenon, as refugees had been coming to Europe for many years and are still coming, however the numbers were particularly high in 2015/2016, when countries in the European Union received over 1 million asylum applications (Hess, Kasparek, Kron et al., 2016).

Hence, while the world being structured according to states can and should be criticized on an epistemological and philosophical level, it is a reality and consequently it makes sense to use states – in this case Israel and Switzerland – as frames of reference for finding interviewees and defining limitations of data collection. Without nations, there would not be much sense in pursuing migration research in its current form at all.

As illustrated above, discussions of transnationalism allow for the examination of different facets and processes of globalization. However, academic and individual ideals of transnationalism sometimes seem to be challenged by still prevalent political streams of renationalization such as changing migration policies and discourses on fixed or traditional national identities. Such contradictions provoke antagonistic tendencies calling for research exploring the present situation of privileged, highly qualified migrants who might be representing transnationalism or multi-sited biographies through their daily life and a discussion of related emotions could further question narrow perspectives on belonging and nationhood.

2.2 Local Context: Two Small Exceptional States

The cases of Israel and Switzerland, specifically, mean that the political and social framework these countries provide is quite unique within their geographic region, which adds an interesting aspect to the daily lives of highly qualified migrants. Interviewees in both places talked about what the specific situation in their current country of residence means for them in various ways, often going beyond simplistic descriptions of what is perceived as "typically Swiss" or "typically Israeli". However, when looking at skilled and especially highly skilled migrants the place should not be overemphasized as there are parallels with the life modes and narratives of highly qualified migrants who live in other regions of the world.

In addition, choosing these two states carries an intrinsic problem. On a theoretical level there is the question of methodological nationalism and justification for choosing these two specific states or any states at all; and on the level of data and empirical material it leads to the fact that, during interviews, there are a lot of comparative assessments made between the two countries or places. In some cases this might lead to stereotypical descriptions: "Switzerland is like this – Israel is like that", however interviewees were always careful to put things into perspective and to not oversimplify comparisons.[13]

---

13 Such comparisons could have been reduced with a different approach, for example choosing people according to their qualification or their profession and not country of origin; however, using comparisons is a very common way of talking about experiences in different places and other contrasting characteristics might have been found in any narrative.

There are 20,900 Swiss living in Israel (BFS, 2020b) and 1,392 Israelis living in Switzerland (BFS, 2020a). Israel has the highest number of Swiss inhabitants in the Near East and is one of the twelve countries worldwide with more than 10,000 Swiss diaspora (mainly due to Swiss Jews making *Aliyah*/Jewish diaspora and moving to Israel, but not only); a large number of them can be assumed to be highly skilled. About 85% of Swiss in Israel are dual citizens (BFS, 2020b), which means that they can easily commute between Switzerland and Israel. Israelis moving to European countries such as Switzerland are often highly skilled young professionals looking for career opportunities (Kranz, 2016). The similarities and differences between the countries as well as the large number of Swiss living in Israel make this project a worthwhile case for research.

The relationship between the two states of Switzerland and Israel has a long history with fluctuating mutual perceptions (Kreutner, 2013). Switzerland and Israel are both small countries with a relatively unique history and standing within their geographical region. Switzerland, a confederation with four official languages, various cultures and a strong direct democracy is often (self-)depicted as a "special" case and seen as a prime example for other democratic states (Hettling, König, Schaffner, Suter & Tanner, 1998). Israel, a relatively young state, founded in 1948, is the only Jewish state in the world and often presented as the only democracy in the Middle East, which is true in many aspects, although the country has a stronger focus on religion and ethnicity than European and American democracies (Illouz, 2015, p. 50 f.). The country has somewhat over 9 million inhabitants (Central Bureau of Statistics, 2019). Israel likes to define itself as a constitutional democracy in the European sense (Kreutner, 2013, p. 27) and an argument could be made that while Israel is not positioned in Europe it "comes from Europe" (Kalir, 2006; Kamil, 2008) due to the role European Jews played in the imagination and establishment of the country.

Like Israel, Switzerland is a small country with somewhat over 8 million inhabitants (BFS, 2019b). It lies in the heart of Europe and was founded in 1848. There is an often-repeated imaginary of Switzerland as a "nation by will" and "special case" ("Sonderfall Schweiz" in German). This is part of its politics; the self-perception as well as the outside image of Switzerland (Hettling, König, Schaffner, Suter & Tanner, 1998). Jonathan Steinberg (2015, p. 1) writes: "The sheer variety of Swiss life, what I think of as its 'cellular' character, makes it hard to write a coherent account of the place." Something similar might be said of Israel, where the Jewish Israeli population is the dominant majority with about 80% of the population, but which is also a highly diverse country with Christian, Muslim, Druze, Armenian, Circassian, Bedouin, and other minorities (Central Bureau of Statistics, 2020). Switzerland's unique political landscape manifests in different ways, one of them being that there are four national languages, German, French, Italian, and Rhaeto-Romance, and cantons have a lot of autonomy (Steinberg, 2015).

The general imaginaries of these two countries are contradictory in some respects. Switzerland is presented and seen as an idyllic island of bliss ("Insel der Seligen" in German) (Hettling, König, Schaffner, Suter & Tanner, 1998, p. 8). This is reflected in the Israeli perspective during interviews as well. Israel is often seen as "problematic" from a European as well as Swiss perspective (Kreutner, 2011, p. 63 f.) due to complex historical entanglements, its creation, or its politics. While Europe and the European view of Israel might be seen with ambivalence from the Israeli perspective (Strenger, 2011, p. 90f), Switzerland itself is usually seen as positive. Swiss living in Israel talk about how they are often asked why they would even come to Israel if they have the possibility to live in "wonderful Switzerland", something also described by Sabina Bossert (2009, 2014) in her research on Swiss Jews making *Aliyah*. These different imaginaries make the choice of the two countries interesting because it would seem that the constructions of reality and frameworks in which the highly qualified migrants live are very different from each other. While Switzerland leads to mainly positive connotations, Israel becomes a place of "everyday struggles" in narratives (see section 5.2). Nevertheless, they do have a lot in common and a strong historical connection which will be explored on the following pages.

2.2.1 Israel and Switzerland: historical and contemporary connections

Israel and Switzerland share one particularly important historical connection: "From an Israeli perspective Switzerland is the actual birthplace of Zionism, tying the two countries intrinsically since before the foundation of the state of Israel. In 1897 the first Zionist Congress took place in Basel. Even the Zionist founding father, Theodor Herzl, was convinced he had founded the Jewish nation-state after the first Zionist Congress. Through the organization of this congress, he thought he had managed to provide the ideological and institutional base for the creation of a Jewish state"[14] (Kreutner, 2013, p. 23). In his own words, Herzl wrote in his diary: "… that our movement has gone down into the annals of history. If I were to summarize the Baseler Congress in a few words, words that I would never say out loud, I would say this: in Basel I have founded the Jewish state. If I were to be overheard I would become a laughing stock, but maybe in five years' time, or at

---

14 Original citation:
"Die Schweiz ist zudem aus einer israelischen Perspektive der eigentliche Geburtsort des Zionismus. In Basel fand im Jahr 1897 der erste Zionistenkongress statt. Selbst der zionistische Gründervater Theodor Herzl war nach dem ersten Zionistenkongress überzeugt, er habe bereits in Basel den jüdischen Staat gegründet. Indem er durch die Organisation des Zionistenkongresses die ideologische Grundlage und die institutionelle Basis für die Schaffung eines künftigen jüdischen Staates gelegt habe."
(Kreutner, 2013, p. 23)

least in fifty everyone will understand" (Theodor Herzl as cited in Heiko Haumann, 1997, p. 2).

While Theodor Herzl's Zionism is a topic of its own and cannot be discussed extensively in the context of this thesis, it is important to acknowledge the historical bond, as well as symbolic connection, between Israel and Switzerland, and Israel and Europe as a whole. Theodor Herzl even used Switzerland as an example for some aspects of a potential Jewish state, for instance, the question of language. "He supposed that the Jews in Israel would all speak their native languages. He imagined his Jewish state as a nation of Jewish immigrants: 'In the Land of Israel, too, we will remain what we are now, just as we will never cease to love, with regret and longing, the countries of our birth from which we were expelled,' he wrote. That's exactly what happened, to the disgruntlement of some of the founding fathers of Israeli Zionism" (Theodor Herzl as cited in Tom Segev, 2001, p. 16). This does not mean that nowadays there is no such thing as "Israeli culture and identity" or "cultures and identities".

According to Jonathan Kreutner (2013) the histories of Europe and Israel are linked in such a manner that it leads to a reciprocal effect in – occasionally conflictual and ambivalent – perspectives on each other. Here, one also has to acknowledge that *Mizrahim*, or Jews who migrated from North Africa and the Middle East faced discrimination by European Jews from the beginning of the foundation of the state of Israel and can have a very different relationship to Europe and Israel (Kamil, 2008), and that, while Israeli culture is based on European principles, it does not mean there are no internal tensions and conflicts due to ethnic and historical realities (Kreutner, 2013, p. 29). "The Zionist movement never represented all the Jewish people. Israeli Zionism had a different set of interests than the Zionism represented by Theodor Herzl, the movement's Austro-Hungarian founder. The Zionist dream has always produced turbulent ideological, political, and moral disagreement. Among other contradictions, the reestablishment of the Jewish nation in its land was not only an act of transcendent historical justice; it also prompted war, displacement and misery" (Segev, 2001, pp. 6–7).

In a long essay on Israel, the Israeli-Swiss psychologist Carlo Strenger (2011, p. 12 f.) argues that modern Israel can only be understood when analyzing its specific historical and political position before the Six-Day War in 1967. Most Israelis saw the war as a coup or act of liberation that would bring security from hostile neighbors and political opponents. However, looking back, the conquest led to an ethical and political disaster, and isolated Israel even more. Still, during the war the strong sympathy for Israel within Switzerland was relatively unique in Europe. This was reflected in the news coverage and due to several reasons including military connections between Swiss army officers and the Israeli military, and a general sympathy between the two small, liberal states (Kreutner, 2013, p. 85). While it shows a certain connection or solidarity between the countries, it should also be looked at in light of an almost colonial standpoint, presuming the necessity to "civilize" the Arab world (Kreutner, 2013, p. 88).

Like Israel, Switzerland invokes strong imaginaries of uniqueness. Switzerland's history goes back to the Middle Ages and the creation of a voluntary and egalitarian republic leading to the foundation of the Swiss Confederation ("Eidgenossenschaft" in German) in the 19th century. Today, one of its central political characteristics is its neutrality, which of course was never absolute (Hettling, König, Schaffner, Suter & Tanner, 1998) but still majorly impacts Switzerland's self-conception. Swiss politics are strongly shaped by direct democracy and a give-and-take culture concerning major and sometimes minor political changes and decisions.

Historically projected causes such as recessions and high national unemployment rates play a negligible role when looking at Switzerland and (to some extent) Israel as places of departure. Arguably, most emigrants from both places can be assumed to be privileged and educated, or in other words highly skilled (which does not mean that financial incentives and considerations do not play a role for individual decision-making on emigration).

Switzerland is one of the richest countries in the world and a highly popular migration destination (OECD, 2018a). About 25% of the Swiss population is foreign, most of them having lived in Switzerland for at least ten years or having been born there (BFS, 2020b). Israel has a rising GDP and a relatively low unemployment rate about 5% (OECD, 2018b) – even though the cost of living has been rising steadily over the past few years (OECD, 2018b). Poverty is deepening and today about 20% of households are below the poverty line (OECD, 2018b), leading to massive protests over the cost of living, for example in 2011, and some emigration movements pushed by economic struggles of young qualified people, making Israel the Western country with the highest emigration of skilled individuals, or brain drain (OECD, 2018b).

Both countries invest a rising and comparatively high percentage of their GDP into "research and development": Israel: 4.95% and Switzerland 3.37% (OECD, 2020, figures from 2018) and consequently are professionally and economically attractive to highly skilled people who can easily move to take part in an increasingly competitive global labor market where states compete with each other to attract the best "brains". Both countries have well regarded universities and research institutions attracting academics from around the world (for example the *Swiss Federal Institute of Technology/ETH* in Zurich or the *Weizman Institute* in Rechovot) (Epstein, 2016). The bilateral relationship between Switzerland and Israel at the level of research and education is strong, mainly due to initiatives by researchers or individual universities (Tachles, 2014).

As advanced economies, the service sector plays an important role. The main industries in Switzerland are watch production, banking, and pharmaceuticals (Handelskammer Schweiz-Israel, 2018). In Israel, the "Start-up Nation" (Senor &

Singer, 2009), the technology and high-tech sector attracts highly skilled individuals. The countries have strong trade connections, for example, in the food-sector (through *Nestlé* and *OSEM Food Industries*). The main goods exported from Switzerland to Israel are pharmaceutical products, gemstones, and watches, and from Israel to Switzerland, gemstones, electronic products, and mechanical machines (Handelskammer Schweiz-Israel, 2018).

2.2.2 Migration in Israel

Israel and Switzerland are characterized by different migration regimes which will be discussed in the following sections. Emigration out of Israel is a complex topic when taking Zionism into account as a form of nationalist ideology, as migrants are often described as abandoning Israel, which then in turn is a form of brain drain from the state's perspective and has been a prevalent topic in the media (e. g.: Alexander/Haaretz, 2014, 2015; Peretz/Haaretz, 2016).[15] As one interviewee puts it: *"you're not supposed to leave"* (Transcript Daniel, p. 12).

Zionist politicians and the media largely discuss issues of brain drain (Fialkova & Yelenevskaya, 2013, p. 17). "Criticism [of emigrants to Germany,] as well as of emigrants in general, has been rife in the newspapers and magazines that engage with the political arena. Lately, a controversy between emigrants and 'stayers' – who surprisingly left Israel not only geographically but linguistically – broke out, the original missives were partly authored in English" (Kranz, 2016, p. 14). Emigration out of Israel is mainly discussed in connection with this issue but there are other approaches as well, namely by Steven Gold (2018), looking at Israelis in California's Silicon Valley. The topic of Israelis living in Germany, particularly Berlin fascinates the media (e. g.: Münch/Süddeutsche Zeitung, 2013; Shumsky/Haaretz, 2013; The Economist, 2014, Uni/Neue Zürcher Zeitung, 2013) and is also a topic of research (Gromova, 2013; Kranz, 2016; Oz-Salzberger, 2016).[16]

As in most Western states, labor migrants are necessary for the Israeli economy (for example in agriculture, construction, and nursing) (Kalir, 2006).[17] Israel's

---

15 This also leads to heated media debates arising out of specific issues, shown, for example, through the "pudding case". The "pudding case" started when a young Israeli living in Berlin shared a post with a supermarket receipt showing how an Israeli pudding was cheaper in Germany than in Israel. Many newspapers in Israel and Germany reported on the issue. For example, the German magazine *Spiegel* (Salloum, 2014, October 11), the Israeli newspaper *Haaretz* (2014, October 19), and the Swiss newspaper *NZZ* (Dachs & Mertins, 2014, October 19).

16 Additionally, there is a conference report by the German Historical Institute looking at the "exchange" between Israel and other countries: Germans and Americans in Israel – Israelis in Germany and the United States (Hilgert, 2013).

17 The discussion around labor migration into Israel is interesting and can be looked at in connection with the Middle East conflict since many labor migrants came into the country after work permits

profile as a migration state is unique in that the aspect of being a "migration state" only applies to the Jewish diaspora and thus could be seen as an "ethnic republic" (Rabinowitz, 1997; Sabar, 2010).[18] Israel, building on particularism (Kalir, 2015), traditionally perceives migration critically (Shokeid, 1988), referring to those who leave as *Yordim* – those who descend (Cohen & Kranz, 2014, p. 4), as opposed to the *Olim* moving to Israel and making their *Aliyah* – meaning going up or ascending. These terms are in stark contrast to the Swiss term for citizens living abroad, which is *Auslandschweizer* or "Swiss abroad".

Existing research about migration and Israel has not specifically focused on highly skilled migrants (Joppke & Rosenhek, 2001; Shuval, 2006; Willen, 2007; Yonah, 2007), however there are a few exceptions, some from an economics perspective (Cohen & Kranz, 2014; Kranz, 2019; Razin, 2018; Schäfer & Henn, 2018). There is a large body of research on the different *Aliyahs* in connection with the history of the country (Ben-Sasson, 2007; Lipshitz, 1998) and Jewish migrants from the former Soviet Union who came to Israel in the late 1980s and 1990s (Hacohen, 2002; Fialkova & Yelenevskaya, 2007, 2013), which could also be discussed from the perspective of highly skilled and highly qualified migrants. Research on non-Jewish migration and Israel mainly highlights the issue of asylum seekers from Africa or labor migrants (Fleischman, Willen, Davidovitch & Mor, 2015; Kemp, 2004; Kalir, 2006, 2015; Sabar, 2010).

Israeli emigrants are generally highly mobile, highly educated, secular, and politically left-leaning (Kranz, 2016, p. 15). Many academics from all disciplines leave Israel for at least a few years (Zwischenzeilen, 2013a, 2013b, 2018). This has led the state to start the "Israel Brain Gain" program in 2010 to motivate emigrants to move back. While other countries such as Germany and France also have return programs for their citizens living abroad, these are more subdued and pragmatic. Israel uses a national rhetoric "appealing to migrants' strong psycho-cultural bond with the homeland" (Cohen & Kranz, 2014, p. 7) and uses measures such as tax incentives to motivate émigrés to move back.

For highly skilled immigrants (Jewish as well as non-Jewish), Israel still provides interesting opportunities, for instance, through research positions at universities

---

for Palestinians from the West Bank and Gaza were revoked, and the Israeli government's attempt to promote the jobs as "Israeli" failed. Also, as in many European countries, it was expected that the migrant workers would only stay temporarily, which was not the case.

18 The Arab-Israeli conflict and the situation of the Palestinians as well as Zionism and Arab nationalism as conflicting powers are not part of the project, though they are part of and influence the research field. With regard to migration, Israel's self-definition as a Jewish state can be problematic when taking into account the 20% of the population who are Arab and the various issues, one of them being that many Palestinians from East Jerusalem are seen as immigrants by the law, strongly complicating their daily life (Schmid/NZZ, 2017, December 27).

or the *Weizmann Institute* and jobs in the high-tech sector. Privileged migrants moving to Israel, such as Swiss, can move to Israel relatively easily (on the basis of a job or education) even if they are not Jewish, but the duration of their visa might be limited. However, there are restrictions in place for non-Jewish migrants or self-identified Jews who do not fit the Chief Rabbinate's definition of Jewish identity. One example are the strict marriage laws, which prevent religiously mixed weddings from occurring on Israeli territory (Burton, 2015).

2.2.3 Migration in Switzerland

Research and diplomatic institutions, as well as high quality of life, are structures attracting highly skilled migrants to Switzerland (Hercog & Tejada, 2014). In the past, Switzerland was a refuge from wars and conflicts: the first time for the Protestant Huguenots in the 16th and 17th centuries. Switzerland was attractive to migrants, either as a safe haven due to its neutrality, as a place of investment, or to find work due to its early industrialization (D'Amato, 2008).

Migration regulations in the 1990s were changed from highly restrictive to more selective ones. This means that while it is generally difficult to migrate to Switzerland permanently, there are many exceptions to the rules, mainly connected to economic needs (Cattacin & Chimienti, 2009; D'Amato, 2008; Hercog & Sandoz, 2018b). This does not mean that immigration is not a contested field. For example, there was a referendum "against mass immigration" in February 2014 due to fears about the growing size of the foreign population in recent years. It was successful, which was strongly criticized by economic and educational institutions (such as *Économiesuisse*, the Swiss economic corporate union and *CRUS*, the organization representing Swiss universities), fearing a future lack of highly skilled individuals in the country and disadvantages in terms of European and global competitivity (Pfister/Tagesanzeiger, 2015).

For certain EU-citizens and highly qualified or skilled migrants in specific fields, it is relatively easy to come to and settle in Switzerland (Cattacin & Chimienti, 2009; D'Amato, 2008; Müller, 2013), in part thanks to migration contingents allotted to economic sectors according to need. However, it is difficult to gain Swiss citizenship, even for migrants who have lived there many years or were born in Switzerland. Switzerland is one of many OECD countries that have implemented skill-oriented policies such as spending more on research and development (Gross, 2011). These types of policies attract migrants and might also lead to constant movement amongst highly skilled migrants. Young, highly skilled migrants, in particular, benefit from a global labor market and consequently might move transnationally several times throughout their career (Eichhorst, 2011, p. 232), as is also the case with some of my protagonists and other informants I interviewed in the field.

As mentioned, Swiss living abroad are called "Swiss abroad". The Federal Department of Foreign Affairs is responsible for them and regularly publishes statistics and information about Swiss registered as living abroad. The Swiss abroad are sometimes called the "Fifth Switzerland" in reference to the four languages of Switzerland (Swiss Forum for Migration and Population Studies, SFM, 2010). They represent about 10% of the overall Swiss population and many Swiss abroad are dual citizens. In 2014 a law was passed regulating the rights and duties of Swiss abroad. The *Organization for Swiss Abroad/ASO*, a special interest group with chapters in several countries is recognized as representing Swiss abroad by the government. About 24,000 Swiss return to Switzerland every year and there are infrastructures in place to support them (Eidgenössisches Departement für auswärtige Angelegenheiten, EDA, 2020). There are several recent and ongoing studies on the topic.[19]

2.3 Defining the Main Terms through Research and Literature

In this section I am going to introduce and define the main terms and concepts used throughout the dissertation which are "(highly) skilled migrants" and "emotions". Both terms are extensively discussed in the literature, and are complicated, fluid concepts closely related to other terms. While it is challenging to find and formulate a fixed definition, the following section describes how the terms were used in the context of this study as a way to reduce the complexity of the emerging narratives.

2.3.1 Who are skilled and highly skilled migrants?

"The story of mass migrations (voluntary and forced) is hardly a new feature of human history. But when it is juxtaposed with the rapid flow of mass-mediated images, scripts, and sensations, we have a new order of instability in the production of modern subjectivities" (Appadurai, 1997, p. 4). Highly skilled migrants are part of these immense numbers of people moving around the globe, while showing distinct features and (sometimes) privileges. Their narratives, of course, differ, from the migration narratives of forced migrants or refugees, who are often prevented from crossing borders easily or can only stay in a country for a limited amount of time under specific circumstances.

Researching high skilled migration and highly skilled migrants is relevant as the process and the participating migrants have long been overlooked by migration

---

[19] It is one of the main research fields of the *Institute of Cultural Anthropology and European Ethnology* at the *University of Basel* https://kulturwissenschaft.philhist.unibas.ch/de/forschung/globalisierung-migration-mobilitaet/, accessed: September 5, 2023.

studies. High skilled migration has recently gained recognition within migration studies after decades of being overshadowed by topics such as low skilled migration, purely economic push-and-pull factors, refugees, crime issues, and legal restrictions. Current research on skilled migration tends to focus on social, cultural, political, and economic dimensions of knowledge-based societies within a globally multifaceted context.

Often, policy debates concerning highly qualified migration tend to be over such topics as brain gain vs. brain drain, brain circulation, and brain waste (Luft, 2011). Losing skilled professionals to host countries is considered a challenge to sending countries, a perception that turns the issue into a political one. Host societies not only gain knowledge and skills (Lowell & Findlay, 2001) through migration but also face immigration-related challenges, such as the closing of borders and the fear of negative economic impacts among portions of the population (Liebig, Kohls & Krause, 2012). Paradoxically, migrants abroad are considered important agents contributing to their host countries and considered a loss towards the development of their home countries (Lowell & Findlay, 2001). Due to this, migration becomes a politically charged topic, and policies tend to divide migrants into "good/wanted" and "bad/unwanted" groups (Boucher & Cerna, 2014; Cranston, 2017; Hercog & Sandoz, 2018a; Sandoz, 2019; Tani, Guo & Hugo, 2010).

The definition and list of characteristics describing highly skilled migrants is still a debated topic and remains fluid (Parsons, Rojon, Rose & Samanani, 2020). Usually, the starting point of the definition is the one used by the *Organisation for Economic Cooperation and Development* (OECD, 1995, p. 16). There, individuals are described as "highly qualified" if they have the following features: "a) successfully completed education at the third level in an S&T [science and technology] field of study, b) not formally qualified as above, but employed in a S&T occupation where the above qualifications are normally required." A further subcategorization into five labor categories can be made: professional and managerial, engineers and technicians, academics and scientists, entrepreneurs, and students, who have varying motivations or push-and-pull factors guiding their move in the form of better salaries or gaining international work experience (Mahroum, 2001).

It is essential to make a strong distinction between *highly skilled* and *highly qualified* migrants according to several authors. The former is about abilities such as work experience, the latter about certifications such as educational degrees (Csedö, 2008; Koser & Salt, 1997; Williams & Baláž, 2005; Zaletel, 2006). In this project I have chosen to talk about "highly skilled or skilled migrants" (depending on education or profession or self-definition) because the term is more useful through its inclusion of experience instead of only qualifications and it can be applied to professions outside the science and technology domain. Beyond that, skills are always unequivocally related to the body and the person being mobile (Cranston, Schapendonk & Spaan, 2018), consequently adding an important aspect of embodiment to the terminology, as the skills inevitably move along with the migrants, while the value of qualifications might change from place to place or over time.

Nevertheless, the definitions remain ambiguous and all skills, qualifications, or equivalent experience are not valued in the same ways, making the definition of who counts as "highly skilled" or "highly qualified" malleable (Kõu, Van Wissen, Van Dijk & Bailey, 2015, p. 4). The geographical context of skilled migrants can play a defining role in how the distinction between skilled and unskilled or qualified and unqualified is shaped and constructed (Jagannath, 2014). Who is truly perceived as highly qualified and granted migration privileges is strongly connected to economic needs and current policies and can consequently always be adapted and change.

In addition, the categorization of migrants along these terms is problematic, as it is highly gendered, highly excluding, and based on certain documents not available to everyone, with some certifications and skills valued more than others. Additionally, salaries can be an important factor and can play into the definition. Looking at the discourse around the terms, one can see that it is mainly an economically driven instrument or category (Randeria, 2016).

Therefore, one could argue that the root of the discussion is essentially about class, and from the perspective of a state, it is moreover about who will or will not be a burden on the state. For instance, refugees are generally excluded from the discussion around "highly qualified/skilled" migrants by governments, unless we specifically discuss how they are excluded or how their qualifications are not recognized (Sontag, 2018b).

Nevertheless, a focus on highly skilled and/or qualified migrants is a good starting point as it produces different experiences from other forms of migration, such as forced migration. The issues faced by individuals who move freely from country to country due to work, education, or a partner are worth further exploration. The privilege they have due to their free mobility – generally not facing issues with immigration offices in terms of entering and settling in a country – makes their migration experiences very different from someone with a refugee status or irregular migrants. Their skills and qualifications as well as their nationality make it possible for such migrants to move as they wish, without generally having to seriously consider many visa restrictions. Additionally, in the case of employed highly skilled migrants, the employer often organizes visas as well as the move and accommodation.

For example, there might still be annoyance at bureaucracy or complications, but overall, there are no major legal issues preventing the physical act of moving from one country to another, as reflected in the following quotation from the interview with Alexander:

I think I'm very comfortable in this regard. 'Cause, uh, I have people who do this for me and help me so far. Now, I don't know how difficult it is to go to the next level [organizing a visa for a spouse and/or staying permanently].
(Transcript Alexander, p. 15)

Related to the processing of one's official migrant status, my own edited fieldnote on a small issue with my Swiss residence permit ("Ausländerausweis" in German – literally "foreigners identification") in 2018 further illustrates how easy things can be, if one is the "right" kind of migrant from a state's perspective:

During the final phase of the project, my employment at the university ended and with that, my residence permit for Switzerland. Having had stayed in Switzerland for 8 years, 5 of those employed but still seen as a student by the immigration office due to doing my main status as a PhD student, the time one can stay in Switzerland for educational purposes was up. I did not get any notification or information and started to panic, mostly, because a non-European friend who had done their master's degree in Basel and had planned on staying (they had already found a job) had been asked to leave the country recently, which their potential employer could not prevent. Thinking about this, my slightly panicked thought was: "But I have an apartment and all my stuff is here!". As this was during Easter break, the immigration office was closed and there was no way for me to get any information right away beyond what I found on their website. I knew, as a highly educated European citizen there would probably be a way for me to stay in Switzerland one way or the other, but I still suddenly felt like I was here illegally and I was going to have to leave from one day to the next. On the first workday after the holidays, I went to the immigration office in Basel, a place where I had already spent some time in the very beginning when I originally moved to Switzerland for my master's degree. I talked to a very friendly lady, whose colleague just had been less friendly to an (I assumed) old Turkish man who hadn't understood where he was supposed to wait, who told me that she could not make the decision about my status, was as confused as I was about why I had not received any notification about the end of my permit, and told me that there were special rules for PhD students and Postdocs and that the issue would be resolved quickly. When I got home, I emailed the responsible department, immediately got an answer, and got asked until when I wanted to stay in Switzerland. I replied and a few days later the new permit was in my mailbox – valid for the rest of the year, allowing me to work if I wanted to, just as I had asked. This experience was "very easy" just the way interviewees had described their contact with immigration offices and illustrated once again, how different migrants' experiences can be.

As mentioned in the section on globalization and transnationalism, the world is not borderless for everyone: "Just as – contrary to the prediction of some observers – globalization itself has not produced a smooth, borderless, integrated global order, transnationalism has not entailed consistent kinds of social formations or practices" (Vertovec, 2009, p. 2). This becomes exceedingly visible in the distinction among "highly skilled" migrants, "regular/other" migrants, refugees, or other groups of migrants. While many states actively want to attract highly skilled migrants, depending on citizenship and visibility, highly qualified migrants can still experience discrimination. For example, Ganga Jey Aratnam (2012) completed a study on highly skilled migrants in Switzerland and showed that participants experienced discrimination and racism, and had difficulties finding suitable employment, which led to a discussion about brain waste. This was not an issue in the study at hand, as the interviewees had all moved specifically for a job or education and were not part of a visible minority. That these forms of discrimination and distinctions between categories of migrants is not only problematic from a human rights perspective but additionally not always useful for new economies in a globalized world is correspondingly something of which economically liberal organizations and authors are aware (Aiolfi/NZZ, 2015; Bertelsman Stiftung, 2010; Feldges/NZZ, 2015; Neue Zürcher Zeitung, 2016, 2018; Rist/NZZ, 2013; The Economist, 2013). "[H]ow many skilled migrants are being overlooked every day because migration is regulated with planned-economy approaches reminiscent of the post-war period and not the flexible approaches increasingly adopted by human resource departments in the private sector?" (Collett & Zuleeg, 2010, p. 337)[20]

Summarized, this means that while many people migrate, migration is not the same for everyone. Taking the ambiguity and context of the definition into account, Israelis are generally seen as "good migrants" (Kranz, 2016). The same can be said of Swiss and other Western European migrants, especially highly skilled ones (Cranston, 2017). Discourses around both groups of migrants, if existing at all, are rarely negative. Both groups of migrants exist in small numbers, are often educated and can be seen as "useful" for an economy in knowledge societies reliant on highly skilled migrants. Even though there has been a growing number of studies on topics of high skilled migration, it is still worth adding insights to the existing research, especially on the experiences and meaning of migration for individuals and particularly the emotions of specific groups, in this case, Swiss in Israel and Israelis in Switzerland.

2.3.2 What are emotions?

But emotions are especially interesting precisely because they do not fit easily into these dichotomies [of nature vs. nurture]. On the contrary, it is precisely emotion terms and

---

20 The authors look at the topic from a purely economic standpoint as a waste of skills and resources for society.

> concepts that we use to refer to experiences that cannot be categorized in this way and that inherently involve both meaning and feeling, mind and body, both culture and biology. To give a simple example: what we describe as a fluttery feeling in the stomach may be anxiety about a public presentation or the result of an unfortunate lunch, or it may be some horrible combination of the two. But we will not call that feeling the emotion of anxiety if we are convinced that the lunch is the only factor involved: to call an experience anxiety, or anger, or happy excitement, it must be associated with a series of culturally defined *meanings* that go well beyond the digestive. At the same time neither a definition of anxiety nor an appraisal of an anxiety-provoking situation is the same thing as being anxious: to be anxious is to have a *feeling* associated with a meaning.
> (Leavitt, 1996, p. 515).

Emotions are a central, complex part of the human experience and consequently of migration experiences and narratives. But who defines what emotions are? According to the historian Jan Plamper (2012, p. 20 f.) the normative power of what emotions are has changed over time. While currently it is mostly a psychological or neuroscientific research field, in the past, it was mostly a theological or philosophical one. However, according to his analysis of emotions in history: "No discipline has unsettled the imagination that feelings are timeless and the same everywhere as strongly as anthropology" (Plamper, 2012, p. 173).[21]

In anthropology or ethnology, emotions have long been a research topic. Influenced by the emergence of poststructuralist approaches in literary studies and new social movements from the 1970s questioning the notion of a "natural" gender (such as women's and LGBT movements), a social constructivist approach challenging and historicizing different categories and terms became prevalent. Emotions were one of the categories discussed, leading to a number of diverse publications on the topic during the 1980s (Plamper, 2012, p. 135).

Accordingly, there is a different way of talking about emotions before and after social constructivism (Plamper, 2012, p. 115 f.). The cultural turn also brought a paradigm shift in the treatment of emotions. Before the 1970s emotion research argued that emotions always stay the same at core and simply manifest differently in different cultures. Just a few years later discussions about emotions were about radically different ways of feeling emotions within different cultures. Hence, emotions were then seen as "cultural experiences".

It has been shown how concepts of emotions changed during the course of history and that the notion of universal or "pancultural emotions" is not as clear

---

21 Original German:
"Keine Disziplin hat die Vorstellung, Gefühle seien zeitlos und überall gleich, so nachhaltig erschüttert wie die Ethnologie." (Plamper, 2012, p. 173)

cut as one might think (Plamper, 2012). For example, one historical analysis shows how certain fears and dreads changed over time. Jan Plamper (2012, p. 93 f.), who looks at emotions from a metalevel, uses the example of how the epidemic fear of being buried alive during the end of the 19th and beginning of 20th century suddenly disappeared after about 20 years with the beginning of World War I. This fear was due to the conflicting discourses of the time on death and the question what happens after death (there were disputes on the topic between morticians, physicians, and religious figures), which took a back seat once mass deaths occurred on battlefields and, ironically, the fear of being buried alive in a dugout would have been quite justified (Plamper, 2012, pp. 94–95).

"Emotion" is everchanging through time and space and a travelling (or migrating) concept – even languages which originally do not have a word for it, know and integrate "emotion", such as Tibetan (Plamper, 2012, p. 21). This movement or processuality is reflected in the term itself. Etymologically, "emotion" or the German "Gemütsbewegung" (literally: movement of the mind or temper) comes from the Latin "movere" – to move, or rummage.[22] In English the word used to mean "cause to move".[23] This puts the notion of *motion* or *movement* in the term itself, which is quite fitting for a term that is so difficult to pin down with a definition and reflects its processuality. It creates a connection to migration, which involves the physical, and one can argue also mental, movement of individuals across borders.

Discourses around emotions reflect divisions between universalism and social constructivism, and are consequently related to discussions of nature vs. nurture (Plamper, 2012, pp. 15–18). Like Jan Plamper (2012, p. 17) and others, I do not think a clear-cut distinction between the two is necessarily productive, especially when discussing emotions. Emotions simply do not fit neatly in either category from an anthropological perspective (Leavitt, 1996, p. 515), as the introductory quotation illustrates figuratively. While it complicates the issue of defining the term one is working with, it is also what makes emotions in migration narratives an especially interesting, if somewhat processual and intangible, topic.

All these issues show why a precise definition of emotions is notoriously difficult to formulate or find. Actually, in the literature on the topic, one of the first things usually mentioned and discussed as the main characteristic of emotions is the problem of definition (Beatty, 2014; Plamper, 2012, p. 21). This is mainly due to the changing notions of the category across places, cultures, and time as well as

---

22 *Duden Fremdwörterbuch*: https://www.duden.de/rechtschreibung/Emotion, accessed: August 8, 2023.
23 *Oxford English Dictionary*: http://www.oed.com/view/Entry/281674?rskey=CuEOk9&result=2 &isAdvanced=false#eid, accessed: August 8, 2023.

disciplines.[24] It is additionally due to the difficulty of grasping the difference between emotions, feelings, sentiment, and affect. Following Jan Plamper (2012, p. 22), I use "emotion" and "feeling" interchangeably as this makes the most sense with regard to the analysis of the data at hand and the existing literature.[25]

Migration lends itself to an analysis connected with emotion, first, because it is another term connected to movement. "For a long time, emotions have been present in studies of migration, not least inherently in the language of belonging, homeliness, and displacement" (Walsh, 2009, p. 44). The multifaceted experiences of highly qualified migrants offer themselves to an analysis with an emphasis on emotions that goes beyond the recognition of its presence in language. Here, emotions are not seen as opposite to instrumental dimensions (e. g., economic theories of push and pull or brain drain vs. brain gain) and decisions, but as a complement or an additional aspect intersecting with all facets of migrants' experiences and ensuring a multidimensional analysis (Boccagni & Baldassar, 2015).

As mentioned, following John Leavitt (1996, p. 515 f.) and Maruška Svašek (2013, p. 69 f.), I look at emotions as complex everyday concepts that involve bodily as well as cultural dimensions. In other words, emotions are not only reactions to something; they are also produced by contexts such as cultures, nations, states, and the constraints put on one's subjective position within society. "[E]motions are biographical: primed by evolution to be sure; shaped by culture; constrained by subject position; but given personal relevance and intensity by individual history" (Beatty, 2014, p. 552).

During interviews on migration experiences, emotions play a crucial role as a way to describe and give meaning to experiences and express subjectivities. "[H]uman beings are fundamentally emotional beings, also when recalling life experiences and translating them into narrative performance" (Svašek, 2013, pp. 87–88). For example, it is common that interviewees use different levels of emotional intensity when reflecting on their experiences and telling their life stories, looking at some topics or periods in a neutral, straightforward manner, while becoming more emotional about other topics, for instance, expressing anger or frustration about some situations/memories of some situations (Svašek, 2013, p. 74).

It could additionally be said that the way highly skilled migrants make use of emotions to narrate and give meaning to their particular migration experiences and perceptions of a globalized world gives us the possibility to understand more about

---

24 Of course, "emotion" is also a term used in neurology, psychiatry, and psychology. In these disciplines, various definitions are used and emotions are usually looked at in connection with affective and cognitive processes (Kleinginna & Kleinginna, 1981; Niedenthal & Ric, 2017).

25 The term affect does not play a role in my analysis, as it has a strong neurological connotation (Plamper, 2012, p. 22) relating it to bodily reactions, something not observable in a qualitative interview setting or the other data used.

migration not only from the individual's perspective, but from a wider "cultural" or contextual one as well. Or, as Maruška Svašek (2013, p. 70) writes: "[R]estrictions and opportunities that limit or allow people's geographic mobility influence the content of their autobiographical accounts." Of course, as an anthropologist, I do not see individual stories as merely singular accounts, but as narratives that can be interpreted and contextualized, and, through this, can tell us a lot about humans and "cultures" (Beatty, 2014, p. 552; Fialkova & Yeleneskaya, 2007; Svašek, 2013, p. 70).

Talking about emotions as changeable and adaptable, or from a social constructivist perspective, leads to questions about the formation and position of the self. One could even say it becomes the superordinate category of the whole discussion (Plamper, 2012, p. 121), as it means one has to take into account the subjectivity and particularity of (narrated) feelings (Beatty, 2014; Svašek, 2013), in addition to contextualization within society. "Emotions might be third-person constructions, a collective product, but they are first-person experiences and not reducible to any of their ingredients. Their particularity is to do with their subjectivity, their me-focus" (Beatty, 2014, p. 551). Emotions are thus biographical, given meaning through individual stories (Beatty, 2014, p. 552), and an instrument to emphasize the meaning of such stories. Besides, in the case of this study, emotions also arise in the narratives due to the nature of the interviews. As the highly qualified migrants are asked to reflect on their lives and decisions, they also evaluate and justify their past (Svašek, 2013, p. 69) in a manner they perceive as acceptable during an interview with a stranger, who then interprets their story.[26]

This is why I take a multidimensional and processual view on emotions throughout the study and see them as a tool to better transmit the significance of migration experiences. Instead of trying to pinpoint exactly what emotion applies to exactly what formulation, transcript passage, or code, the aim is to understand how the emotions are used in the shared stories and narratives of identity, as well as what role they play in the other forms of data integrated in the study, such as fieldnotes and newspaper articles. Within the scope of this thesis, I use "emotions", therefore, as a lens through which I can grasp experiences of migration the same way my interview partners used them as a tool to better share their experiences in their narratives.

Throughout this, the guiding points were the following two important characteristics of emotions: firstly, particular/first-person experiences/self-referential or reflective, and secondly, biographical – while certain biological, historical, and cultural aspects structure them, they are still shaped by personal history and embedded

---

26 Emotion comes up in face-to-face contact more than in written contact – at least in Western societies (Plamper, 2012, pp. 134–135).

in interwoven lives (Beatty, 2014, pp. 551–552). This means that they represent two dimensions of experience: an inner dimension in the form of consciousness and an outer dimension in the form of lives and stories. Or, as Maruška Svašek (2010, p. 869) sees it, emotions can be seen as "discourses, practices and embodied experiences". Through this, emotions can be used to tell us something about the subjectivity within migration experiences (Svašek, 2005, 2006, 2008; Walsh, 2012).

In summary, while difficult to strictly define due to their processuality and multifariousness, emotions are still an ever-present phenomenon in migration narratives. Sometimes they are inherent in the language and themes (e. g., in topics of belonging and biography), other times they are directly expressed within narratives (e. g., when talking of happiness, hope, and regrets), or they are more hidden as reflections of subjectivities and constructions of identity (e. g., when talking about migrating as an adventure and form of self-fulfillment). I understand emotions as multifaceted processes which become visible in various ways through the narration of migration stories by highly skilled migrants and lead to a better understanding of the migratory self within specific contexts, thus helping to reduce the complexity of human experiences.

2.4 Approach and Methods

In this section I will discuss the approach and methods used for the study. I will explain what techniques were used to collect and analyze empirical data and why. There are always limitations to what a scientific study, such as the one conducted for this book, can and cannot achieve. Time is limited, as are available data and resources. There is logistically no way to include all aspects and interview all highly qualified migrants, as the topic itself is vast and multifaceted. The focus on emotions and migration meant that other questions, narratives, and aspects had to be left out, and the design of the study brings with it some delimitations which will be touched upon in this section too.

A qualitative approach consisting of a combination of interviews, fieldwork, including documenting conversations and observations, and the collection of additional contextual data such as newspaper articles and blog entries forms the data basis for this thesis. This comprehensive material was chosen in order to achieve a rich context for the final text. The approach of the study is influenced by various qualitative methods from a social constructivist tradition. The main influence is *grounded theory*, which I understand as a research style (Charmaz, 2000, 2006; Glaser & Strauss, 2008; Götzö, 2014; Strauss & Corbin, 1997) and adapted to my field, data, and topic accordingly. This means that empirical data was approached in an open manner with the goal of providing a dense picture and developing a (tentative) theory or new approach that is grounded in the collected data as a final step.

While literature on globalization, transnationalism, (highly skilled and qualified) migration, and emotions was being considered throughout the process and included as frame of reference, the starting point for the research was a general interest in the "exchange" of highly skilled migrants between Israel and Switzerland and the construal of meaning and subjectivity among these migrants, and not a specific theory or single starting point of truth. Already deciding on a fixed theoretical framework at the beginning of the research process would have been contradictory to the openness required by an approach in the sense of grounded theory.

2.4.1 Fieldwork and data collection

I carried out fieldwork in Israel and Switzerland from 2015 to 2018. During this time, I regularly visited Israel and lived in Switzerland. Some less systematically collected material from the time before and after the official conclusion of fieldwork was incorporated into the final text as well.

In the time frame, in which preparations and data collection took place, some events occurred that might have shaped perspectives on migration in the field and were discussed in interviews and conversations. As mentioned, there was a federal popular initiative "against mass immigration" in Switzerland in early 2014.[27] Later in the same year, the case of over 50 highly trained musicians from non-EU-states who were asked to leave Switzerland, some of them from Israel, led to discussions about migration laws and a petition.[28]

In summer 2014 a war broke out between Israel and Gaza (also known as Operation Protective Edge), delaying my first long-term stay in the field, and it became a topic I used systematically in interviews to learn more about interviewees' experiences and perceptions. While I was in Tel Aviv in March 2015, the elections for the twentieth Knesset took place, which was won by the conservative party Likud and Prime Minister Benjamin Netanyahu. This event was highly emotional and made many of the more left-leaning people I met in the field feel hopeless for the future of the country, for instance, making some Swiss in Israel reconsider if they should move back to Switzerland or another country.

---

27 The results of the vote were published on February 9, 2014. For further information see René Zeller (2014, February 10) in the newspaper NZZ.

28 The musicians were ordered to leave Switzerland due to visa issues, mainly due to not having fixed employment and being freelancers. Apparently, the visas some of them were issued by the responsible authorities were illegal, due to not having fixed employment. Some of the people affected had been living in Basel for many years. For news reports, see e. g.: Peter Bollag (2014, November 24), Yaël Debelle (2015, May 11), taz (2014, December 19).

From 2015 to 2018 I conducted twelve long semi-structured biographical interviews, several additional shorter interviews and informal, unstructured conversations during fieldwork, visited events related to the research project (for example embassy functions and meetings and presentations organized by the *Chamber of Commerce Switzerland-Israel*), spent several months in Israel (the longest stay was for three months at a stretch, other stays lasted one to two weeks), and collected data related to the research topic from various media sources, such as newspaper articles, blog entries, and radio programs.

Sampling for the project was purposeful. I specifically looked for highly qualified and skilled migrants (for a discussion of the term see section 2.3.1) from Israel who moved to Switzerland and vice versa through various channels. I accepted self-definitions as "(highly) skilled migrant" from informants reacting to my call for participants as I wanted to avoid becoming the normative instance deciding who is highly qualified or highly skilled and who is not. This ensured that I met a diverse group of people in terms of age and profession (for example, not all informants are in the science and technology sector, as the OECD's original definition proposes). It also means that in terms of qualification and current profession, some informants would probably fit into the description of "highly skilled", while others are "skilled".[29] In terms of qualification, all participants did have at least a bachelor's degree, but not all of them work in the field of their original degree. The purposeful sample was explicitly decided on because, as mentioned above, I wanted to ensure a diverse range of age, profession, qualification or skills, and locality and consequently chose interview partners accordingly to reflect the heterogenous profile of highly skilled migrants. The heterogenous profiles of the protagonists reflect the complexity of the term "highly skilled".

Interviewees were chosen when they fit the profile or self-defined as highly skilled or highly qualified, and when their main motivation for the transnational move was professional, though, as will be discussed later, the motivation for the move was often a mix of several factors. The fact that none of the Israeli interviewees were non-Jewish (though some are non-religious) was not deliberate. It might have to do with the channels used to contact participants. Participants were either Swiss, Israeli, or Swiss-Israeli dual citizens. Some had additional passports. While being aware that it can be seen as restrictive to choose such a framework (see section 2.1.3 for a discussion of methodological nationalism), I argue that using specific nation-spaces and specific groups based on nationality can be a useful containment as long as one asks relevant questions and stays open during analysis to thinking across and beyond those containments. Additionally, as mentioned earlier, due to their political structure, Israel and Switzerland do provide very specific frameworks and

---

29 I sometimes use the terms interchangeably in the text for simplicity.

circumstances. So while this is not a research project about a confined locality such as Israel or Switzerland but rather a project about specific protagonists in these places (Geertz, 1964, p. 32), the particular context and circumstances of the two countries always played an indirect role and should not be disregarded.

Participants were found through an existing contact list from the *Institute of Cultural Anthropology and European Ethnology* at the *University of Basel*.[30] In addition, social media, especially *Facebook* groups, proved to be useful for finding interviewees and contacts. I posted calls for participants (see appendix B) in the *Facebook* groups "Austrians, Germans and Swiss in Israel" as well as "Israelis in Switzerland" and "Israeli Women in Switzerland", which led to several people contacting me, though not all of them were available for a formal interview. Other interviewees were found through personal contacts: one person in particular, a highly qualified Israeli-Swiss friend of a colleague, served as a gatekeeper and informant. Another originally planned strategy to contact multinational firms such as *Hoffman-La Roche* or *Novartis Pharmaceuticals* in Basel to distribute the call for participants proved less useful. Alternatively, I tried to find interviewees working there through private contacts, however, I was not able to gain access for actual full interviews.[31]

In Switzerland interviews took place in the German-speaking regions of Basel, Bern, and Zurich. In Israel interviews took place in the cities of Tel Aviv, Haifa, Jerusalem, and their surroundings. While in Switzerland it would have been interesting to find interviewees in the metropolitan area of Geneva or Lausanne, none were available. This limited choice is partly related to the fact that highly qualified migrants are usually residing in urban, economically strong areas of a country due to their jobs and partly due to accessibility and availability of interview partners.

Interviews took place in cafés, in my university office or at people's places of work, or homes and were carried out in German, Swiss German,[32] French, and English. While I did learn Hebrew during the study, my knowledge was not comprehensive enough to complete a whole interview in the language. This is relevant, as it means that in some cases, interviews and conversations were in neither my

---

30 The list had been used before for a student excursion to Israel, where several Swiss people living in Israel were contacted in order to talk about their experiences and provide information to the students.

31 This might have been due to timing or luck. In one case, for example, the potential interviewee from *Roche* ended up being too busy to meet me for the interview, and we only had a short talk on the phone. In another case I only had contact information of the partner of a highly qualified Israeli researcher working for *Novartis*, who did not call me back after asking me to send them the call for participants to forward to their partner.

32 I do not speak Swiss German, but some interview partners found it easier to answer my questions in Swiss German.

nor the interviewees mother tongue. While everyone spoke English very well and regularly due to their professional context and education, it sometimes might have made it more complicated to express thoughts and emotions and influenced the overall atmosphere of the interview. The long interviews were semi-structured by an interview guide containing the main themes in the form of central issues or stimuli. These consisted of 1. A biographical section asking about the story of the move or relocation, 2. Questions about professional skills, outcomes, and transnational activities, 3. An ethnographical section asking about the impact of surroundings and frameworks (see appendix C and D).

The overall guiding qualitative, biographical approach (Picard, 2014) to the interviews meant that interviewees were sometimes very moved or affected by the unfolding narrative of their own biography (Svašek, 2013, p. 74). This situation, which led to an exchange between interviewee and the interviewer, does not only happen with words, but also with expressions of laughter or surprise and affirmations of empathy through nodding or various fillers.

Before the qualitative interview was started, interviewees were asked to fill out a basic questionnaire (see appendix E) in order to collect general information on age, education, and other overall biographical data. This proved useful for two reasons: a) it added another kind of material to the data and b) it was an "easy" interview start for the participants and provided information that could be integrated into the narrative interview that followed. Long interviews lasted between 1.5 and 3 hours. Directly after each interview I took notes on my impressions and thoughts as a way to document first reflections on the collected data.

Towards the end of the data collection phase, I additionally interviewed an expert to add a meta-perspective to the study. I met Professor Dr. David Horn,[33] a physicist and member of several committees for international research infrastructure at *Tel Aviv University* to talk about his committee work, Israelis abroad, and the Israeli state-sponsored return program. Prof. Dr. David Horn is the chairman of the advisory committee for research infrastructures of Israel and was part of the *European Strategy Forum on Research Infrastructure/ESFRI*,[34] which is developing a strategy to improve the European research infrastructures and its connections abroad, for example with Israel. During the interview he not only talked about Israel as a research site but his own emigration and return as well: He worked in university administration and was the *Israeli Liaison Officer* at the *European Organization for Nuclear Research/CERN*[35] in Geneva, Switzerland during the 1990s. The interview

---

33 For more information about Prof. Dr. David Horn and about projects on research infrastructures see: http://horn.tau.ac.il, accessed: September 5, 2023.
34 For more information on ESFRI see: https://www.esfri.eu, accessed: September 5, 2023.
35 Israel is the only non-European country with full membership of CERN. For more information on CERN see: https://home.cern, accessed: August 11, 2023.

confirmed the main result of the study, namely the significant role of emotions in migration biographies located in Switzerland and Israel.

2.4.2 Data analysis

Besides the transcripts of the twelve long qualitative interviews, the expert interview and shorter interviews and conversations, additional material consisted of media publications (mainly newspaper articles and blogposts), fieldnotes (on observations and conversations as well as visited events), as well as my research diary entries. In order to approach the data, I coded it in a pragmatic and intuitive manner according to grounded theory guidelines and the guiding principle that "[T]he idea in coding is to link what the respondent says in his or her interview to the concepts and categories that will appear in the report" (Weiss, 1994, p. 154).

Coding took place in several stages. After a cursory first reading of the transcripts and notes or "open coding" to identify recurring themes and formulations, later coding and analyses were more focused. First, external codes based on the central issues of the interview guide and corresponding subcodes were created (such as "migration strategy" or "expectations concerning migration"). However, as the first readings had revealed the broad recuring theme of "emotions" within the language and focal points of the narratives, additional internal codes were developed, which specifically focused on emotions related to a topic (such as "feelings of home" or "feelings of freedom"). In further readings I thus put a stronger emphasis on emotions – while attempting to stay as open as possible, consequently without "searching" for emotions or looking at emotions as the only possible narrative – as they emerged in interview narratives and conversation fieldnotes. Through this approach, I developed the main themes or feeling categories of belonging; nostalgia, irritation, expectation; and going abroad as an accomplishment, as discussed below.

Emotions were not something I specifically looked for in the early stages of the project or analysis. The discovery of them being a common theme was quite surprising, as I had naively assumed my interview partners would be more "neutral" when talking about their professional biography and migration experiences due to them being relatively privileged migrants, seemingly detached from local space. This made the decision to focus on emotions as a main theme even more interesting.

The results rely on my interpretation of the emotions of others as I found them through analyzing transcripts and notes, as is done in other projects on emotions (e. g., Leavitt, 1996, pp. 514–518; Walsh, 2012, p. 46). Sometimes the emotions are explicit (for example, when talking about a specific feeling such as hope or anger), while other times they are more subtle (for example, expressed through intonation of speech or abrupt endings of a sentence). Other times the narratives show equivocal signs that still shape the migrants' subjectivity and migration experience or more than one emotion at once. Something similar was discovered by Katie

Walsh (2012, p. 47) in her research on British transnationals in Dubai when she talks about the "mixed emotions" shown by her interviewees.

As suggested by Katie Walsh (2012, p. 47), my approach to emotions during the analysis was one where I did not only rely on "people naming or claiming particular emotions" in their speech acts, but also my interpretation of "emotional performances" during interviews and fieldwork. Individual emotions (such as "happy" or "sad") were not used as codes or categories during the analysis and not specifically looked for, as they are too diffuse and processual for that.

Overall, as is often the case with qualitative studies, the process of analysis was circular instead of linear, with a lot of going back and forth between my own material and literature, and several readings of transcripts and notes, as well as making continuous changes to the final report. While the sample of main interviewees is small, we can learn a lot about a topic from individual stories and "main characters" or "protagonists" of a study (Fialkova & Yelenevskaya, 2007; Svašek, 2013). Additional shorter interviews, conversations and other materials were used to weave a rich picture out of various fragments of information in order to provide a dense and diverse story. This study can thus provide a snapshot of the lives of highly qualified migrants from Israel in Switzerland and vice versa that is contextualized in a broader context of globalization and transnationalism. As a qualitative study it remains an interpretation of the topic by the storytellers and me without claiming to represent all highly skilled migrants from Israel or Switzerland.

2.4.3 The researcher's position in the field

As anthropologists working on the interpretation of other's experiences, we talk about the emotions of others, making inferences on their feelings and actions. "The roles qualitative investigators play are not strictly and exclusively of their own choosing. The mistaken belief that the researcher's role is unmitigated by those whom he or she studies, remains the positivist's unachievable hope" (Mitchell, 1993, p. 12). Qualitative interpretation is always a complex endeavor, where it is important to be reflexive (Leavitt, 1996, pp. 514–517) and aware of one's own emotions, assumptions, and biases as well.

Within a broader research field this project should be positioned as a migration study with a focus on the emotions of highly skilled/qualified migrants. This focus does not negate the fact that emotions are not the only important aspect one can find in migration stories, which are always complex narratives consisting of various elements. The study is not what could be called a traditional "ethnography of emotions" in which a crucial part of the material consists of "ethnological soul-searching" (Plamper, 2012, p. 111). Emotions and the researcher's subjectivity while doing fieldwork have become their own subject of study within anthropology, working with various layers of self-reflexivity (Massmünster, 2014; Plamper, 2012, p. 136).

During the research process emotions came up not only in others' narratives, but also as my own emotions in research situations. Being a migrant myself might have deepened my empathy for the stories of my interviewees (Svašek, 2013, p. 70) and undoubtedly shaped my perspective. However, it might possibly have prevented me from asking some questions due to having presumptions or biases. It certainly put me in a specific role of empathizing strongly with my interviewees and always being able to create a quick first connection on the basis of transnational biographies and migration experiences.

As a way to create rapport, I often used my own migration biography to confirm my understanding of the experience or shared a similar experience of my own. I did not use this personal migration experience to systematically shape each of the interviews, but used it when it seemed appropriate, sometimes in the very beginning, other times as a way to keep the interview flowing, or as a manner to provide a break to the interviewees when it seemed necessary, such as after an emotionally complex passage or when I believed they held back with their honest opinion because they thought I might not be able to understand their experience (for example, feelings of detachment from the country one lives in or irritations about Israel or Switzerland).

I identified with many things my interviewees told me. This is good: the emic perspective cultural anthropologists like to create through participant observation came naturally. However, this can also be something of an obstruction because, while I was careful and self-conscious, it still might have led to me assuming a lot of things or stopping me from pursuing explanations of issues I saw as self-evident at the time of the interview.

Throughout the research my own position in the field oscillated between familiarity – my own transnational experiences and multi-sited biography, myself being, in a way, a highly qualified migrant, or at least an "international student" – and detachment – and my irritations with my research fields of both Israel and Switzerland. One entry about my connections to my research fields reads:

Even though I lived in Switzerland for several years and feel local in Basel, I'm not sure how long I will stay here. My stay is very connected to my work. Almost like an expat or some of the protagonists of my study. Am I a "migrant"? I do live and work here, I have an apartment, I have friends, a daily life. Still, my status in Switzerland is somewhat temporary. Not only on an emotional level, also on a legal level. My being here is tied to my employment and my status as a PhD researcher and I have to renew my residence permit once a year. Like some of my interview subjects, I am a "typical" highly qualified migrant in the sense that I am here because of my job, that this is a temporary affair, that I will quite possibly leave

> again at some point – to another place, to another job, to another place for a few years. Still, I do have a long-term connection to Basel. Partly growing up across the border in Alsace, I have known Basel since being a child. I also speak German and understand Basel-German. So, Basel was never completely foreign.
>
> In Israel, things are much clearer in that I am an obvious outsider. I'm non-Israeli and non-Jewish. My Hebrew is basic. Additionally, my status as researcher makes the temporality of my stay obvious. I'm a visitor. A visitor who participates in daily life, but a visitor, nonetheless. I have a snapshot view of Israel. I was never there during a war, but during the first visit, from my Western European perspective, the numerous security controls and visible weapons were a constant reminder that "the conflict" is there, that "something could happen" anytime. In a way, this was the most striking aspect, as it was so unfamiliar. After several visits, the security controls and weapons didn't bug me anymore. I got used to them quickly. They are part of daily life there. Even the notoriously harsh airport security controls don't shock me anymore. I understand. But mainly: been there – done that.[36]

While not a typical ethnography where self-reflexive material is part of the design, my own emotions and migration story and possible biases should not be concealed. In a contemporary anthropological qualitative study, self-positioning is relevant in the name of transparency (Erez, 2013; Flick, 2011, p. 29; Said, 1995). In order to be aware of and systematic about this I used a research diary throughout the research process.

2.5 Conclusion and Outlook: Swiss in Israel and Israelis in Switzerland

In this chapter I provided some contextualization of the research project on a global, local, theoretical, and methodological level. I discussed why globalization and transnationalism are important concepts for this research, as well as provided concise economic, political, and social descriptions of the two research fields, Israel and Switzerland. In order to understand the realities of highly skilled and skilled migrants and the meaning of emotions in their narratives, it is necessary to understand the context and daily life of these individuals.

As described, globalization as an empirical reality shapes today's world. One of the many processes of globalization is the transnational mobility of skilled individuals. These migrants take part in a global job market and often have the privilege to move across borders easily. For a long time, this group of migrants was left out of research on migration, which mainly focused on push and pull factors and unskilled labor migration. Only in the past years was the field widened and there has been more

---

36 Excerpt from fieldnote entry Summer 2018. The text has been shortened and edited for clarity.

research on highly qualified or skilled migration. While there have been studies on Israelis in Germany and Swiss living abroad, there has not been a case study on Swiss in Israel and Israelis in Switzerland like the present one. While the number of Swiss and Israelis abroad is small, these migrants deserve attention. Additionally, Israel and Switzerland provide interesting frameworks due to their political and historical profiles.

Empirical data was analyzed and contextualized according to the research field, and was "translated" and brought together to discuss the topic of emotions in migration narratives. The focus on emotions emerged out of the material. As argued earlier, a better understanding of the complexities of human mobility necessitates a focus on emotions, as they are a central aspect of transnational migration experiences (Svašek, 2010, pp. 867–868). "[E]motions are unified *experiences*; and this subjective unity, which bears heavily on social processes, is due to their conceptual or narrative structure as construals of personal situations. … Our job [as anthropologists] is to get the experience right and to work out its significance in the stream of life – to recover the imponderabilia" (Beatty, 2014, p. 559).

This recovering of imponderabilia is what is attempted in this thesis, using emotions in various ways to better understand the self and subjectivity of highly skilled Swiss in Israel and highly skilled Israelis in Switzerland. As discussed, in interview narratives, such as in reality, emotions are often mixed, interlinked, and related. They can be integral in the language used and topics chosen, directly expressed within narratives, and specific reflections or interpretations of subjectivities and constructions of identity. However, in order to present the results in a more structured manner, the following chapters are divided into sections along the lines of specific emotions and corresponding themes of a) belonging, b) nostalgia, irritation, and expectation and c) narratives of identity and accomplishment connected to going abroad and staying on the move. Before these themes are discussed in detail, the twelve main protagonists of the research project are presented.

3. Ethnographic Portraits

Keeping in mind that: "[E]motions are particular or they are nothing" (Beatty, 2014, p. 551) selected characters, or using another term, the main exemplary protagonists of the research project are now presented. Portraits of main informants[37] whom I met for biographic interviews are given below. All stories have their individualities and different profiles, as they were chosen to reflect variations in narratives of skilled and highly skilled migration. Yet, there are also some similarities and common themes found in other stories and literature on highly skilled migrants.

It is important to note that none of these interview partners had any issues with their visa or migrant status and could probably be seen as middle class in terms of income and habitus. All of them moved for either professional or educational purposes or due to a combination of professional or educational purposes and personal relationships such as their spouse being from the country to which they moved. Interestingly, the similarities in the emotions and experiences revealed in the stories cannot be reduced to single categories like nationality, gender, education, or age. This does not mean that similarities and common themes are not found at the level of skills, professional field, or experiences as well. None of the individuals were completely detached from their local space, but some lived in a highly skilled professional "bubble" that might be very similar to the ones existing in any other country. In their narratives, the informants give meaning to their biographies through use and emphasis of various emotions, and narrate their individual, successful self.

3.1 Swiss in Israel

Simon

This protagonist was highly skilled. He was in his mid-60s, a Swiss-Israeli citizen and had been living in Israel for over 30 years. He had an international academic career, taught at several European and North American universities and was a tenured professor at a large Israeli university. He and his wife lived in a town house, and I interviewed him at his home office full of books and papers, a professor's office just as one imagines it. He was passionate about his work, but described himself as very pessimistic in his views on Israel and its future. During the interview he made it repeatedly clear that he did not move to the country due to any ideological or

---

37 The names of the protagonists are pseudonyms, personal details have been anonymized.

Zionist notions, but because his former spouse wanted to live there. He was mainly interested in a position at a university with a good department in his field.

He made a strong distinction between Israeli Jewish culture and the liberal Eastern European/Swiss Jewish culture with which he grew up, for instance, saying that while he might have gone to the synagogue on high holidays in Switzerland, he never did so in Israel as he always remained a foreigner or stranger here. A similar feeling was expressed by Doron, a skilled Israeli in Switzerland. Simon stated very clearly that he did not perceive himself as living "in Israel" but in a convenient academic bubble (he calls it a *"Hochschul Ghetto"* in German, meaning "university ghetto") while the rest of the country remained foreign and exotic. He and his wife had an apartment in Switzerland and he also continued to pay into the Swiss pension system,[38] thus keeping various personal and financial ties to the country.

Hannah

Hannah was in her late 20s and worked in museum management while doing her master's degree part time. She was additionally planning to start a small business with her husband. She speaks four languages and moved to Israel several years ago after she met her Israeli husband in Switzerland. She had decided to move abroad to study after high school at a young age but in the end the decision fell on Israel as a combination of meeting her future husband and wanting to leave Switzerland, at least for a while. I interviewed her at her workplace, a beautiful small museum.

Being from a Swiss Jewish family, she already knew Israel from previous visits and spoke some Hebrew before moving there. Still, she, at first, did not make her *Aliyah* but moved to Israel with a student visa. For her, the move to Israel led to what she saw as more freedom as a woman and in her career than she would have experienced had she stayed in Switzerland. She described the Swiss middle-class female biography as very straightforward with few possibilities for individual, creative career development and was sure her professional life would look extremely different right now if she had not gone abroad. The impact of migration on gender roles is a topic discussed in literature. Some women are enabled to attain greater agency and power through employment-related mobility. Even if they work in low-paying, precarious fields that reproduce gender hierarchies, many migrant women

---

38 The Swiss pension system consists of three main pillars. The first is the basic state "Old Age and Survivor's Insurance" (*OASI*), or *AHV/AVS* in German/French. The second pillar is based on obligatory company pension schemes. The third pillar is based on occupational pensions and private investment schemes. Contributions and paybacks from the *OASI/AHV* are related to being a resident of Switzerland. However, Swiss abroad can contribute voluntarily or make private investments, which many people choose to do. For more information see: https://www.ahv-iv.ch/en/Social-insurances, accessed: August 9, 2023.

are also able to put these gender norms in question and to overcome contradictions (Morokvasic, 2007).

Gabriele

The initial contact Gabriele and I had was on social media, and she messaged me that she had led an "eventful life" and had lived in Israel since the 1980s. She was a skilled migrant in her late 50s and we met at a small French café in a hip part of Tel Aviv. Her husband is Israeli, and she had lived in the country for over 30 years. Her professional biography includes several major changes and transitions. She has a professional M.A. degree and was currently self-employed in the tourism sector. Prior to that she worked in the high-tech sector for many years and originally, she studied a social discipline and was a teacher. She described her years working in the high-tech sector as varied and challenging but after a near burnout, decided to change industries.

Interestingly, in this story, the informant defined herself as a migrant in the sense that she repeatedly mentions "*migrating being hard*" and how learning Hebrew and studying at an Israeli university helped her integrate into a society that constantly saw and treated her as a tourist upon her arrival. In a way, she consequently reproduced a traditional view on migration as leaving one's country of origin to completely settle into a new country and society. In the course of her story, however, she challenged this perspective and made it clear how processual and complicated the notion of "integration" is. Her work in tourism made her feel especially "de-integrated" as she now dealt mostly with foreigners in her daily life and revisited Israel as a tourist. She planned on buying a vacation house in Switzerland for herself and her family in retirement in order to occasionally escape Israeli summer heat.

Matt

Matt lived in a southern city with his wife and children, and we met during his lunch break. He was a skilled migrant in his 30s. He started working at a school recently, but used to work in high-tech and the private sector before that. The career change to education was partially an ideological one in that he sees it as his contribution to society and a way to teach tolerance. This came up when I asked him about his views on the future of Israel, and he told me that he sees himself as rather conservative and that for him, the only solution for peace lies in learning to live together and in strengthening moderate views instead of radicalism on all sides. The war and conflict researcher Stacey Gutkowski (2019) calls this approach of emphasizing moderateness and rationality an "emotio-political antidote".[39]

Matt grew up in a large Swiss city in a multicultural and multilingual environment. He knew Israel from yearly summer holidays before moving there. While the reasons for moving to Israel are multifaceted and his career was part of it, it became clear in the course of the interview that the move was also related to his Jewish identity (he made his *Aliyah*). He told me that he liked that being Jewish is nothing special in Israel (a feeling related by other Swiss Jews who moved to Israel as interviewed by Sabina Bossert, 2009) and recounted anti-Semitic experiences during his school years in Switzerland as the beginning of the wish to emigrate to Israel. While his extended family was secular, he is religious and after attending a religious school in Israel for a year, he confirmed his plan and decision to one day emigrate to Israel. He did this after finishing university and working in Switzerland for a few years. For him, going abroad was always connected to Israel specifically as a long-term strategy and a way to explore his religiousness in a deeper fashion.

While he complained about Israeli bureaucracy and how he had to get used to the fast pace and stress of daily Israeli life, he enjoys Israel and is still very happy about his move, which took place about five years before our meeting. His Swiss family and friends are often worried about him due to the political situation. He was the only protagonist who moved to Israel due to explicitly ideological reasons, which came up during the interview and was not as clear in the preliminary exchange.

Susanna

I met Susanna at her home in an Israeli city. During the interview we sat on a cozy couch in her living room. She had prepared snacks and something to drink, and told me about how she "landed" in Israel in a humorous manner. She was in her late 40s and, while she was originally a scientist, she now worked in a high position at a library. She had lived in Israel for about 20 years. In her narrative she often talked about the history of Israel and Switzerland, and related her biography and family history to certain events in (Swiss) Jewish history. Some of these details and events were unknown to me and I did not always immediately understand her references, for example, to certain families and their origins and history.

She initially came to Israel in her university years for graduate school, but, in the end, her decision to stay in Israel was a deeply personal one. She framed it with the help of childhood memories and family history, and strongly related it to an intangible feeling of being at home. After travelling to Israel with a good

---

39 The political formula was suggested by Amos Oz in a 2002 lecture titled "How to Cure a Fanatic" and while it resonates particularly with *hilonim*, secular Jews, it also resonates with Jewish Israelis of the center and the right (Gutkowski, 2019, p. 123).

friend as a young adult, having been there the last time as a child, she walked down the airplane stairs and thought, "*Wow, I'm here!*" She laughed about herself when recounting this story, as she said she is usually a highly rational person who did not give into such kinds of esoteric experience or gut feelings. While she is Jewish, she only decided to make her *Aliyah* after over one year in Israel and mainly because she wanted to be able to participate politically. She said that she enjoys living in Israel but is open to moving to another country if an interesting opportunity arises.

Margot

I met Margot in a café in a suburb of her hometown, where she went regularly with her laptop to get some work done. Margot worked in the high-tech industry and communications for many years, but decided to become a freelancer in order to have more flexible hours as she had small children. She has lived in Israel for over ten years, is married to an Israeli, and aside from voluntarily contributing to the Swiss pension system and regular visits, she is very settled in Israel and does not plan on moving again. Like Hannah and Gabriele, she saw her move to Israel as bringing her more freedom, flexibility, and choice than she would have had, had she stayed in Switzerland, for instance, in terms of starting her own business and being able to work while also being a mother.

Margot's story about her move to Israel was closely related to her family story in that she found out that her father was Jewish more or less by accident as he had not talked about his childhood to her. She tried to discover more about her family story through talking to relatives and organizations and found out about her Eastern European Jewish ancestry. After completing her first university degree she travelled to Israel with a friend, where she was able to meet a distantly related aunt; this was a pivotal experience for her as she immediately felt a strong sense of family and belonging. She went back to Switzerland and worked there for a while, but then ended up deciding to move to Israel for a second degree after a relationship with an Israeli boyfriend and another visit. Within a month she had moved there and stayed.

3.2   Israelis in Switzerland

Alexander

This protagonist was a highly skilled migrant in a leading position of an international organization which has its main office in Switzerland. He moved to Switzerland about a year before we met for the interview. Switzerland was a chance destination, as the key reason for the move was the position (as is the case for other Israelis I met in similar positions in Switzerland). Before this he worked in the private sector for large international firms and, originally, he started his career as a scientist. Before moving to Switzerland, he and his family lived in the United States. His wife stayed there and came to visit, or they met in Israel. Their children lived in Israel and the United States respectively. He was in his mid-50s, and his biography was typical for a highly skilled transnational migrant as he moved from Israel to the United States for graduate school and later moved several times within the United States due to work. He is an Israeli-American citizen.

The interview was very comprehensive, and he offered me a lot of his time, while being an open and reflective interview partner. We met in a coffee shop at a Swiss airport, which seems fitting for an interview with a highly skilled migrant – a transitional space, for someone with a multi-sited biography and a transnational life. Thomas Hylland Eriksen (1992, p. 2) argues that airports can have their own cultures but are also "intermediate nodes", which connect societies by "virtue of not belonging to the societies themselves" (especially their transit lounges, can be seen as non-lieu, or non-places (based on Augé, 1992, see also Coleman, 2007)).

Alexander lived in a sort of bubble within Switzerland – his apartment was provided by the institution that hired him, his direct neighbor worked with him, his work life took place in English and includes international travel and meetings, his private life took place mainly outside of Switzerland, and he only moved to the country due to the opportunity of this particular position he holds. He described his ties to Israel and the United States as stronger than the ties he has to Switzerland and while he left Israel very consciously in order to "*take a break*" from there, he now would take a similar position to the one he has in Switzerland immediately, if it were offered to him in Israel.

Rhea

Rhea was an academic in her mid-30s. She and her husband have young children and moved to Switzerland for work. Her husband, a scientist, was offered a job, which prompted them to move and made her look for a job herself. They had been in Switzerland for about two years when I met her for the interview. We met in a café at a major train station, another transitional space, for a story of transnationalism. Her answers were particularly reflective and detailed, which made for an interesting and rich interview.

She was a leftwing political activist, a topic she talked about passionately. While she described her family's stay in Switzerland as the realization of a long-term plan of living abroad for a while due to professional reasons for herself and her husband, as well as a much-needed break from Israeli politics, she felt very conflicted about having abandoned Israel. This notion of abandoning Israel, while coming from a liberal and leftwing person in this case, is also reflected in Zionist discourses about brain drain (for example: Alexander/Haaretz, 2014, 2015; Peretz/Haaretz, 2016 and footnote 15 on p. 29).

Being abroad restrained her possibilities for being politically active and might mean that the Israeli identity of her children will become less important for them, something she struggled with. Raising her children in Switzerland consequently created an internal conflict. On the one hand, her children were safer in Switzerland, on the other hand they seemed happier and freer in Israel. This conflict was something she had not been able to resolve, and we touched upon this several times during in the interview. It is repeated in conversations about childhood memories with others as well.

Daniel

This protagonist was an Israeli scientist in his late 20s. He had lived in Switzerland for less than a year when we met. Before this move to Switzerland, he lived in another European country. His wife was from Europe and leaving Israel to go abroad was due to a combination of love and career opportunities for the both of them. We met at his university office. He replied to my call for participants, but immediately told me he was not sure he actually migrated. This shows the issue mentioned earlier: that many migrants, especially highly skilled ones, do not see themselves (or are not perceived as such by others) as migrants but as transnational citizens or as cosmopolitans (Friedman, 2017; Hannerz, 2002), or describe migration simply as "going abroad" (Hage, 2005) or a relocation.

While the interview itself took place in an agreeable atmosphere, it was sometimes hard to find out what exactly Daniel thought about a topic. Questions were often taken very literally and thus answered concisely by him. Overall, his story highlights how for young skilled people one international move often leads to another international move (Kōu & Bailey, 2014) and how identities are not always linked with one locality but can be transnational or multi-sited. Moving becomes a manner in which one can find professional self-fulfillment and personal adventure. Daniel did not plan to move back to Israel, unless specific circumstances forced him to do so. Instead, he preferred to move to another country in a few years, to experience another place. Like Simon, he reflected on the fact that he lived in an academic bubble and both he and his (also highly qualified) wife had professions that allowed them to move freely within a global job market, which is something they would have liked to take advantage of.

Doron

Doron, a skilled Israeli migrant living in Switzerland, moved due to a mixture of love and professional development. We met in a coffeeshop in the city center. His story resembled Gabriele's in the sense that he framed it in a way that he was a successful migrant, learning the language, liking the country, and, in the end, remarked how he is going to integrate better and better over the years, even though he did not believe that he could ever fully "integrate". When I asked him about his future as a last interview question, he reflected on how he will always stay a stranger in Switzerland. He met his Swiss wife and abroad while travelling. They lived in Israel for a few months but, in the end, decided to get married,[40] settling in Switzerland, and had been there for somewhat over two years at the time of the interview.

Doron related his contentment with being in Switzerland to his own personality which he saw as more suited to Swiss mentality than to Israeli mentality, which is faster and more stressful. And while Israel is "*always an option*" it was not something he and his wife were considering at the moment because he would prefer to stay in Switzerland. Transnationalism in this migration story is much less prominent than in other stories, at least as an activity or part of an identity. One moves once and then stays. Currently he and his wife did not plan to move and a third country was not an option they seriously discussed as they preferred that at least one of them has family and friends close by.

Isabella

Isabella was an artist and educator in her early 30s who grew up in Switzerland, lived in Israel for several years and recently moved back to Switzerland. She is an Israeli-Swiss dual citizen by birth. The recent experience of moving back to Switzerland after having been away for almost ten years was something of a culture shock for her. At the same time, being in Israel made her notice her "Swissness" very strongly. She went to Israel for her art studies, as she felt that Switzerland was a place that blocked her creativity. She had a unique profile in the group of protagonists due to her dual citizenship by birth, as she was neither a migrant in Israel nor is she one in Switzerland. Nevertheless, she described both moves (from Switzerland to Israel and back to Switzerland) the same way as others talked about migration. In addition, she described her move to Israel to attend university as a way of finding or confirming her identity.

We met on a strangely cool and windy June day in a popular café in a city area with a high migrant population. She told me she was a bit tired but, after a while, we found a good interview rhythm. The main theme throughout the interview was her struggle to find an identity or space within which she could include her Swiss and her Israeli worlds, something she also worked on in her art. We extensively talked about the feeling of homesickness, a condition originally seen as an illness

---

40 Interfaith marriage is not possible in Israel, as mentioned earlier in the text, as there is no arrangement for civil marriage (Burton, 2015).

mainly associated with Swiss soldiers stationed abroad and famously discussed by Karl Jaspers (1996, original 1909) in his dissertation, but often analyzed from an anthropological and literature or cultural studies perspective, for example, by Simon Bunke (2006).

Jacob

Jacob studied business and was a journalist and educator in his 30s. He is Israeli, but, before moving to Switzerland, he and his wife lived in another European country. His (also highly skilled) wife found a job in Switzerland first, and he worked in the pharmaceutical industry at the time of the interview. He additionally worked as a journalist and was currently in a transitional phase, about to start a new job. Jacob already lived in Switzerland for a few years as a child, giving him a view of Switzerland, where he often compared the country's current state to past memories. According to him, these memories and his knowledge of Switzerland also meant he quickly felt at home, especially as he speaks some Swiss German and knew his way around.

Like Doron, he argued that his character fitted in better to Switzerland than it did to Israel in many respects, framing the move as a positive personal decision. However, he still missed Israeli flexibility and creativity; he also remarked that in Switzerland, emotions are less important than in Israel, as individuals in Switzerland are seen as carriers of skills and knowledge. While living a secular life in Israel, the move abroad and living with his more traditional wife changed this. He was the only interview partner who reflects on a strong change in his personal religiosity through the move to another country.

3.3 Conclusion and Outlook: Twelve Protagonists in two Places

These main exemplary protagonists are at the heart of the study and were chosen to better illustrate the importance of specific stories and variations for the following analysis of the connectivity, use, and meaning of emotions in migration narratives, while considering the frameworks or localities of Israel and Switzerland and how they are part of the told stories. The protagonists additionally reflect the diversity of trajectories amongst highly skilled migrants.

During interviews and conversations, the individuals had an opportunity to share their life stories and experiences, which created a reconstruction of memories, decisions, and events. These reconstructions are not only about the past but also reflect the present in which they are told. Within a story, occurrences are given meaning and purpose, sometimes retrospectively, sometimes forward looking. For migrants (as well as non-migrants), storytelling it is a way of making sense of "their (sometimes ruptured) lives" (Svašek, 2013, p. 72). During interviews, "… interviewees tend to move between descriptive, argumentative, and reflective narration, and may 'work through' confusing life events, as they try to unravel and understand earlier experiences" (Svašek, 2013, pp. 73–74).

This "unraveling" in turn leads to various situations in which emotions are either highlighted or used as way of telling a story in a convincing and sequential manner in the present. While telling the story, events are remembered, re-experienced, interpreted, and evaluated. New emotions can emerge through the narration as well. This biographical construal of meaning achieved through the use of emotions in narratives can tell us more about the realities of highly skilled migrants, as we learn about their construction of a self, as well as their perceptions of the frameworks of Israel and Switzerland as places of living and within the world. This will be explored in the following chapters, focusing on the main (narrated, experienced, reflected on or constructed) feelings of a) belonging; b) nostalgia, irritation, and expectation; and c) accomplishment connected with going abroad or staying on the move, that are part of the (one could say) "multi-sited" biographies and migration stories of the protagonists.

4. Narratives of Belonging in Multi-Sited Biographies

In this section I will focus on emotional dimensions of belonging in a detailed manner and discuss the ways this feeling and the discourses surrounding it play a role in the lives of skilled and highly skilled migrants. The transnational life of migrants can lead to narratives of what was earlier called "multi-sited biographies" with attachments to various places and people, which complicates the notion of belonging to one place or group only, and demonstrates the complexity of notions of belonging: "… belonging is always a dynamic process, not a reified fixity, which is only a naturalized construction of a particular hegemonic form of power relations" (Yuval-Davis, 2006, p. 199).

Of course, non-migrants are also not necessarily territorially rooted in their local place or surroundings only. However, the transnational activities and experiences of mobility of skilled and highly skilled migrants might lead to interesting narratives, emotions, and combinations of belonging. Being highly skilled or skilled and having citizenships and migrant statuses that allow for free movement moreover brings up categories of power in terms of belonging to an educated middle class and actively being part of knowledge-economies and distinguishing oneself from "other", less qualified migrants, for example. However, one should not assume that this automatically makes them purely privileged migrants who do not struggle with various aspects of their migration or daily life.

The sociologist and migration researcher Nira Yuval-Davis (2006) argues that it is crucial to differentiate between *belonging*, which is about emotional attachment and the *politics of belonging*, which is comprised of specific political initiatives which aim at constructing specific forms of belonging for particular groups. Questions of belonging (including notions of "home", often an indirect topic in migration research) and the politics of belonging have been studied by various social science disciplines from numerous perspectives, often relating to questions of displacement due to alienation or migration (Yuval-Davis, 2006, p. 198). An in-depth analysis of the politics of belonging of Israel and Switzerland, while interesting, would go beyond the scope of this study, as the focus lies on the migrants' stories themselves. However, belonging in the sense of emotional attachments – partly in terms of citizenship, national, or cultural identities but mainly as a sense of attachment or belonging to a place or (imaginary) group – is relevant when discussing skilled migration.

It is difficult to look at belonging without emotions, while keeping in mind that emotions often are an important factor connecting individuals to other people or places in an everchanging globalized world. Emotions are used by the highly skilled migrants to construct a life anchored in place as well as in transnationalism and multi-sitedness in their narratives.

4.1 Putting the Self in Place

Somebody asked me "what are you?", I said mostly from Israel.
(Transcript Alexander, p. 38)

In a world divided into nation-states, citizenship is often perceived as one of the main containments or identifiers influencing feelings of belonging among migrants, which disregards the complexities of how belonging is created and maintained. Early migration literature "… generally assumes that migrants will gravitate towards co-ethnics with whom they share a language, similar cultural values and religious beliefs" (Wessendorf, 2017, p. 2). Highly skilled migrants (one could argue many other migrants as well) disrupt this notion. For instance, highly skilled migrants might perceive themselves as cosmopolitans (Hannerz, 2002), or belonging to a transnational social class (Cranston, 2017; Sklair, 2002; Vertovec, 2007; Weiss, 2006) and living flexible, transnational lives.

The analysis shows no indication that there is necessarily a strong communal sense of belonging amongst highly skilled migrants from the same region or that they have universal aims; however, attachment to place is discussed. This aspect of non-existing community is, for example, discussed by Ghassan Hage (2005) in his research on Lebanese emigrants from two small villages dispersed across several countries. It is also discussed by Avtar Brah (1996) and, based on this and theories of Bruno Latour, by Neha Vora (2008, 2013). Avtar Brah (1996) and Neha Vora (2008, 2013) both argue that the concept of "diaspora" is not applicable to every group. This means that not every group that crosses borders and settles somewhere assumes a joint "diasporic subjectivity" with the aim of achieving "integration" and/or citizenship of the place of settlement. In the case of the Indian middle class and highly qualified migrants in Dubai researched by Neha Vora (2008, 2013), for instance, the "diasporic subjectivity" is achieved through racial consciousness due to lived discrimination and distinction from others through economic citizenship in the sense of consumption practices, such as belief in a globalized free market and buying certain products denoting a middle-class status.

In other words, simply being abroad and coming from a common place does not lead to belonging and community from itself or to a joint wish for settlement and achieving citizenship in itself. Especially with highly skilled migrants, this has to be considered, as other factors having nothing to do with country of origin or birth might be more important and assuming a communal feeling of national belonging is misleading. Instead, belonging to a certain (transnational) class, professional group, or other form of community might become more important (Korpela, 2009; Scott, 2006; Weiss, 2006).

In the case of highly skilled Swiss in Israel, for example, none of the Swiss in Israel interviewed participate in the existing *Swiss Club* or similar organizations for Swiss abroad in Israel.[41] The clubs might be used as a resource for information upon arrival at the beginning or for bureaucratic questions but are not seen as a vital factor for one's stay in the country or as place to find meaningful ties and connections. For example, Gabriele talks about how she only had contact to such a group when her husband applied for Swiss citizenship (Transcript Gabriele, p. 8) and Margot sporadically had contact to other Swiss mothers in Israel through an internet forum (Transcript Margot, p. 10).

There is moreover not necessarily any strong connection to Swiss Jewish communities simply because someone is Israeli and Jewish. The following response by Daniel, a highly skilled Israeli in Switzerland, illustrates this, when asked if he has any ties to any other Israelis or the Jewish community in his current hometown, rhetorically distinguishing himself from other, "traditional migrants" who stay "*immigrants*":

> *Mh no, it could be nice if I would meet someone from Israel just to complain about our Prime Minister would be a joy but, um, I'm not willing to actively search for it 'cause then it might solely absorb you in the category of immigrant that stays immigrants. Actually, it's exactly the wrongest thing, that, at least for me.*
> (Transcript Daniel, p. 10)

None of the interviewees in Israel specifically look for other Swiss people, e. g., Hanna has some Swiss friends, however, she says this is usually a coincidence or are people she knew before moving and who now live in Israel as well:

---

[41] There are several organizations connecting the two countries and organizing meetings and events: https://www.eda.admin.ch/countries/israel/en/home/living-in/clubs.html, accessed: August 9, 2023; the *Swiss Community Israel* has existed for several decades, http://www.swissil.com, accessed: August 9, 2023; the *Swiss Israel Association* focuses on strengthening the bilateral relationship between the two countries http://israel-schweiz.org.il, accessed: August 9, 2023; the *Chamber of Commerce Switzerland Israel* focuses on economic aspects and connections, https://www.swissisrael.ch, accessed: September 5, 2023; there is also the official Israeli chapter of the *Organization of the Swiss Abroad* and various *Facebook* groups where people can connect. For Israelis in Switzerland the *Chamber of Commerce Switzerland Israel* can provide opportunities to network and there are also several *Facebook* groups or other local groups on expat forums.

> *But not really, that I searched for something Swiss here. You rarely see me at these kinds of events* [embassy or *Swiss Club* meetings] *[laughs].*
> (Transcript Hannah, p. 3)[42]

Could this be something that distinguishes highly skilled migrants from other groups of migrants? It is true that highly skilled migrants are not reliant on traditional networks to organize migration. However, they might have help from employers and they might use social media platforms such as *Facebook* or other applications to inform themselves about their destination and find contacts in advance, for instance. Is it important to them to differentiate themselves from other groups of migrants, particularly non-highly skilled ones? Some quotations and narratives of identity seem to suggest so.

Anja Weiss (2006) interviewed highly skilled Germans in Asia, Africa, and South America, as well as highly skilled migrants from these countries working in Germany in order to find out about the emergence of a transnational social class. Working with a theory based on Pierre Bourdieu, distinctiveness, and using few interviews with chosen protagonists to maximize potential differences, similar to the way it was done in the present study, she found out that the migrants themselves saw belonging to a new transnational social class as more crucial than belonging to or living in a specific country. This is partly reflected by the protagonists, but they are not detached from place, and the local frameworks in which they live do strongly matter in the narratives around daily life of some of the interviewees.

For the protagonists of this study, belonging is narrated through ties to and feelings about such things as certain places or neighborhoods, landscapes, connections to friends and family or professional groups, but indeed rarely through citizenship or national identity. If citizenship or nationality is mentioned, it is made to illustrate a specific point. This does not mean that the protagonists do not use distinction from others, such as lesser qualified migrants, for example – the ones contradictorily perceived as planning their migration with the aim to completely integrate into a host society, but simultaneously trying to maintain strong networks with other migrants from the same country of origin in their new home.

As will be discussed in section 6.1, this distinction from other migrants is often a way to frame their migration story as "going abroad" rather than talking of "migration". Citizenship is seemingly seen in strategic and pragmatic terms. It is simultaneously seen as a "calming" document with regard to emotions concerning the future, such as anxieties about political upheavals and changes. Other aspects

---

42 Translated from German:
   "(...) (A)ber nicht wirklich, dass ich das Schweizerische hier gesucht habe gross, ja. Sehr selten siehst du mich an solchen Events [lacht]."

of belonging, such as national identities, are also sometimes contradictory and show very different ways of dealing with experiences and surroundings by the protagonists.

4.1.1 National identities and flexible citizenship

Citizenship as a flexible and strategic possession in connection with globalization and economic benefits based on the interests of capitalist accumulation (as opposed to purely political rights and duties) has been documented by research since the 1990s. Aihwa Ong (1999) coined the term "flexible citizenship" in her research on Hong Kong business elites and their acquisition of foreign passports in light of the political uncertainty concerning China. Through this, one can look at narratives of identity: "The multiple-passport holder is an apt contemporary figure, he or she embodies the split between state-imposed identity and personal identity caused by political upheavals, migration, and changing global markets" (Ong, 1999, p. 2).

In his comprehensive research on citizenship, Yossi Harpaz (2019) looked at how dual citizenship is in demand due to a global hierarchy of citizenship and how a second citizenship from a Western or EU country, a "compensatory citizenship", can be a strategy for non-Western elites in a globalized world or an extension of a capitalist "field of struggle". In the case of Israel (though his findings are similar for US-Mexican and Hungarian-Serbian cases), an additional, European passport became something "cool to have" surrounded by discourses on investment, restitution, or understood as a luxury product, while being seen as awful and unwanted in the past. Through these strategic approaches to passports, citizenship becomes something one can achieve, as opposed to something that gets ascribed randomly by parents or place of birth.

This is also reflected by the protagonists and most other informants with whom I spoke during research. Alexander, for example, who is an Israeli-American dual citizen, uses his American passport depending on what country he travels to for business; while saying he might have felt ashamed about this in the past, he now takes a more pragmatic approach (Transcript Alexander, p. 35). The acquisition or retention of passports is an issue that has to do with current feelings about potential future uncertainty for the interviewees and becomes something that can promote a sense of security and preparedness in the present. Hence, making it not only a "compensatory" but also a "calming" citizenship.

For instance, while Margot talks about feeling very integrated and rooted in Israel, when talking about conflicts in the region, Palestine, and the future of Israel, she says she hopes the secular part of society goes on to make decisions about the country. However, she then mentions in passing that she and her children still have their Swiss passports "*just in case*" things get "*too complicated*" (Transcript Margot,

p. 36[43]). Gabriele applied for a Swiss passport for her husband (Transcript Gabriele, p. 10), also out of a sense of being prepared for the future, *"just in case"* something happens. The acquisition or retention of a citizenship then becomes something related to anxieties about the future and a strategy to manage them. It is mainly related to Israel as a surrounding framework in these examples. The framework of Switzerland does not require such feelings of preparedness for potential future political upheavals or turbulences leading to different transnational activities.

Citizenship in the form of a passport is overall is not only seen as something pragmatic and acquired in a strategic manner, but also as something related to the future, as the above examples suggest. It is not an aim in itself, but something used and gained for practical reasons in the present, such as travelling easily for business and being able to participate politically, or for potential future events, such as worries or fears about the uncertain development of Israel (making Switzerland a constant place of stability and security, in contrast). The document itself is not what creates belonging, which is rather produced and maintained through activities and connections with individuals, but it might provide a calming feeling of security when discussing the future.

Susanna, who made her *Aliyah* only after having already spent some time in Israel as a student, also had practical concerns about gaining her Israeli citizenship and connects it to a desire for a future, politically active self, that she has not yet made authentic:

> *But – actually, it had pretty much practical reasons, because, because I was staying such a long time and I had to renew (the visa) every three months or something, and the elections (…) – because when Netanyahu was elected for the first time, I couldn't vote here. Yeah, and I kind of wanted – I wanted to vote here and had this resolution to be more politically active, which I'm still not [laughs].*
> (Transcript Susanna, p. 12)[44]

Gabriele was politically active when she was younger and still positions herself as very left on the political spectrum, arguing that the current political situation in

---

43 Translated from German:
   "Ja und sonst haben wir immer noch den Schweizer Pass …".

44 Translated from German:
   "Aber – eigentlich war's mehr so aus praktischen Überlegungen, weil, weil's so lang war musst' es so irgendwie mit dem – also äh alle – ähm, drei oder vier Monate oder so was erneuern, und ähm ja und die Wahlen – wie war denn des? (…) (D)ie waren wie ich das erste Mal angekommen bin, da konnt' ich noch nicht wählen. – Weil, weil, die Wahlen, wie Netanyahu das erste Mal gewählt wurde, konnt' ich nicht wählen, da. Ja und ich wollte halt, dass ich – ähm wählen können würde, ich hab' mir auch vorgenommen, mehr aktiv politisch – zu sein, was ich bis heute nicht wirklich bin, aber – ja. [lacht]"

Israel is often frustrating for her. Talking about the war and the rising tensions in the summer of 2014, she says the situation made her feel foreign in Israel, even though she had no longer felt like a stranger for many years (Transcript Gabriele, p. 24). This reflects the complexity of belonging on a small scale and how highly skilled migrants might feel belonging at one point in time; however, a change of circumstances in the surroundings or interactions can lead to irritations and to questions about belonging. Gabriele started planning to own a second home in Switzerland, especially for summers when it is very hot in Israel, and also after the elections of 2015, which reconfirmed this idea, leading to the transnational activity of buying a second residence (Transcript Gabriele, p. 8). Simon and others continue to pay into the Swiss pension system, participating in transnational activities, which is also a strategy to keep ties to Switzerland and act in light of future eventualities (Transcript Simon, p. 15).

4.1.2 Brain drain and brain gain

One aspect that is part of the emigration discourse for Israelis leaving the country is the heated discussion around brain drain.[45] Dani Kranz (2016, p. 15) writes about Israelis living in Berlin: "Certainly, the immigrants expressed longing for home, and homesickness (*ga'aguim*, literally yearning) for Israel, but their notions compared to those of other immigrant groups. What sets Israeli emigrants apart was their repeated encounter with the specific Israeli reproach expressed at them that they should not have left – that is, betrayed – Israel, and in consequence, the question when they will return." This Israeli reproach is not comparable to the way Swiss abroad are perceived in Switzerland, where, like with many other European countries, emigrants in the public discourse are rather seen as "agents", positively and (especially in the past) patriotically representing the home country (Swiss Info, 2016), and only subtly encouraged to come back, or as individualists or adventurers exploring "exotic" foreign places.[46]

When discussing the discourse around brain drain, the protagonists made sure to put into perspective and individualize the topic with regard to their own narratives, emotions, and biography and additionally to demonstrate their education and understanding of complex processes, distancing themselves from ideologically

---

45 While not as extreme in English language publications, Hebrew media and publications are often very opinionated on the topic, accusing emigrants of betrayal etc. (Kranz, 2016, personal communication/translation). The case of Israelis in Berlin is, of course, particular, as Berlin is the capital of the country that planned the Shoah, but Israelis moving abroad to other countries are sometimes also confronted with accusations.
46 As can, for example, be seen on television shows about Swiss abroad: https://www.3plus.tv/adieu-heimat, accessed: August 9, 2023.

nationalist or Zionist discourses. As mentioned, Alexander, when discussing citizenship, also talks about how, in the past, a lot of shame was felt by Israelis living abroad about not being there, something he struggled with as well. However, over time he became more pragmatic about it (Transcript Alexander, pp. 38–39).

Concerning brain drain, Gabriele says that she understands there is a discussion and sees it with one of her own children who is thinking about moving to Europe (Transcript Gabriele, p. 41), but says one has to consider all the highly skilled immigrants who came to Israel, for example, from Russia and who built up important parts of the Israeli economy, such as the high-tech sector due to their good education (Transcript Gabriele, p. 27). And Daniel says:

> *Even though I have a higher education degree, I'm not sure I would be what you call the brain drain, and maybe or not maybe because of the brain drain, because I met a lady, fell in love and then you leave. (…) I don't think I am part of the brain drain, I can imagine that Israel is, it's a bit of a special society, ok, not special, maybe in Europe there would be less people concerned about brain drain phenomena as such. Because I think Israel is a bit, a bit more nationalist than European societies. Partly because of the constant war but I care less about it. I don't think I'm part of it and it also doesn't bother me on the conceptual level.*
> (Transcript Daniel, p. 14)

Simon, who came to Israel as a highly qualified migrant and could be seen as part of a brain gain process from an Israeli perspective, makes it clear that his decision to move there was not an ideological one. Through this he is also distancing himself from the brain-drain-gain discourse and the idea of a communal diaspora:

> *The only thing I can say, is, I didn't have Zionist, Zionist feelings. It would not have mattered to me, if I, I could have been in France, or in Italy, or in America, or in Germany. Israel as well, but not due to – The choice to be here was because it was going to be a good university, not because it was Israel.*
> (Transcript Simon, p. 13)[47]

Rhea, also an academic, relates the topic to the current situation for highly skilled Israelis, especially academics, showing understanding for everyone who leaves and consequently for her own trajectory:

---

47 Translated from German:
"*Das Einzige, was ich sagen kann, ist, ich hatte keine zionistischen, keine zionistischen Gefühle. Es ist wirklich äh – äh es wäre mir egal gewesen, wenn ich, wenn ich, ich hätte in Frankreich sein können oder in Italien oder in Amerika oder in Deutschland. Eben auch in Israel, aber nicht aus – Die Wahl war hier, weil es eine gute Hochschule wurde, nicht, weil es Israel war.*"

There's, um, there's no future in Israel. For highly educated, um, people, for left-wings, absolutely. First of all, if we look at the labor market for professionals like me, (an) academic, (there are) four universities and (a) few colleges and that's it, there are very limited places. That's A). B), the budget is like phhh. You cannot compare the budget for research. I mean, I think everyone who's-, every scholar (who has) an option to be at the ETH [Swiss Federal Institute of Technology in Zurich] or be in L.A. or Berkeley whatever, and who goes to, I don't know, Tel Aviv, I mean, he's a Zionist because he wants to go to Israel because of Israel. He doesn't go – He will have a low budget, no funding, no, I mean, it's, it's an ideological decision, it's not professional, one hundred percent.
(Transcript Rhea, pp. 17–18)

Nonetheless, earlier in the interview, she describes her own job in Israel as better than the one she currently has as a visiting scholar in Switzerland, but she still wanted to go abroad for various reasons. Her description also draws a contrast to Simon's above.

Beyond these subjective positionings of the self, one can look at the topic of brain drain from an ideological as well as an economic or anthropological perspective, two perspectives, which are often enmeshed. While Israel is a special case in this regard, due to its history and structure, current conservative streams, and the Zionist discourses around the Jewish diaspora, the topic also can be looked at from the perhaps more neutral perspective of a competitive job market in a globalized world – in which case Israel is comparable to other small, industrialized countries. Put simply: "As qualified individuals become ever more mobile, they are highly attractive for a large number of countries, including their own" (Cohen & Kranz, 2014).

Hence, while overall, Israel might have high emigration rates compared to other OECD countries in some years, this should not be weighted too strongly as one has to consider economic fluctuations among other things. As the demographer Sergio DellaPergola (2011, pp. 16–17), who compares emigration rates of Israel and Switzerland, puts it: "As the assumed collapse of Zionism cannot explain the Swiss migration patterns or the Swiss-Israel migration differential, it should plausibly be dismissed as the chosen explanatory paradigm for the comparatively less frequent Israel emigration." He argues – adding yet another aspect to research on high skilled migration – that when looking at migrating populations from small countries, there often is a surplus of educated individuals in certain areas. "Here, not unlike Switzerland and other societies of similar size and quality, Israel faces the dilemma of providing efficient training facilities, including highly developed higher education systems. Such countries tend to produce talented individuals whose numbers are appreciably larger than the absorption capacity of the respective local markets" (DellaPergola, 2011, p. 17). Of course, the infrastructures of these countries might also attract highly skilled migrants from other places in return, as discussed earlier and as seen through the exemplary protagonists' stories.

Interestingly, Swiss in Israel sometimes have to justify why they have decided to leave Switzerland, however only on an individual level and in consequence, without any ideological expectations. Sometimes these interactions occur with Israelis, because of the very positive images of Switzerland that makes some people wonder why one would want to leave, or with other Swiss, who do not understand why one would want to live in Israel due to the surrounding threats and conflicts, and negative, sometimes anti-Semitic, imaginaries. This is not the case to such an extent for Swiss who move to a neighboring European country. Generally, the protagonists themselves, while aware of the discourses around brain drain, prefer to position themselves as singular cases, narrating their migration story and decisions on individual terms, while showing an educated awareness of the discourse.

4.1.3 Self-descriptions and distinctions

Talking with people about their life makes questions of the self and constructions of identity an issue that leads to complex and sometimes conflicting feelings. Even if one looks at highly skilled migrants as a privileged group of people focusing on the fact that they migrate voluntarily and (often) as a way to self-realization (Benson & O'Reilly, 2009), they still produce singular emotionalized narratives of migration experiences that include contradictory and sometimes "middling" (Camenisch & Müller, 2017) self-constructions.

In this study terms such as "home", "belonging", "identity", and "self" are understood as fluid and processual, and were not used as codes since the focus is on the narratives and construals of meaning during interviews. Discussing these terms becomes as complex as discussing "culture" itself. As Lila Abu-Lughod writes about the self (Abu-Lughod, 1996, p. 468): "First, the self is always a construction, never a natural or found entity, even if it has that appearance. Second, the process of creating a self through opposition to another always entails the violence of repressing or ignoring other forms of differences."

For highly skilled migrants one opposition often used as distinction are other, less skilled or qualified migrants, sometimes locals, and other places and surroundings. For example, as will be discussed in the section on religion and tradition, protagonists create opposition or distinction from other Jewish traditions – Rhea perceiving the Swiss Jews as different due to their religiousness or Simon only feeling belonging through rites in a Swiss synagogue (examples in section 4.2.2). Concerning places, for instance, in the course of their narratives, the protagonists relate being happy or content to be in a certain place or leading a "good life". They connect this with their individual character, and position themselves within the place in which they live through discussions of their personal traits. In other words, a way of constructing parts of the self is describing why one is satisfied or happy with living in a place and connecting these emotions to personal character traits.

For instance: "*So, it, to my character, I think* [Swiss city] *fits a bit less*" says Daniel, who lived in major cities in Israel and European countries before coming to the smaller Swiss city he lives in now (Transcript Daniel, p. 4). Doron has a similar approach in relating his individual character to a place. While he says he needed to get used to the way "*things work*" in Switzerland, for example, that "*there are no shortcuts, everything goes by the book, by the rules, there are rules*", he also adds that this is something he likes as it fits his character better and makes him feel much more relaxed than circumstances did in Israel (Transcript Doron, p. 5 and p. 11). When we later talk about his pessimistic view of the future of Israel as a country and I connect this to general happiness about living in Switzerland, he corrects me, relating it to his own character again:

> *Question: So, is this (the negative future of Israel mentioned by him earlier) also part of why you're happy to be here (in Switzerland)?*
> *Doron: No, actually not.*
> *Question: Ok?*
> *Doron: No, I'm happy to be here because I feel people respect each other more, I have more space. In Israel, the mentality is so aggressive, I really don't like it. You have to fight for everything, it's not related to the political situation at all, and not to the security situation at all. It's more the mentality. Here, people are nice, considerate. Considerate, that's why I feel more – the society is better.*
> (Transcript Doron, p. 22)

Similarly, at another point of his story he says:

> *So, we have the opportunity (to go to Israel). I, if I would want it right now, no, I like it a lot in Schweiz* [he is speaking in English but using the German word for Switzerland, Schweiz]. *Um. We, I miss my family, friends, also some other nice stuff in Israel, good food and (…) but I feel much more comfortable in Switzerland. I really feel more relaxed, I like it a lot and I think I would prefer to live my life here, basically. But officially we didn't really decide yet and so, maybe we'll see…*
> (Transcript Doron, p. 11)

Additional forms of differentiation and self-positioning can be seen in the following quotation from Simon's interview:

> *But in the Switzerland that I know, there is a civilized way of conducting oneself amongst strangers. I mean, when a person from the city comes to the Alps and meets a herds- and*

dairyman, who brings in his cows, then you're obviously not each other's peers but you have a ritual of how you behave. So, the townsman asks about the weather, about how the harvest was, or something, right, and the dairyman asks, and well, you're still infinitely foreign to each other, because the city person is not an alpine herdsman, but you have a way of dealing with the strangeness. And this doesn't exist in Israel at all. Well, foreign is fundamentally repellent and friend is fundamentally embracing.
(Transcript Simon, p. 53)[48]

There is a strong distinction between "civilized" Switzerland and "other" Israel. The projection on Israel as "other" can be seen as a way to deal with frustrations about interactions in daily life and maybe also a reproduction of European colonial perspectives on the Middle East (Kreutner, 2013; Walsh, 2012). It might additionally be that the structuring effect of class consistently stays relevant in the narratives and self-positionings (O'Reilly, 2009, p. 103) of highly skilled migrants.[49]

Rhea does something similar to Daniel (in his quotation on immigrants and meeting other Israelis mentioned above), to position herself through an indirect class distinction when talking about the Swiss school system and what she perceives as shockingly early division of professional paths of life:

I mean, I would have died if my daughter went to vocational school. No really, it would be really hard for me. I mean, it's not that I'm that competitive, that I want her to be a professor, I don't want her – I want her to be happy. She can be happy as a, I don't know, a hairdresser, it's ok. But the idea that in the fourth grade or the fifth grade they decide it, I mean, it's decided, which is of course not, you can change it, I know, I know, but that's really–
(Transcript Rhea, p. 48)

The various examples discussed above demonstrate how migration stories make tensions or dichotomies around emotional connections to "'here' and 'there'"

---

48 Translated from German:
"*Aber die Schweiz, die ich kenne, dort gibt es eine, eine zivilisierte Art, sich gegenüber Fremden zu benehmen. Also ein Städter kommt in die Alpen und, und trifft da einen Sennen, der seine Kühe reinholt, dann ist man natürlich nicht seinesgleichen, aber man hat ein Ritual, wie man sich benimmt. Also als Städter fragt man, wie ist das Wetter, wie war die Ernte, oder irgendetwas, oder, und er halt auch, der Senne, fragt (auch). Also man ist sich schon unendlich fremd, weil Städter ist kein, kein Älpler, aber man hat eine Art, mit dieser Fremdheit umzugehen. Und das gibt es in Israel überhaupt nicht. Also fremd ist dann grundsätzlich abweisend und Freund ist grundsätzlich umarmend.*"

49 To be more explicit about this a somewhat different, more sociological approach with information about income etc. of the protagonists would have been necessary. In this study only information about education and professional status is available. However, there are several instances of "distinctiveness" visible, sometimes very subtle, in the narratives and working with Pierre Bourdieu's theories might also have been a feasible approach.

(Boccagni & Baldassar, 2015, p. 74) and in some cases also past, present, and future tangible. Places become relevant for the construction of a mobile self within narratives of identity. A – not always convincingly presented – emotional detachment from the local, questions of citizenship, and issues of brain drain is created to present a pragmatic, educated self. Still, transnational connections and multi-sited biographies connected to specific places remain important. This will be further explored below.

4.2 Bubbles, Cheese Domes, and Ghettos

> *I live in a ghetto, I live in an academic ghetto, I don't know Israel. I mean, uh, Ashkelon is as exotic for me as Morocco. I, uh, live in this liberal milieu and not in Israel, emotionally.* (Transcript Simon, p. 12)[50]

"Bubbles" in several variations, as a way of non-belonging to place and instead belonging to a class or professional group, or a way of protected, privileged belonging is regularly brought up by the protagonists, either directly or indirectly. It can be positive detachment, or more negative alienation and in some cases is also related to feelings of happiness and freedom. In the following examples, the language and images used are very strong. "Bubbles" are connected to the privilege of emotional detachment, feelings of happiness, and taking a break from one's former, regular life. Interestingly, the "bubbles" in different manifestations are something that the interviewees are extremely aware of and which they discuss in detail, seemingly either as a way of distinguishing themselves from other migrants, mainstream society, or as a way to acknowledge their privilege. This is further reflected in the fact that highly skilled migrants tend not to use the terms "migration" or "migrant" when talking about their activity of moving transnationally (Sontag, 2018a). As mentioned, they rather talk about "living somewhere" or "being somewhere", a "relocation" or "going abroad". The term "migrant" has a somewhat negative connotation, as can be seen in the results of this study (section 6.1), maybe because being a migrant carries the expectation of integrating and behaving a certain way and evokes the wrong kind of "bubble" (for example, the creation of a "parallel society").

---

50 Translated from German:
  "(...) Ich lebe in einem Ghetto, in dem, ich lebe im Hochschulghetto. Ich kenne Israel nicht. Also, ähm, Aschkelon ist für mich so exotisch wie Marokko. (...) Ich lebe in diesem liberalen Milieu (...) und nicht in Israel, emotional."

Alexander talks about the comfortableness of living in a professional "expat"[51] bubble and the privilege of detachment from one's place of living and also acknowledges that after the initial agreeableness of having a break from Israeli politics, he did get more involved in the US after moving there. However, he does not see this happening in Switzerland beyond staying informed on a general level:

> *So. When I left Israel, one of the advantages of going to study in the US was to take a break (from) our very dense and depressing politics. So, from a very young age I saw my advantage there. In the fact that I can avoid (…), not to care and not to get involved. Um, but it happens on its own, you know, after a while you find yourself in a party one day, one way or the other, and before you know it, you are a registered Democrat. So, um, so by the time I left to the US, I already (knew) what I'm for and what (I'm) against. I don't think it will happen here* [in Switzerland] *any time soon. One of the, one of the effective barriers is the fact that I don't know shit of German. So [laughs]. So that gives me some kind of, um, isolation. Um, which is comfortable, you know.*
> (Transcript Alexander, p. 14)

Also feeling comfortable in detachment from daily politics in Switzerland, Rhea says something very similar:

> *It's like, I feel like, yeah, they have this Ninth of February* [the above-mentioned referendum "against mass immigration"], *everybody was so upset, who gives a fuck? It's not my problem. Like, I find (Swiss politics) interesting but only gender questions, I find it for me. All the other question(s) here, it's your problem, you solve it. It's not me. In Israel, everything is so personal, it's so political, it's, every, everything in you, you feel, like, strong, politically. Mhm. We built a shelter. We built a house, and we built a very strong shelter. It's not good. But we did it. – Life is very easy here, (from) a lot of perspectives, you know. And in Israel it's a struggle, it's an everyday struggle. They even have a Facebook group (on) how to survive the, the 'Israeli Jungle'. And it's, it's about everyday. How to stop to (having) cable. They have like this post: how do you deal with the cable people?*
> (Transcript Rhea, pp. 42–43)

She feels strongly about having had to build a shelter in their house in Israel and the privilege of not having to care about immigration politics in Switzerland, as it gives her a break from her political activity in Israel. Further, she describes Switzerland as a "*public bubble*" (Transcript Rhea, p. 35) which makes her reflect on the happiness

---

51 The term "expat" or "expatriate" was not used in this study. It is generally understood as describing highly skilled individuals or specialists, often white and from English-speaking countries, who are sent abroad temporarily by companies (Aratnam, 2012).

and future of her children, as well as her own feelings of security and identity, and could be a question many migrating parents (highly skilled or not) might have to ponder in one way or the other:

> *I mean, so what is more important, what makes you more happy. To live with your, um, community, like origin community with all this unconditional love, or (to) be safe on a, I don't know, on a physical basis with everything that comes from that racist blablabla* [of essentialist notions of "home" and "roots" discussed at another point during the interview], *you know. But there's another axis here, for me to live here. (…) (On) one hand because I'm less worried. I mean, (I worry about) the car accidents you have in Switzerland as well. But people stop – and in Israel they don't. In Israel, they shout, here they don't shout. In Israel, kindergarten is thirty-two children and one teacher. Here it's fifteen with four people. I mean, I'm less (anxious) on a very basic term about my children and I also think, from all these objective opportunities, they are better here. And in Israel it's not the same. Although I'm a middle-class, privileged, semi-rich person, I mean, it's a, it's a bubble. They can live in a bubble, I lived in a bubble. They can do that as well. But here it's, it's public. The bubble is public.*
(Transcript Rhea, pp. 34–35)

Isolation or non-belonging can be seen as a comfortable situation for highly qualified migrants and they are generally not strongly criticized for it compared to the way other groups of migrants might be criticized in public discourses. It is also one of the stereotypical images one has of highly skilled migrants, particularly "expats" who live in their own, mainly English-speaking world within a country (Bracher/NZZ, 2018; Brönnimann/Tages-Anzeiger, 2013; Kunz/Tachles, 2014; Vögeli/NZZ, 2014). Moreover, living in "bubbles" is sometimes criticized or discussed as "wrong behavior" by Western lifestyle migrants in non-Western regions, even though their own reality is not always that different, due for example, to language barriers (Benson, 2009). In the narratives presented, being in a bubble is not necessarily negative for the protagonists, as it provides a way to be detached and independent from what is happening around oneself, and the distance of not getting emotionally involved might also come naturally when one has moved many times already or knows that the stay will be only for a certain period of time. However, the emotional status of "comfortable detachment", such as in the form of not knowing the local language, is a privilege that is not conceded to all groups of migrants. Others, such as migrants from non-Western countries, might be under more pressure to integrate in the public discourse.

Gabriele, who describes herself as "*integrated*" in Israeli society still sees herself as living in a bubble – she uses the image of a "cheese dome" – as well, due to her profession in tourism. Being a tourist guide and thus interacting a lot with tourists and Palestinians makes her feel a growing distance from mainstream Israeli society:

> *The (job in tourism), yes, that's something new for me and, and it actually also leads me back to my roots on a cultural level, back to Switzerland, yeah. Because (when) you're travelling with a German group, well, then you usually have a Palestinian bus driver and, in the hotel, there are a lot of Arabs as well, but then culturally you're – I actually always picture it like being under a cheese dome, yeah. This then leads me back culturally as well, and I have a lot of new connections through this. Actually, new connections to Germany, which I never had before, to Austria and also connections to Switzerland and this leads me, uh, a bit further away from Israeli society.*
> (Transcript Gabriele, p. 46)[52]

These narratives of belonging within "bubbles" invariably lead to other, related narratives of belonging such as home or creating and maintaining ties through traditions and language, for example.

4.2.1 Reflections on home and homesickness

While I did not directly ask about it, the topic of "home", as it does often with migration stories, came up in most interviews, often in the form of self-constructed belonging to a place in one sense or another. Alexander talks about the sentiment and the difficulties arising through it in a broader sense when he melancholically reflects on "home" and "going back home":

> *I don't think you can leave – you cannot leave home, you cannot return home 'cause that's (the) catch of this (…). There is no such thing as, uh, as going back home. And I like to (say) that (that's because) after you left home and you're trying to come back, um, home has changed so it doesn't meet your expectations anymore. And when you are coming back home there (are) expectations from you, but you have changed so you don't meet home's*

---

52 Translated from German:
   "*Das [Arbeit im Tourismus], ja, das ist ja für mich etwas sehr Neues und, und das führt mich eigentlich auch kulturell wieder etwas zu meinen Wurzeln, zur Schweiz zurück, ja. Weil (wenn) du mit einer deutschen Gruppe unterwegs bist, also dann hast du äh meist einen palästinensischen Busfahrer und im Hotel gibt es auch viele Araber, auch Israelis und Araber, aber dann bist du eigentlich kulturell bist du dann wie ähm, ich stelle mir das immer vor, du bist so unter einer Käseglocke, ja. Das führt mich dann auch kulturell etwas wieder zurück und (ich) habe dadurch auch viele, viele neue Beziehungen mit, ja, eigentlich neue Beziehungen mit Deutschland, die ich nie hatte, mit Österreich, und auch Beziehungen mit der Schweiz geknüpft und die führen mich dann auch etwas weiter von der israelischen Gesellschaft äh weg.*"

expectations either. So there never is a coming back home.
(Transcript Alexander, pp. 14–15)

Or as Anne-Sigfrid Grønseth formulates from a theoretical perspective: "… there is no return to home other than to the existential experience of the initial self-in-the-world" (Grønseth, 2013, p. 11). This will also be seen in the discussion of memories (section 5.1.1), where the current mobile self is constructed with the help of incisive memories lived by the initial self while at the same time creating distance to a former "home" of which one is no longer a part.

Margot talks about being distanced from her family, which is something, in her words, "*no Israeli can understand*", and, which in the course of her story, illustrates some of her frustration or sadness in dealing with family and friends she maintained in Switzerland. For example, she mentions with a certain resignation and dejection that her direct family in Switzerland and most of her former Swiss friends did not check on her during the war in summer 2014 (Transcript Margot, p. 34). She describes this summer period as an incisive time and "*really something*" as the distance between herself and her Swiss ties grew even wider than it had in the years before. She says it led her to close up a bit, not wanting to continually clarify the local situations for friends and family in Switzerland in the future (Transcript Margot, pp. 34–36).

As mentioned, Margot's case is in itself a unique biography, as she discovered she was Jewish almost by chance and later decided to move to Israel. These circumstances and discoveries made her feel a deep sense of belonging once in Israel. She does not talk about "bubbles" or detachment, and her transnational ties and activities are mainly professional. Her feelings of belonging in Israel are mainly illustrated through two experiences. First, she talks about belonging to a family she had not known until meeting an older, distant aunt who lived in Israel for the first time. Second, her university roommate's stories and jokes about family made her realize who she was, as, like her, the roommate was from a Swiss and Eastern European Jewish family. These short reflections and exclamations in the course of telling this story illustrate the deep impact these meetings had for her understanding of identity and as experiences:

> *Wow, ok. I'm actually Swiss, that is what I always believed but these* – [above events], *ok, I finally understand who I am.*
> *And this experience that you can belong to something that you didn't even know about …*
> *And wow, we felt like a family – and it was well, ok, there was a connection …*

And suddenly – there was someone like me –
(Transcript Margot, pp. 6–9)[53]

In discussions of home, the protagonists usually narrate emotional connections to Israel as a place and not to notions of a Jewish diaspora. Similar to Margot, Isabella says: *"(I) immediately from the very beginning had the felling, I'm really in the right place"* (Transcript Isabella, pp. 2–3).[54] A little bit later in the conversation she relates this specifically to her university and the town it is located in, which, for her, was its *"own world"* in which she found her place over time.
She says:

Um, well, yeah. I believe on the one hand I felt very quickly that I've arrived at a place where I would like to be. However, I believe that it has a lot to do with my school and the people there, who surrounded me, and this intellectual and spiritual enrichment, um, but I believe, I mean, I wasn't a complete stranger. But still I felt very strongly that I had grown up in Switzerland and that I'm somewhat different, or, this being different was quite in the foreground. And I think, I needed about three years, until I kind of found my place in society. (Transcript Isabella, pp. 5–6)[55]

Susanna tells a similar story of expectations and feelings of belonging, but with a less specific connection to people or places:

---

53 Translated from German:
"Wow, ok, ich bin ja eigentlich Schweizerin, das hab' ich bis jetzt geglaubt, aber diese [beschriebenen Ereignisse], ok, ich versteh endlich, wer ich bin."
" (...) (S)o die Erfahrung, dass es, dass man zu irgendwas gehört, von dem man eigentlich nichts wusste..."
"(U)nd das war schon Wow und wir fühlten uns wie eine Familie (...) Und das war schon, ok, es gibt da irgendeine Verbindung (...)."
"(...) und auf einmal sagte jemand, war (jemand) eigentlich so wie ich."
54 Translated from German:
"Und (ich) hatte gleich von Anfang weg das Gefühl, ich bin einfach am richtigen Ort gelandet."
55 Translated from German:
"Ähm, also, ja, ich glaube einerseits fühlte ich sehr schnell, dass ich an einem Ort angekommen bin, wo ich sein möchte. Ich glaube, es hat aber auch extrem viel mit meiner Uni zu tun und den Leuten, die mich einfach dort umgeben haben und diese intellektuelle und spirituelle Bereicherung ähm aber ich glaub', ich mein, ich war ja nicht komplett fremd. Aber trotzdem hab' ich ganz stark gemerkt, dass ich halt in der Schweiz aufgewachsen bin, und dass ich irgendwie anders, also das Anderssein war schon sehr im Vordergrund. Und ich glaub', ich hab' schon sehr circa drei Jahre gebraucht, bis ich so meinen Platz in der Gesellschaft gefunden habe."

Um, and when (I) arrived, I hadn't been here for several years and then I really had the feeling, I can't explain it even today, because I'm not usually like that, hm, I landed at Ben Gurion [Airport] and had the feeling: 'Wow, I've arrived'.
(Transcript Susanna, p. 2)[56]

Later in the story, Susanna recounts how she was told by an uncle that her father would have been very happy that she is now living in Israel, also tying the story to her Jewish identity even if it might not have been in the foreground or the main reason for moving to Israel. Isabella says that while she observes that many people do not define themselves through places nowadays, she believes that places are very influential on the "*imprints*" (Transcript Isabella, p. 32)[57] of one's identity and relationships, and that, as a dual citizen, she sometimes feels conflicted and under pressure:

I kind of realized, that I always had the feeling that I have to decide where I'm going to be and settle. That is so much pressure. And then, I think I have to make myself a place, no matter where I am geographically, where I can connect both worlds, and that is really something which I had to negotiate and decide with myself.
(Transcript Isabella, p. 27)[58]

Isabella regularly comes back to questions of identity, home, and belonging during the narrative, and having one Swiss Christian parent and one Israeli Jewish parent seems to be a factor that adds to the described identity-crises she experienced during her life, as illustrated above. She describes going back and forth between Israel and Switzerland as exhausting ("*sehr anstrengend*" in German) and "*emotionally stirring*" (Transcript Isabella, p. 26). However, she adds that she is working on herself and "*her situation*", and is trying to find a way to make going back-and-forth easier and trying to create a space of her own, no matter in what place she is in. Being a dual citizen who lived in both countries seems to make her acutely aware

---

56 Translated from German:
"Ähm, und wie wir dann angekommen sind, da war ich schon mehrere Jahre nicht mehr hier und ich hatte wirklich so das Gefühl, ich kann mir das bis heute nicht erklären, weil ich dann normalerweise nicht so, mh, bin in Ben Gurion [Flughafen] gelandet und hatte das Gefühl und 'wow, ich bin angekommen'."

57 Translated from Swiss German:
"Ich glaube ebe scho dra, dass de Ort dich sehr prägt oder, wo du ufgwachse bisch (...)"

58 Translated from Swiss German:
"Ja, (...) ich glaub, ja. – Ich han wie so gmerkt, dass ich han immer s Gfühl gha, dass sich müse entscheide, wo ich mich jetzt festlege, das isch so en Druck. Und denn, ich mues mir glaub wie so en Ort schaffe, egal won ich bin, geographisch, won ich diä zwei Wälte chan mitenand veriibare, und das isch würkli öpis, wo ich mit mir sälber ähm mues mache."

of the processuality of identity, and she sees it as one of the big questions of her life. She also discusses homesickness, and in the following long quotation shows the melancholy that sometimes seems to be an inherent emotion to some migration narratives. Isabella is the only protagonist who uses the actual term "homesickness" and talks about it the most, relating past definitions of the term with herself as she exists in the present. Due to her current career and financial status, it might not be as easy to travel back and forth regularly, but she emphasizes that going back and forth too often is exhausting for her, disrupting the image of highly skilled migrants who not only cross borders easily physically but also emotionally. About homesickness she says:

> *Yeah, but the feeling of belonging and well, roots, and home, (and) identity is kind of, yeah, it's a bit the story of my life* [she is using the English term "story of my life" also in original Swiss German], *right. And, um. The* [art project] *I wanted to make about homesickness, is well, in the past homesickness was actually seen as an illness (…). And that really made me think a lot. (…).* [reflections on former views on homesickness, apologies about talking about homesickness].
>
> *And then, in the past they thought it's an illness that cannot be healed and that people can die from it, and in the beginning, it was called Swiss illness, because it mainly affected Swiss mercenary soldiers, who were often young boys or men who grew up on farms surrounded by family (…). Everything that was written about it and also what doctors wrote about it in this time is that it's something that besets you and that you cannot do anything about it, that you're, like, completely possessed and the only thing that one can do about it, is to send the people back home to get better. (…) Otherwise they would stop eating.*
>
> *And there really are medical statements, where it says the blood flow in the brain is too strong, and that, well, it really concerned me, how strong the meaning of your geographic roots is. And even more today, in a globalized world, where (…) many people do not define themselves according to a place. (…) I really believe that the place can have a strong (cultural) imprint, or, where you grew up. (…) And I also believe that nowadays we kind of have this longing for, or are always looking for a place to belong to in the mess of being able to be everywhere, and yeah. And I mean, that really is a topic I think about a lot and that I find interesting.*
>
> (Transcript Isabella, pp. 31–32)[59]

---

59 Translated from Swiss German:
"*Ja, aber das Zugehörigkeitsgfühl und ebe, Wurzle und Heimat, Identität, isch scho, ja, isch so chli the story of my life, oder. Und ähm. Dä* [Kunstprojekt] *won ich ha wele mache über Heiweh, isch ja, Heiweh het me früener gmeint sisch e Chranket. (…) Und das het mich denn sehr beschäftigt. (…) Und denn, früener het me gmeint sisch e Chranket, wo nöd heilbar isch und d Lüüt chönd dra sterbe, und am Afang hets ja die Schweizer Krankheit gheisse, wil's vor allem Schwiizer Söldner betroffe hät. Und me erchlärts so chli damit, dass es meistens so chli Buuresöhn gsi sind, wo sehr so – Ja und de Familie*

While one might miss certain places or people, homesickness as a specific feeling in the sense of a strong, sad emotion is not necessarily a major topic in the narratives except for Isabella's. However, this does not negate the sometimes strong feelings of longing and missing discussed in a more abstract manner in the stories of other protagonists. The feeling of longing associated with "homesickness", as she mentions, is also touched on by other protagonists, mainly in ways of talking about missing certain *"green landscapes"* or wishing for *"warm climates"*.

Dani Kranz (2016, p. 16), who did research on highly skilled Israelis in Berlin writes: "Missing Israel or feeling in exile are two emotions to which he [her interviewee Ran, a highly qualified Israeli living in Berlin with his German wife] does not relate. Owing to cheap air travel and a high level of education, and hence earning power, the overwhelming majority of all Israeli immigrants can afford a somehow transnational lifestyle, which supports the lack of feeling in exile, and which diminishes the feeling of homesickness." This physical accessibility of different places is also reflected by the protagonists, for instance Alexander or Simon, who can regularly visit and have several homes, or a highly skilled Israeli businessman I interviewed at an event, who explains that daily life is not only happening in Switzerland but at his second residence in Israel too, in a way making Switzerland the workplace and Israel his (emotional) *"home"* (Field Diary, September 2014).

Moreover, for example, Rhea and Matt talk about how easy it is to stay in touch with friends nowadays thanks to modern technologies, and Matt argues that not staying in touch is rather due to friends and family being busy with work or young children as opposed to lacking opportunities to travel or contact each other. Nevertheless, as the quotations above show, there are sometimes feelings of nostalgia or melancholy in the narrations around home and its emotional accessibility beyond an existential experience of a passed self (Grønseth, 2013, p. 11). Even when one wants to avoid essentializing migration stories as extraordinary due to individuals being mobile and crossing borders, one has to admit that they do provide an interesting approach to discussing feelings of belonging and narratives of identity

---

a *eim Ort ufgwachse sind und denn so für zwei Jahr id Fremdi gschickt worde sind, und dänn ähm, und alles, was me drüber schriibt oder was au Ärzt drüber gschriebe händ in dere Ziit, sind würkli, dass es so öpis isch, wo dich heimsuecht, und du wie so gar nöd chasch dägege mache, das isch so fremdbestimmt wirsch, und s'Einzige, wo me denn chöng mache, isch die Persone wieder heischicke als Genesig und süscht würdet si ufhöre esse und s'git dänn au würkli so medizinischi Befund, s Hirn sigi z'fest durbluetet, und was, und das het mich denn sehr, ähm beschäftigt, ebe, was das eigentlich so füre Begütig het, so dini geografischi Wurzle. Und hützetags umso meh, ebe in däre globalisierte Wält, wod du eigentlich, vili definiered sich ja gar nüm so würkli nacheme Ort, aber ich, ich glaube ebe scho dra, dass de Ort dich sehr prägt oder, wo du ufgwachse bisch und dass du so starchi Beziehige häsch und ich glaub au, dass mir ois hützetags wie denaa sehned oder immer au de Zueghörigkeitsort sueched, in dem, in dem Durenand vo chli überall chöne z'si und ja. Und das wär, das isch so würkli es Thema, wo mich sehr beschäftigt und intressiert."*

often brought up by the protagonists themselves. Or: "Migrant stories are linked with the experiences of adjustment, settlement, nostalgia, a shattered sense of belonging, renewal, loss, discrimination, abrupt endings, new beginnings and new opportunities – all potent sources of emotions" (Skrbiš, 2008, p. 236).

4.2.2 Tradition and religion

Overall, highly skilled migrants are not very religious. While there are Swiss Jews migrating to Israel specifically due to religious or ideological reasons, most of the selected protagonists and people interviewed in the field differentiated themselves from this group. Nevertheless, when asked about religiousness or the perception and maintaining of religious traditions and holidays, the protagonists – secular as well as religious ones – use the question or prompt to discuss feelings of belonging, family ties, as well as issues of maintaining a Jewish identity. For example, Alexander who describes himself as *"religiously non-religious"*, mentions Jewish holidays as family meetings (Transcript Alexander, p. 29).

The exception to the more secular highly skilled migrants is Matt, the only interviewee who describes himself as *"very religious"*, which, as mentioned, did not come up in the first exchange, and who strongly frames his narrative with his Jewish identity, which was difficult for him to live to the extent he wished in Switzerland, where there are fewer Jewish institutions and no kosher supermarket, and where his extended family is not as religious as he is. In his narrative, Israel becomes *the* place one can belong in a way that is not possible in any other country and which fulfills a wish of being "normal" in the sense of being part of the majority, which is reflected in the very short sentence below:

> *Here I'm not special.*
> (Transcript Matt, p. 10)[60]

Normalcy there becomes a way of belonging and a state one can achieve (Lopez Rodriguez, 2010), similar to how citizenship can be achieved. Matt later uses this image again when talking about how he can connect closely to his Arab friends in Israel because *"they know what it means to be a minority"* (Transcript Matt, p. 21), thus reflecting on the wish to belong or to be part of a majority within society. Susanna describes how she did not become more religious or *"more Jewish"* through her move to Israel, but she did change some of her traditions and, like Matt, took advantage of the numerous opportunities related to Judaism available

---

60 Translated from French:
    "*Ici, je ne suis pas spécial.*"

in Israel, such as classes on Jewish history or interreligious meetings (Transcript Susanna, p. 31 f.).

In Switzerland, Judaism is something one has to consciously think about, as is also noted by Rhea and Hannah during their interviews. Hannah, who mainly wanted to "go abroad" and not necessarily to Israel originally, says that in Israel her being Jewish simply becomes less important than it is in Switzerland, illustrating the changing importance of aspects of belonging depending on place and surroundings and the processuality of feelings of belonging:

You are less made to feel that you're Jewish, because here it simply is the norm.
(Transcript Hannah, p. 5)[61]

In contrast to Matt, who refers to his own self within a place, Hannah refers to how the surroundings make her feel about herself at first and later reflects on the meaning of being Jewish without being religious.

I would say that the holidays for me in Switzerland, well, the Jewish holidays in Switzerland were much more meaningful than they are today, uh, they are here. Because it really is, I mean, when you're not even connected to tradition in Switzerland, then you're not connected to anything at all anymore. I mean, what else is there then, right? Um, and here you don't need this.
(Transcript Hannah, p. 34)[62]

Mirroring this from Switzerland, where the existing local Jewish communities are rarely joined by Israelis, Rhea says:

Now, I mean, (my) question of Judaism, which didn't have to be a question at all in Israel, because I was just Jewish and that's it, I didn't need to do anything. It was like, it was like (being) heterosexual, it's like, obviously. Yeah, I mean, if you are not, you need to really say (it). And here, it's not like that. Here, I need to ask myself again: 'Am I Jewish?' But I'm not of Jewish religion. So, what is Judaism? Because in Israel, it's also a nation, it's not really a religion. And here, I am (of) Jewish (nationality) but not Jewish religion, so how do I pass

---

61 Translated from German:
"*Du kriegst es weniger zu spüren, dass du jüdisch bist, weil das hier einfach die Norm ist.*"
62 Translated from German:
"*Ich würde sagen, dass es, die Feiertage für mich in der Schweiz viel, also die jüdischen Feiertage in der Schweiz viel bedeutungsvoller waren, als dass sie heute das hier sind. Ich ähm, weil es wirklich, also wenn du in der Schweiz die Tradition, nicht mal mit der Tradition verbunden bist, dann bist du eigentlich nicht mehr verbunden. Also dann, was bleibt dann noch, ok? Ähm und hier brauchst du das nicht.*"

> this thing (on) to my children? Oh, it's holidays, so it's religious. This (complexity), and all those questions are very typical for immigrants. (…) I mean, I didn't put my child into the Jewish, uh, school, I didn't do that.
> (Transcript Rhea, pp. 20–21)

In this reflection on religiousness, she relates herself with "*immigrants*", a group she differentiates herself from again when discussing other topics and experiences.

While religion in an orthodox sense did not play a major part for the other protagonists, traditions and ties, to family, for example, maintained through religious ceremonies, as well as a Jewish identity remained important no matter where they lived. Some of the traditions were changed, adapted, or emerged only through migration, while others stayed the same. And even if the interviewees themselves were not religious, religion still sometimes played a role in their stories in other contexts, for instance in arguments with family or friends. Margot (Transcript Margot, p. 23) recalls a painful memory about fighting with a friend about her converting to Judaism and her friend suddenly talking about "*Christ-killers or something*" (original: "*Christverbrecher oder so*"), making the distance she feels towards Switzerland grow larger.

Gabriele mainly converted in order to fit in better, demonstrating how migrants in a marriage with a local are often most committed to ideas of integration or assimilation (Scott, 2006, p. 1115). Conversion is something many non-Jewish spouses of Israelis living in Israel do if it does not contradict their own beliefs, due to the fact that immigration structures in Israel do not provide a lot of infrastructure for non-Jewish migrants (Kranz, 2019). Gabriele explains that while she sometimes thinks about religious questions, she is generally not a religious person and the only rules she follows are some of the dietary ones. She converted because she was constantly asked if she was Jewish when she moved to Israel several years ago and sees it more as a cultural adaptation (Transcript Gabriele, pp. 18–19). However, like Margot she recalls a painful memory, when talking about the reactions to her conversion:

> Um, my mother was so – she never could understand: 'Why, and why are you in Israel and why did you have to convert there?'
> (Transcript Gabriele, p. 31)[63]

---

63 Translated from German:
   "*Ähm, meine Mutter war so, die konnte das nie verstehen. Warum und warum bist du in Israel, und warum musstest du da auch konvertieren?*"

Most of the people I met in the field are secular or, if they are religious, it was not seen as a crucial aspect of their migration decisions or daily life. With the exception of Matt and Jacob (who became more religious through his marriage), religion consequently played a minor role in daily life, but did play a more prominent role, sometimes serving as a backdrop, when discussing and reflecting on identities and experiences.

Simon explicitly ties traditions and going to the temple to memories and feelings of "home", saying these activities have nothing to do with religion in itself for him. Others do this as well, but less directly. He says:

It has nothing to do with it (religion), but with memory.
(Transcript Simon, p. 37)[64]

Earlier in the interview when talking about belonging to Israel and his personal contradictions he says:

No, I don't have feelings of belonging (here), because the Judaism which I, of course, grew up in, is marginalized here. Quite extremely. I feel, I go to the synagogue on Yom Kippur (in Switzerland) and here I don't go to the synagogue. That is uh – the European liberal Jewry is marginalized here, right. I have little to do with other forms of Judaism. (…) I'm an atheist, that's a contradiction.
(Transcript Simon, p. 17)[65]

In these formulations staying connected to traditions or "origins" can be seen as a way to create emotions of well-being and belonging in the present through agreeable memories and connections to a past self. It is additionally a way for the protagonists to differentiate themselves not only from other migrants but also from other groups, such as various Israeli religious traditions for Simon and the Swiss Jewish community for Rhea:

Because they're a pain in the ass, the Jewish Swiss. I mean, I'm not religious and they are, so they look at me differently. And I'm Israeli, I'm not Jewish Swiss and they look at me

---

64 Translated from German:
"*Es hat nichts mit dem* [Religion/religiösen Ritualen] *zu tun, sondern mit der Erinnerung.*"
65 Translated from German:
"*Nein, ich hab' das so, ich hab' kein Zugehörigkeitsgefühl, weil das Judentum, in dem ich natürlich aufgewachsen bin, ist hier marginalisiert. Und zwar ganz extrem. Ich fühle mich, ich geh in* [Schweiz] *an Jom Kippur in die Synagoge und hier geh ich nicht in die Synagoge. Das ist äh - Das europäische liberale Judentum ist hier marginalisiert, oder. Ich habe mit den, mit den anderen Formen des Judentums wenig zu tun. (…) Ich bin ich Atheist, aber das ist ein Widerspruch.*"

differently. And they are so competitive. I mean, they, everybody goes to [specific school] *and they are so distinct upon themselves.*
(Transcript Rhea, pp. 22–23)

Daniel also very clearly states that he is not religious and, when asked a second time, says, the only way he would see himself as religious is in the sense of *"being a humanist"* (Transcript Daniel, p. 17). This is similar to how he distances himself from being a citizen of Israel earlier in the interview and emphasizes his individuality and transnational identity. He also did not change his manner of dealing with major holidays since migrating; he is reminded of them by family, but he did not celebrate in Israel and does not celebrate in Switzerland.

Religion and tradition can become something the protagonists think about more consciously through migration experiences, but it is not necessarily something crucial for everyone's processes of identity. However, as mentioned, it is connected to memories and personal connections. Doron, for example, says he is not religious but misses the family gatherings and recalls childhood memories that usually happen on holidays when he says:

My [Christian] *wife and her family try to help me to do some family stuff, but they were surprised to see that when they don't, then it's just a regular day. That makes me a bit sad, I somehow felt (something was) missing, I miss it. (…) I think it's more traditions, stuff you knew from childhood, family time for me. I try to go to the synagogue, which I don't do in Israel. I tried to go but I still didn't feel comfortable there, so…. I wouldn't say my view has changed.*
(Transcript Doron, p. 10)

This approach to religion might change when one becomes a parent, as was further illustrated above by Rhea, who struggles with how to transfer a secular Jewish Israeli identity to her children while living in Switzerland. Discussing the future, Doron later says that depending on where their (potential) children will grow up they will be more Christian (Switzerland) or Jewish (Israel) (Transcript Doron, pp. 16–17), which again shows how religion and tradition is discussed as something that can be flexibly adapted or reinvented according to circumstances, like other (transnational) practices. Religion is often looked at in regard to a globalized world or a transnational field with multiple identities (Levitt, 2003b). Like citizenship, it is partly viewed in very practical terms and as a strategy to make life "simpler" in one's locality. Hannah also describes how major religious holidays are mainly a family thing, which is why she usually tries to be in Switzerland then (Transcript Hannah, p. 4 and pp. 33–34).

Looking at religious holidays and activities as tradition or as mainly a way to keep family ties and something one can maintain while still being secular is important for most of the protagonists. Margot, for example, says that she and her husband are not religious at all but that they strongly believe in the credo that one can be *"Jewish and secular at the same time"* (Transcript Margot, p. 33). Others use different formulations:

> Question: Did you grow up religious?
> Isabella: No, but I would say traditional.
> (Transcript Isabella, p. 24)[66]

"As Anne Marie Fortier (2000) and Ahmed et al. (2003) note, migrant attempts to engage with homeland traditions are always marked by distance from the homeland, and should not be understood as direct replications of identity" (cited in Grønseth, 2013, p. 85). Relying on descriptions of certain activities as direct identity markers amongst migrants might thus be too easy an explanation, even though it sometimes is the approach the protagonists themselves use to reflect on religion. However, generally the activities are rather ways to keep or maintain emotional connections upright through memories or to create new ties through participating in different activities, for example. Here, one also has to consider again that highly skilled migrants often have sufficient financial means (or at least earning power) to travel to see family and friends if they wish to do so; therefore, there is not always a need for strongly maintaining (religious) traditions from afar in their current place of residence or a need for the networks religious activities might provide for other, less privileged groups of migrants.

4.2.3 Language as a strategy of (non-)belonging

Language can be one way through which (non-)belonging is created and maintained. Either through non-learning and consciously staying in a bubble or through acquiring strong skills. Depending on what perspective on migration the protagonists have, either the wish of "integrating" on their personal terms or simply navigating daily life better, learning the local language plays a major or minor role in their story. Language can lead to a number of emotions, such as discomfort or irritation about hearing German due to Jewish history, for instance. The Swiss in

---

66 Translated from Swiss German:
"*Nei, aber scho traditionell, würd ich säge.*"

Israel all learned Hebrew, but it was not a vital aspect of their narrative. In part probably because they already had been in the country for an extended period of time and had taken advantage of the extensive structures in place in Israel to learn Hebrew or had knowledge of the language before migrating.

The exception is Gabriele, who is from a German-speaking part of Switzerland and who used language as an explicit strategy to create feelings of belonging. She thinks that if her mother tongue had been Russian or English as opposed to (Swiss-)German, she would have found it much easier to form relationships and find a local group of friends upon arrival in Israel. In the beginning of the interview, she emphasizes several times how important it was for her to learn Hebrew and that she learned Hebrew "*very well*" in order to be able to integrate, feel accepted, and not be seen as tourist (Transcript Gabriele, pp. 1–5). Being a tourist has a negative connotation for Gabriele, as it means that one is constantly accosted for something or swindled. Her being married to an Israeli, of course, leads to a different situation than those of Rhea and Alexander in Switzerland, who do not have Swiss partners and consequently might have different expectations towards their lives in their country of destination.

For Gabriele, starting studies for her second degree at an Israeli university was another part of the strategy to integrate and stay in the country. These two activities – learning and speaking fluent Hebrew, and matriculation at and attending university – however, were not only a way to "integrate" (as mentioned, not all interviewees use that concept as not all of them have this aspiration due to the duration of their stay, stronger feelings of belonging to another space, or lack of outside pressure to integrate, for example) but also, maybe even more importantly, a way to establish her own life, independent from her Israeli husband and family and from her own family back in Switzerland.

Her husband did not learn German and they spoke English at the beginning of their relationship (Transcript Gabriele, p. 10). She spoke Swiss German to her older children but the youngest one does not understand or speak it at all. This is similar to Margot's experience who raised her first children bilingually but did not do it with the younger ones. For Gabriele, permanently moving to Switzerland was never an option based on her husband's strong attachment to Israel. She quotes him as always saying: "*I was born here; I'm staying here and I'm certainly not moving to Switzerland*" (original German: "*Ich bin hier geboren, ich bleibe hier und (gehe) sicher nicht in die Schweiz.*" Transcript Gabriele, p. 4). However, as mentioned above, her whole family has Swiss citizenship in addition to Israeli citizenship.

Where to move can, of course, often lead to negotiations in a couple (something also described by other interviewees and explored by Dani Kranz, 2019 in a paper on highly skilled, non-Jewish female partner and spousal migrants to Israel) even if sometimes the motivation for the original move is love. It is interesting to consider the gendered aspects of migration in cases like the ones presented. Some highly skilled migrant women in Israel, even if better qualified than their Israeli husbands and able to leave easily in theory, describe feeling trapped occasionally and talk about the crucial aspect of learning Hebrew to be less vulnerable in the work as well as family sphere (Kranz, 2019). Also, "… Israel has some very specific, local characteristics: career options not only depend on the inner-Israeli, inner-ethnic subgroup, but also in many cases on the position one attained in the Israel Defense Forces (IDF). … This militarization of civil society contributes to a specific economic structure: the high-tech sector drives the economy of the country" (Kranz, 2019, p. 7). Both, Gabriele and Margot (who says: *"in Israel high-tech is (…) like the banking sector in Switzerland"* (Transcript Margot, p. 36), worked in the high-tech sector but for many (non-Jewish) immigrants, even highly qualified ones who speak Hebrew, it can be difficult to find access to the well-paid jobs in this area.

As research for this study was limited to the German-speaking parts of Switzerland, one has to consider that German has a unique standing for Jewish Israelis in that it was the language of the National Socialists. Dan Diner (2017) describes how from a certain Jewish perspective German was or is seen as "contaminated commando-language".[67] While the relationship and migration mechanisms between Germany and Israel are very different to the ones between Switzerland and Israel (Sibold, 2020), which has a completely different historical connection to Judaism (Picard, 1997), Switzerland shares a border with Germany and the various Swiss German/Alemannic dialects spoken there are versions of German. Rhea says she did not expect language to be such a strong issue before coming to Switzerland, where she is now surrounded by German, even though she is not in Germany. She became very aware of this in the course of living in Switzerland. She talks about sadness and the unexpected complex emotional reactions she had to hearing German in daily life, tying it to her complex, pessimistic feelings about the future of Israel:

> *I see Israel as a country without hope now. Um, I'm saying it very sadly 'cause, um, well you know, to be in a German-speaking country, (…). I think maybe there will be a different (perspective from Israelis living in non-German-speaking parts of Switzerland). Um. Because it is true, I mean it's not so much about the German language, the German language is just to remind me what (it) means, being close to Germany, and to go shopping in Germany and to go for vacation in Germany, just because it's so cheap. It's really, you know, it really confronts you with the Jewish history. Which is, you know, an everyday thing in Israel. Not every day, but you know, it's very up in (the forefront of) your head. And, um, I mean, (on the one hand) I know, I think, there's no other country for Jewish people than Israel. But on*

---

67 The contemporary image of Germany in Israel is also discussed by the historian Fania Oz-Salzberger (2016) in a book about Israelis in Berlin.

the (other hand), I, I think Israel is the most dangerous place for Jewish people.
(Transcript Rhea, p. 20)

Concerning the geographical closeness to Germany and being confronted with Jewish history while being in Switzerland she also says:

And here nobody died. (…). I mean, I'm not sitting in a HB [main station] and (look at) it and - - and I think like ok, if I'm in Berlin and I'm sitting in the Hauptbahnhof [main station], which I did, it's like, ok, over there they collected the Jews, ok, here's (where) my grandparents came to the train, and I don't have this problem. I don't have this every day here in Switzerland. And I think (that's) quite important about Switzerland, actually. But, um, it is (easier) for me to be here and for my partner. I didn't expect it to be this issue about Germany because I was like 'Germany has done so much', in remembering and in, in paying and, uh, paying on (a) symbolic and mat- (material level), so it's actually solved. But, um, and I did (come) to the idea that this is important to me. That was a surprise. To (be) confront(ed) with all these feelings.
(Transcript Rhea, p. 28)

While in her discussion of the decision to migrate, the major motivation is a general idea of "going abroad" and Switzerland as a country seems irrelevant in the course of the narrative; experiences, interactions, complicated feelings about the German language and the influence of the locality in which she lives, Switzerland as a place becomes relevant because it is "not Germany". Hence, the destination country itself gains importance and meaning that goes beyond simply being the place where an interesting job was offered, where one can gain international experience, or take a break from stressful surroundings.

Jacob has a different connection to the German language and describes his strong feelings of belonging to Switzerland as partly related to already knowing Swiss German thanks to parts of his childhood spent in Switzerland:

So, because of the language, because I ('ve lived here before), I feel (good) here. I have to say, that actually, we left Switzerland when I was a child, I have, in all these years in Israel felt a bit like a fish out of water, uh, out of the pond. Even though Israel also was a home for me, but, for me, Switzerland, the transition was very easy, (it was very easy) to integrate here. I didn't find it hard for myself. Simply, um, the financial situation or the work situation is still a challenge for me.
(Transcript Jacob, p. 4)[68]

---

68 Translated from German:

Jacob is in a professional transitory phase as we meet for the interview, which stresses him a little bit and creates feelings of unrest, as he mentions. The last part of this quotation shows that simply because someone is highly skilled or highly qualified does not mean they are not sometimes confronted with professional anxieties and challenges.

Simon, whose mother tongue is (Swiss-)German humorously recalls an upsetting experience he had in Israel due to the German numberplate on his car:

One time when I was here on a visit (before moving here), I was faced with hostility because I spoke German. When in, when in Switzerland there were parallel experiences of an anti-Semitic nature, but here I also had an experience. My tires were slashed twice, because I had German number plates, when I was, here, uh, for the fourth time. So, therefore, [laughs] the friendliness was the same –
(Transcript Simon, p. 18)[69]

Overall, learning or not-learning language plays a role in the daily life of the highly skilled migrants that leads to very individualized emotions, such as feeling more confident in the case of Gabriele, irritation in the case of Rhea, agreeable familiarity in the case of Jacob, and conflictual interactions in the case of Simon. Still, depending on the profession of the highly skilled migrant, learning the local language might not be necessary – Alexander, for example, does not need to know German as his work environment is English-speaking and his main ties are in other countries. The approach to language moreover has to do with the spouse or a personal decision or aptitude for language.

"Also wegen wegen der Sprache, wegen, weil ich hier also, ich fühlte mich hier, ich muss sagen, dass eigentlich (als) wir die Schweiz verlassen haben, als Kind, habe ich mich all diese Jahre in Israel ein bisschen so wie ein Fisch ausser Wasser, oder aus dem Teich quasi, äh, gefühlt. Obwohl in Israel hatt' ich natürlich auch immer ein Zuhause, aber für mich war die Schweiz einfach-, der Übergang war eigentlich relativ leicht. Also sich zu integrieren hier, hab' ich nicht schwer gefunden für mich. Einfach, ähm, die finanzielle Lage, oder die Arbeitsmässig-, arbeitsmässig ist es hier noch eine Herausforderung für mich, ja."

69 Translated from German:
"(Bei einem) Besuch wurde ich angefeindet, weil ich Deutsch sprach. Wenn ich in der, wenn in der Schweiz war, gab es parallele Erlebnisse antisemitischer Natur, aber hier hab' ich auch ein Erlebnis gehabt, man hat mir zwei Mal die, die, die Autoreifen verstochen, weil ich eine deutsche äh Autonummer hatte, wie ich äh, äh zum äh vierten Mal hier war. Also von da her ist [lacht], die Freundlichkeit war dieselbe."

4.3 Conclusion and Outlook:
Narratives of Belonging in Multi-Sited Biographies

Feelings of belonging come up in several ways in the protagonists' narratives. The self is put in place through discussions and reflections on questions of national belonging and citizenship – confirming existing research on flexible citizenship – and conscious distinctions and self-positionings as individual, transnational actors within a globalized world. For instance, issues of brain drain are discussed in a way that reflects the protagonists' education and sometimes feelings of belonging to a cosmopolitan group.

A recurring theme is the issue of "bubbles" with regard to belonging. Often belonging to a specific privileged group or not-belonging to a specific place are discussed as being more important than belonging within classic identifiers discussed in connection with migration, such as nationality or religious group. Religion and tradition are seen from a pragmatic perspective that allows room for individual reinvention and is similar to the perspective the protagonists take on nationality and citizenship. However, the Swiss in Israel do reflect on their Jewish identity and the different manifestation it acquired through having moved to Israel, and Israelis in Switzerland might reflect on how to keep a Jewish identity or transfer it to their children without being religious. Questions of home and homesickness arise in the narratives when discussing the personal meaning of places, in some cases in a melancholy manner.

The chapter demonstrated how migration stories are in need of emotional attachments or belonging to illustrate individual construals of meaning and identity. When reflecting on and retelling migration experiences, belonging can assume various shapes. It can be Swissness, Jewishness, being an academic, having a character that fits in the place one lives in now, learning or not learning a language, differentiating oneself from others, mainly from other migrants but the local population or a past self as well. In the following chapter the meaning of places is explored from another perspective, namely in terms of memories and imaginaries as well as struggles and other ambivalent feelings evoked through migration.

5. Past, Present, and Future, or Nostalgia, Irritation, and Expectation

Feelings of nostalgia, irritation, and expectation are discussed by the protagonists when recounting their subjective (migration) experiences and in their narratives of identity as part of a globalized, interconnected world (Svašek & Skrbiš, 2007). Through this, past, present, and future selves become part of the migration narratives (Walsh, 2012). Some of the themes have to do with imaginaries of Switzerland and Israel and the need to adapt them according to lived experiences, as well as with rather positive emotions such as hope, longing, and anticipation. More negative emotions of regret, melancholy, or needing distance from a place are also discussed (Walsh, 2009).

While collectively emotions are regularly overlooked in migration studies, in terms of expectations connected to migration, feelings of "desire" and "hope" are relatively often studied. Ghassan Hage (Hage & Papadopoulos, 2004) even argues for the perception of subjects in a globalized world as "hoping subjects", in the sense that society can be looked at as a mechanism for the production and distribution of hope and that migrants project dreams of "upward symbolic mobility" (p. 112) onto physical mobility. The specific connection of hope and migration is also discussed, for example, by Frances Pine (2014), who found that Polish migrants perceive migration as an investment and belief in a better future. While they are not labor migrants who might be forced to become mobile for their own economic survival and that of their family, highly skilled migrants also discuss their migration with regard to a future that is "better" in various, individualized ways, such as a more fulfilling career, an adventure, a break from home, a "good, simple life", or the continuation of a loving relationship with a partner, as is the case for many lifestyle migrants as well (Benson & O'Reilly, 2009).

Likewise, there are regrets and more complex or negative emotions within interview narratives connected to a look in the past, which can be relived while telling a story and lead to feelings of nostalgia or distance, which are then interpreted and reflected upon in the present narrative. Further, emotions in interactions with people and places can be relevant when looking at migration stories. As emotions are not only direct reactions to events and surroundings but are also shaped by surroundings, contexts, states, and the constraints put on the individual's subjective position within society, the temporal aspect of past, present, future and the self changing according to those dimensions can become visible in the meaning making of the narratives.

5.1 A Place of Yearning and a Place to Savor

The title for this section comes from the words of the protagonists themselves. Hannah describes Switzerland *"a place to savor"* (original German: *"ein Ort zum Geniessen"*) (Transcript Hannah, p. 4) and Isabella uses the term *"place of yearning"* (German: *"Sehnsuchtsort"*) (Transcript Isabella, p. 1) for Israel, both providing specific images based on emotions for the two research fields. Michaela Benson and Karen O'Reilly (2009) describe meanings and imaginaries ascribed to specific geographical places as "geographies of meaning"; usually these are places where one can "live the good life" one imagines or has planned. These geographies of meaning in the case of the highly skilled protagonists are not necessarily as specific as for other groups of migrants who might need to migrate for pressing reasons such as economic survival, or a distinct image of what their "good life" entails. Instead, the protagonists' "geographies of meaning" have rather abstract, singular qualities, as the idea of "going abroad", rather than to a specific place, is more dominant for most of them.

Still, Israel, as well as Switzerland, are connected to certain imaginaries in the narratives. While the protagonists take great care to present themselves as having a "neutral look", not wanting to think and talk in dichotomies, this is not always possible, and the analytic distance produced at some points in the narratives cannot be sustained throughout the whole story and described actions or interactions. Using comparisons and contrasts as a way to describe surroundings in narratives is a useful tool in storytelling as well.

This means that pictures of Israel and Switzerland come up in sometimes more stereotypical ways than others. The protagonists talk about how others view the countries as a way to avoid becoming too simplistic. Often distinguishing or distancing themselves from simple perspectives of "others" – in general these others are explicitly or implicitly lesser educated people, not the "circles" with whom the protagonists engage, or the "bubbles" they live in. For example, through saying things such as *"it obviously isn't really like that"* (Transcript Isabella, p. 22) after describing what they see as "typical" for a place, they attempt to construct a singular image of the places that hold meaning for them and to connect memories and expectations to their current migration experience.

5.1.1 Memories and hopes

As mentioned, emotions should not only be seen as something emerging and developing through interaction and storytelling, but also as shaped by memories, imagination, and frameworks (Casey, 1987; Harkin, 2003; Skoggard & Waterston, 2015; Svašek, 2010, p. 868; Tonkin, 2006), something often becomes visible in interview narratives. Subjectivities and constructions of a self or identity can not only change depending on place but also in accordance with time. Reconstructions of events take place through emotions and might in turn make the protagonists feel newly emerging emotions. This is particularly relevant in the analysis of migration, as transnational activities and ties might lead to tensions between physical proximity and distance (Svašek, 2010, p. 868), which inhibit or shape direct interactions with people, places, or objects. This distance forces the protagonists to use memories as illustrations for their stories, and additionally can be reflected semantically in the formulations themselves; for instance, talking distantly about "*this country*" when referring to one's country of origin or similar formulations, it creates contradictions and illustrates tensions or dichotomies between images of transnationalism and the meaning of "roots" (Korpela, 2009).

Also, even if experiences and concurring emotions might be negative or ambivalent, it can be difficult to talk about them in purely negative terms, as retrospectively there might be a wish to look at issues in a different light, reflect on a potentially "learned life lesson" or something similar and trying to find a neutral, if not positive way, of talking about experiences in order to narrate a sequentially logical story. This can be described as "meaning making" (Kohler Riessman, 1993). Within the performance and exchange of a co-produced interview about migration experiences, it might seem unfitting to the protagonists to say something purely negative about their current situation, and it might, for example, be easier to frame an experience as an adventure or lesson learned as a way to relativize a negative description and the concomitant emotions. Nevertheless, irritations are also part of the narratives, as will be illustrated later.

Various kinds of childhood or youth memories are used and retold in order to narratively justify later migration and to create preexisting connections to the place to which one has migrated. Even if the stories are negative, the result – the migration, being on the move, and the place one finds oneself in in the present – is framed in a positive manner or at least as having positive aspects (a fulfilling career, a loving spouse, living in a place corresponding to one's character). The stories about the past lead to constructions of a self before and after migration or before and after specific experiences that can then be connected to migration in the story. In order to explain the source of the wish to migrate at some point, pivotal memories are woven into the story and past emotions are connected to more recent activities and decisions.

For instance, Isabella describes how she met Israelis on a backpacking trip through South America and relates discovering aspects of her character through the interaction with these young Israelis. She explains how she travelled with them for several days, how they made fun of her in a friendly manner and how she suddenly felt her own "*Israeliness*" emerge after several days when she started joking, bickering, and teasing back, which led her to discover a different side of herself and, as she says afterwards, made her feel liberated and happy:

And I arrived, I came after my high school graduation (…), and they are there after three years in the army. – And – and I did not understand, well, I understood the words, but I did not understand the mentality, it was really, I arrived there, and I just didn't get it. 'What's up with these Israelis?'

And in the beginning, they thought I was like them, right. I also bantered with them and I also don't have an accent or anything, but it just really made me realize how different their reality was and how they experienced such different things in the past three years compared to me, that I somehow – didn't understand the culture. It was a real culture shock for me.

I stuck closely with one of the Israeli groups and we travelled together. (…) (the) Israelis and I. The first weeks I didn't say anything [laughs]. (…) Yeah, I just didn't get it and I only observed, and they made fun of me the whole time, and then [laughs]. And then suddenly I guess I got it, and then (after) another week (…) I started to defend myself, and then one of the said, um, I don't remember exactly anymore: 'Now your whole 'Israeliness' comes out, it was sleeping for 20 years and now suddenly it comes up!' (…)

Yeah, and it made me discover this side of me – Also, this way of behaving towards each other, it was familiar from back home and so on, but here in Switzerland it wasn't really in the foreground.

(Transcript Isabella, pp. 14–15)[70]

Jacob uses another way of connecting to give meaning to migration. Moving to Switzerland for him was mainly due to his wife's career. They lived in another European country before but, as mentioned, he had lived in Switzerland for some time during his childhood, making Switzerland a place of memory with happy connotations:

---

70 Translated from Swiss German:

"*Und ich chum, ich chum da vo minere* [Matura], *(…) und si nach drü Jahr Militär. – Und – und ich han nüt verstande, also ich han d Wörter scho verstande, aber ich chan d Mentalität nöd verstande, sisch würklich, ich bin döt acho, ich bin eifach nöd drus cho, was lauft mit dene Israelis, und si hend am Afang gmeint, ich seg au esoo, oder, ich bi schön mit mine Sprüch cho und ich han au kän, äh, kän Akzent oder so, ähm, aber döt isch mer würklich eifach ganz fest ufgfalle, dass die so en anderi Realität händ und so öpis anders erlebt händ i däne letschte drü Jahr wie i ihrem Läbe, dass si irgendwie, ich, ich, ich die Kultur gar nöd verstahn. Es isch denn für mich würkli en Kulturschock gsi. Bi denn au sehr intensiv so es paar Wuche mit sonere Gruppe zäme greist, (di) Israelis und ich, ich ha no, di erst Wuche han ich keis Wort gseit.* [lacht] *(…) Ja. Ich bi eifach nöd drum chi, ich han nu beobachtet, si hend sich di ganz Ziit über mich lustig gmacht, und denn* [lacht] *Und denn plötzlich hanis glaub checkt, und denn noch dere Wuche, und denn hani mi afange wehre, und denn het mer de eint so gseit, du, ähm, was het er jetzt gseit, jetzt chunt dini ganzi israelisch-Heit use, wo zwänzg Johr gschlumeret het und jetz plötzlich gots uf.*"

For me Switzerland anyway was always a place of, uh, my past, which I have such good memories of and that's why it also was quite easy, the decision to move here right away.
(Transcript Jacob, p. 1)[71]

Hannah, who starts her story saying that she mainly wanted to "*go abroad*" not having a specific country in mind, later on does relate her family background and Jewish identity giving a deeper meaning to her living in Israel and connecting it to feelings of belonging that developed over time:

It's not just that – how should I put it, it's not just so that one can define everything through the past, I don't do that. But for me, my family is very, very, very affected by the Holocaust from all sides and I think, also for those in Switzerland, for my parents, for my grandparents, it sparks very positive and also proud feelings in them that the daughter then actually came to the country in which, which she can move around freely and live and so, I think this is there as well. I think I feel it as well, this feeling of belonging. I certainly feel it here more. And by the way, this, I know it now, that's funny, it just occurred to me: this was after three years I'd lived here, I was in Switzerland on a visit and on my flight back I realized: 'Wow, this is the first time that I look forward to coming back to Israel more than I'm sad about leaving Switzerland now'.
(Transcript Hannah, pp. 6–7)[72]

Susanna has a similar approach and talks about how her father would have been happy about her move, or at least her spending some time in Israel, as he had thought about it as well. Like Hannah, Susanna ties her being there to family history and her Jewish identity in the course of developing her narrative, which originally

---

71 Translated from German:
   "*Für mich war die Schweiz sowieso immer so ein Ort des-, äh, wo (mir) aus meiner Vergangenheit immer so gut in Erinnerung geblieben ist und deswegen war es für mich auch äh ziemlich leicht, die Entscheidung auch sofort hierherzuziehen.*"
72 Translated from German:
   "*Es ist ja nicht nur so, dass - wie soll ich sagen, es ist ja nicht nur so, dass man alles über die Vergangenheit oder so definiert und das mach', tu ich ja auch nicht. Aber es ist für mich, meine Familie ist sehr, sehr, sehr stark geprägt vom Holocaust von allen Seiten und ich denke, es ist doch auch für die in der Schweiz, für meine Eltern, für meine Grosseltern, eigentlich auch sehr äh, das löst in ihnen sehr positive und auch stolze Gefühle aus, dass die Tochter dann doch in das Land gekommen ist, in der, quasi, in dem sie sich frei bewegen kann, leben kann und so, das ist schon auch da. Und ich denke, das spür' ich auch, also das Zugehörigkeitsgefühl spür' ich sicher hier mehr. Und übrigens, das hat sich, das weiss ich jetzt, das ist lustig, das kommt mir jetzt wieder in den Sinn, es war nach drei Jahren, als ich hier lebte, da bin, war ich in der Schweiz auf Besuch und auf dem Rückflug merkte ich, wow, das ist das erste Mal, dass ich mich mehr freue, zurückzukehren nach Israel als dass es mich traurig macht, jetzt die Schweiz zu verlassen.*"

starts with a cosmopolitan ideal and a general wish of *"going abroad"* without a specific aim (Transcript Susanna, pp. 32–33).

Alexander, who thinks about one day moving back to Israel, explains that going back home is not necessarily easy and does this with an illustration of the past inhabited by nostalgia (Marcu, 2011, p. 11 f.). For example, he has grown apart from many of his formerly close childhood friends. With other friends made later in life, he never created this same form of bond, which he attributes to the time period he grew up in in Israel while comparing it to his later experiences in the United States.

> *So when I was growing up, that's no longer true to the younger generation – when we were growing up we were – trained (and we accepted this) to think about 'we (are) better than me'. And that-, you know, we grew up when Israel was still a semi-socialist country and so forth. So as such, we had some very strong, uh, experiences as a group. And then comes the army. So, you learn the value of friendship, you learn the value of being together, the value of the group and so forth. There's none of this in the US. In the US it's all about 'me, me, me'. – And there are some advantages to that, too. But, uh, I think that the basic difference lies there.*
>
> *So, when you are 'me, me, me' you are less open – to, um, to give, you know, just to give everything, you know. If we're true friends and so, there's no boundaries. Um. That's not the case there (in the US). So it's not that it's superficial, it is a different, uh, atmosphere, a different culture. Uh, and the truth is that – there, because it's like that all around, you have to take care of your interests much stronger than it used to be in Israel where you had a group with you and around you that sometimes helped you and (did) a little of the job for you, so anyway.*
>
> (Transcript Alexander, pp. 28–29)

Reflections on living abroad, transnational perspectives, and childhood memories are visible in the following quotation from the interview with Jacob as well. He is several years younger than Alexander and his present perception of Israel provides an addition and contrasts the description above. He puts his own personality or character in opposition and (economic) competition to "others", who are never clearly defined beyond some friends or schoolmates in the very beginning of the quotation:[73]

---

[73] The interview was in German and while Jacob's German is good, it is not his mother tongue. Due to this his speech was stagnant and disjointed at times, especially when he was trying to find the correct formulations. This is somewhat reflected in this quotation. Additionally, he might have been unsure what to answer or trying not to become too personal in his description.

I was quieter than the other children, um, I could listen better, I also knew another language, which means – my horizon was already much broader than, um, than the horizon of others, of my friends, for example. (…) I think that this shaped me and simply put me on different tracks than others. (…) Uh, I mean, for example yeah, when, when everyone is loud, then I'm actually, I look around (…) and I'm particularly silent (…). I look where I can be comfortable, where it is quieter, for example. Or I stand out because I'm the quiet one and not the loud one.[74]

Through his notion of having a "broader horizon" than others he presents a self that contains the capital and "soft skills" of a transnational habitus or cosmopolitan attitudes (Vertovec, 2009, p. 69 f.). He goes on, using concepts of transnational capitalist competition on a global job market:

(…) Sometimes you can win a competition when you're the outsider and not actually, uh, participating, in a way, and simply this different way of thinking [achieved through migration and transnational experiences]. *I mean, well it just creates something else, even just in relationships with other people.*[75]

A little bit later, but still talking about his memories of living in Israel, where he sometimes felt like "*a fish out of water*" (see pp. 118–119), he says:

(O)r things like 'nouveaux riches', for example, so this, this group, of people, who just became rich. I mean, in Israel, when someone finally earns well, then it is very important, for example, this (idea of) showing off, (…). Well, uh, to show yourself and everything you can and for me it is less important, to prove, uh, what I can, what I've got, that I've got what it takes – (For me this) was never really important, um, because it was more about, that when I have something, then it's not about making others, uh, envious.

---

74 Translated from German: "*Ich war ruhiger als die anderen Kinder, ähm, ich war, konnte besser zuhören, ich konnte auch eine andere Sprache, das heisst – mein Horizont war schon viel weiter als ähm (der) Horizont von anderen, von meinen Freunden zum Beispiel. (…). Ich glaube, das hat, das hat mich auch so geprägt, dass ich einfach auch auf (einer) anderen Schiene gedacht habe als andere. Also (…) in bestimmten Situationen, zum Beispiel äh, irgendwie auch (andere Faktoren) in Betracht genommen habe. Äh, sei es zum Beispiel ja, wenn, wenn alle so laut sind, dann bin ich eigentlich, dann schau ich das an und alle, alle sind laut, dann bin ich extra ruhig und schau eher wo ich mich wohlfühlen kann, wo es ruhiger ist, zum Beispiel. Oder ich (steche) eigentlich hervor, weil ich der Ruhige bin und nicht der Laute.*"

75 Translated from German: "*(…) Manchmal kann man (einen) Wettbewerb gewinnen, wenn man als Outsider (kommt), äh und eigentlich nicht mitmacht (…) und einfach diese andere Denkschiene (fährt). Also (…) schon in Beziehungen mit anderen Menschen, also es kommt einfach, etwas anderes (…).*"

And I think that this is very important in Israel. That when someone achieved something, then they also want, that, not that others are immediately envious, but I do think that people want to stand out. I mean, a bit like, 'I'm so great'. And it's less important, that people, uh, say: 'I feel good now', or: 'I feel good and I also achieved something', or: 'I achieved something, but I want to see that others achieve this as well'. Well, I mean, when you earn something, others can do this as well.

And I think in Israel it should be more about, when you earn (or achieve) something, then, you have to take care that others, I guess, well, that others achieve more.
(Transcript Jacob, pp. 13–14)[76]

As shown, memories, for example, childhood our youth memories are used as a way to frame and justify migration and, in turn, migration experiences are used to present a self that overall benefits from migration in the form of openness, having assets in a competitive global job market, feelings of belonging in several places, or the recounting of an eventful multi-sited biography. As mentioned, in some cases, specific memories are used to create something like a preexisting connection to the place one lives in now or to create a distance to the place one left.

Margot, for example, recalls how, in elementary school, an Israeli-Swiss boy who had just moved to the area joined her class. According to Margot, he "*danced into the classroom*" (in the original German: "*Der ist wirklich so ins Klassenzimmer getanzt gekommen*") and she felt deeply impressed by his openness and perceived freedom: "*he was just so incredibly free!*" (Transcript Margot, pp. 30–31). This memory might have shaped her image of Israel for the future as her recounting of her experiences with her classmate is quite detailed (she tells several anecdotes about him and his family) and she talks about how happy she is that her children can now grow up with the same freedom she saw in her classmate many years ago. As mentioned, through

---

76 Translated from German:

"(O)der, zum Beispiel, Sachen wie 'Nouveaux Riches', also diese, diese Bewegung, (also) Leute, die gerade reich geworden sind. Also in Israel, wenn jemand zum Beispiel endlich mal gut verdient, dann ist es zum Beispiel (wichtig), (dieses) 'Show Off', (…) um sich zu zeigen, (zu zeigen, was man) alles (…) kann. Und für mich ist es weniger wichtig, anderen zu beweisen, äh, was ich alles so drauf habe – es war nie, nie wirklich wichtig, ähm, weil es war-, mir ging es mehr darum, dass wenn ich etwas habe, dann muss es, dann suche (ich da jetzt nicht danach, dass) andere Leute auf mich neidisch sind. Und ich glaube, das ist in Israel sehr wichtig. Dass wenn jemand etwas erreicht, dass er (auch) will, dass andere (vielleicht) nicht sofort, nicht unmittelbar neidisch sind, aber ich glaube schon, (dass) man hervorstehen will. Also ein bisschen so, 'ich bin so toll'. (Und es wird dann weniger darauf geachtet zu sagen) ja, 'ich fühl mich jetzt gut', oder 'ich habe etwas erreicht, aber ich möchte, (dass die anderen auch etwas erreichen)'. Ich möchte, dass andere das auch etwas (erreichen), äh also, das heisst, also, wenn ich etwas verdiene, heisst das, andere können das auch. Und ich glaube in Israel (sollte) es mehr darum (gehen), dass wenn ich etwas verdiene (erreiche), dann muss ich auch dafür sorgen, dass andere, na, an mehr kommen."

the use of these kinds of memories, a temporal aspect comes into the narration. The past is used to talk about present and future situations, and strengthen narrative ties to places, identities, and characteristics. In the course of the narratives, childhood memories or, in some cases, relating to one's own children's experiences often helped to describe an emotion and experience in a clearer manner.

One thing that surprisingly came up quite regularly during interviews with protagonists, and also in several conversations in the field, was the difference between children's birthday parties in Israel versus Switzerland. A strong contrast was drawn between Israel and Switzerland in the narratives at these points, which was usually avoided or relativized by the protagonists when talking about other aspects of daily life. While in Israel it is described as being common to invite the whole class or at least a large number people and to include games and activities, the parties in Switzerland are described as smaller and shorter affairs, that from an Israeli perspective seem to lack joy or openness. During one of my stays in Tel Aviv in Summer 2018, I happened to stay close to Yarkon Park and walked past several such birthday parties. My fieldnote says:

Yarkon Park is a large park with the Yarkon River flowing through, many different plants and lakes, sports facilities, and spacious green meadows where groups can meet and spend the day. One birthday party in particular, seemed to illustrate the discussed difference to Swiss birthday parties. There were little girls in princess dresses, a small stage, blankets on the ground, music playing, a table with a tablecloth and jam-packed with food, balloons, and garlands on trees, and at least 30 children and several adults standing or sitting on the ground talking and laughing. The scene was interesting and fun because it was such a good demonstration of what my interviewees had described. I have to admit that I never walked past a similar scene in a Swiss park, even though many children's parties take place there as well, but it is true that they usually seem to be smaller events. I wonder what the reason might be other than the warmer climate? One could organize the same kinds of parties in Switzerland?

Jacob, remembering children's birthday parties and relating them to how he perceives Swiss society says:

So, it was like this when I was a child: it was always, there always were birthday parties and the children actually always invited their friends. It was always a pretty, uh, small party with about five, six, maximum ten people, but then my mom came to me and said: 'Look when you have a birthday party, then you invite everyone, because that's simply how it's done. You invite everyone. Either no one or everyone.' (…)
I think this is simply where the differences lie, simply, this, that you look at the person and in Switzerland the person is less seen as an emotional being somehow, but simply as a carrier

of skills, knowledge, expertise, and the feelings, hm, are simply less important.
(Transcript Jacob, pp. 27–28)[77]

He draws a connection between the differences in birthday parties and the way individuals are perceived in a country, and, through this, presents Switzerland as a place where individuals are considered as *"emotional beings"* to a lesser extent arguing that feelings are less important in Switzerland. In a way, this again connects his experiences and interpretations to Alexander's image of a more communal Israel of the past. Specific events, such as birthday parties, are used to illustrate these forms of perceived cultural differences.

Gabriele recalls a completely different kind of memory, a crucial political event, the assassination of Yitzhak Rabin in 1995, and connects it to her conditions about staying in Israel, her position there in the present and her view of the future:

Yeah. So maybe the most drastic – uh, one of the most drastic experiences was during, when, at the demonstrations for peace, when Prime Minister Rabin was murdered. So, we were also, we were there, and we were eyewitnesses, and we ran away, and it was, it still is a very, very difficult experience. Yeah. And it – (…) I mean, I'm still an optimist, yeah. Someday [laughs], somehow it has to get better, someday there has to be a change, we just can't go on like this forever. And, uh, there are more and more, uh, circles [activists] in the West Bank as well. (…) Then if we become one state, everyone should have the same rights. So, I always said that I have these red lines and then I leave (Israel). So that's, that's something I always said, but then I also see, that the red lines are somewhat flexible, yeah – And as you get older, it's not becoming easier to come to a decision, yeah, 'now I'm leaving', yeah.
(Transcript Gabriele, pp. 34–36)[78]

---

77 Translated from German:
"Also, das war auch zum Beispiel als Kind so, es gab immer Geburtstagspartys, und die Kinder haben eigentlich äh immer ihre Freunde eingeladen. Und das war immer so, mh, eine kleine Party, so fünf, sechs, maximal zehn (sind) gekommen, aber dann ist meine Mutter zu mir gekommen und hat gesagt: 'schau, wenn du eine Geburtstagsparty machst, dann lädst du alle ein, (…) weil sonst – so etwas tut man nicht. Man lädt alle ein. Entweder niemanden oder alle.' Also, (…) ja, ich glaube einfach, da liegen die Unterschiede. Einfach, dass man auf den Menschen schaut und halt, in der Schweiz wird halt der Mensch weniger als emotionales Wesen irgendwie äh begriffen, sondern einfach als Träger von Fähigkeiten, von Wissen, von äh Expertise vielleicht und die Gefühle, mh, sind, sind (einfach) weniger wichtig."

78 Translated from German:
"Ja. Also vielleicht so der Einschneidenste-, äh, eine der einschneidendsten Erfahrungen war die äh, war während der Friedensdemo (an der wir) teilgenommen haben, wo der äh, Ministerpräsident Rabin ermordet wurde. Also das sind wir auch, wir waren da Augenzeugen, wir rannten davon und das war, das ist immer noch eine sehr, sehr schwierige Erfahrung. Ja. Und es- (…). Also ich gehör' immer noch zu den Optimisten, ja. Irgendwann [lacht], irgendwann muss es doch äh, besser werden, irgendwann muss es eine Änderung geben, wir können ja nicht ewig so weitermachen und äh, ewigs. (Es) gibt auch

As illustrated with the above quotations, emotions are not only shaped and reflected on through direct interactions, they are also shaped by memories and imaginations. Past events and memories of these events can shape the current self and perspectives on migration decisions (Casey, 1987; Svašek, 2010; Tonkin, 2006). However, migration stories not only include the past, questions about the future arise as well. Looking to the future, discussions about moving back to Switzerland, Israel or another country are led in a somewhat uncertain way which tries to be open to future personal and political changes (Benson & O'Reilly, 2009; Scott, 2006) and maybe reflects a globalized world perceived as fast paced and everchanging. Societal and political changes and various forms of hopes and anxieties are considered by Swiss in Israel as well as by Israelis in Switzerland.

Alexander discusses the role emotions play in decisions about moving back to Israel and explicitly talks about the temporality of the moment in which the interview takes place and how his perspective might change at another point in time:

We're considering, we're talking (about) finding a way to go back to Israel because of, more than anything, my wife's family. Uh, we try hard to make a conscious decision, (and) my answer would really be, let's wait for the elections, you know, because I have a difficult, I have a lot of difficulty there. But you know, you may have come across this with other Israelis, that's what I tell you now: ask me tomorrow morning and it may be different. And, and it's not that it's a, an emotional ride, because when I say this (I say it in an analytical way), when I get the emotions involved, I can take the risk of saying you know what, it sucks there, it's shitty, but it's our shit and we all belong here. So yeah, it oscillates between those two [laughs]. And I think that's the case with many Israelis. Uh. So, it's the question if you catch them at what time, part of the oscillation, but that's – you know.
(Transcript Alexander, p. 37)

Similarly, Rhea says:

Now, we're going through a very, it's um, I don't know. First of all, I mean, I don't want to go now as long as Bibi [Netanyahu] is, is Prime Minister, I don't want to. And, I think I would go back because I'm not sure that one day I want my children to be Swiss or German or American, whatever we made up. I think, I mean, for me it's very clear, I'm an Israeli, even

---

zunehmend äh, im Westjordanland Kreise [Aktivitäten]. Und, äh, oder dann, ja, müssen alle, oder dann werden wir ein, ein Staat und alle sollten die gleichen Rechte kriegen. Also ich habe immer gesagt, ich habe so meine roten Linien und dann geh' ich weg (aus Israel), also das, dass habe ich immer gesagt, aber ich sehe dann auch, dass die roten Linien, ja, die sind etwas dehnbar, ja. - Und wenn man älter wird, wird's auch nicht einfacher, eine Entscheidung zu treffen, ja, jetzt geh' ich weg, ja."

if I will live twenty years here, I'm an Israeli. But I know for my children it's not the same.
(Transcript Rhea, pp. 18–19)

Margot, in contrast and from the perspective of Israel says:

Well, the motivation to be in Switzerland is actually really low and I have to say, except for the political aspect, well, I would say, I would be very happy, if my children, would grow up with the political security that we, yeah, that a child has in Switzerland, but society wise I would not want to go back to Switzerland today.
(Transcript Margot, p. 13)[79]

The decisions to stay or leave a place are often tied to a memory or memories and a past self in the course of the narrative, which draw on different emotional registers such as happy childhood memories or nostalgia about bygone events, interactions, or connections. The decision to be in a place is rarely presented as clear-cut as is the discussion of future plans, selves, and hopes. There is always some reflection going on and a questioning of future possibilities to which one might have to adapt, and which leads to a restructuring of expectations and imaginaries, maybe as a way to present a flexible self, adapted to the realities of a place and the demands of globalization.

5.1.2 Imaginaries and realities

Not only memories, but different imaginaries of Israel and Switzerland and the emotions they evoke are at play in the narratives. There are questions of perception from the outside, and also personal observations and preferences, which shape the view of a place by the highly skilled protagonists. The tensions between reality and imagination often documented in migration research (Benson & O'Reilly, 2009) are not an explicit factor for the protagonists, who all present themselves as "realists", different from other migrants, who might have more idealized imaginaries.

Reflecting on the image of Israel in Switzerland and Israeli society, Isabella says:

I have the feeling the image [of Israel in Switzerland] *is so dominated by the media. The image, that well, it's an unjust country and yeah, kind of a 'justification country', where*

---

79 Translated from German:
"Also die Motivation in der Schweiz zu sein ist schon sehr klein und ich muss sagen, ausser dem politischen Aspekt, also ich sage, ich wäre sehr froh, meine Kinder hätten, würden mit der, der politischen Sicherheit aufwachsen, die wir, ja, die ein Kind in der Schweiz hat, aber gesellschaftlich möchte ich heute nicht in die Schweiz zurück."

people are a bit brainwashed and there is no justice. And I think, um, I guess people expect too little of Israelis and most people don't know what kind of society it is, where in the political sphere there is a lot of discourse. Just that it's so diverse, that there is an incredible number of layers, I think. I don't have the feeling that it's looked at in a differentiated manner. I also don't have the feeling that people can imagine that there is the kind of university I attended, and then, for example, that I had classes and subjects with a strong discussion. And I think, it's also a very self-critical country. I think somehow Switzerland is much worse, concerning tabooing, and not talking about things. Um, I find it's a society where there is much more, well, which is much more capable of criticizing itself, than for example here (in Switzerland). Ah, yeah, so that's a bit of the feeling I got. I really have the feeling in Switzerland or in Europe you get the feeling that there are just some European Jews living there, who exiled everyone quickly, and uh, always use the Holocaust as an excuse. That's a bit (of) my image – – which of course is not always true.
Of course, there are some social classes who concern themselves with it more –
(Transcript Isabella, p. 22)[80]

Isabella relativizes her description in the last part of the quotation saying that more educated classes might have a more complex view of Israel. Doron, on the other hand, distinguishes himself as not being *"very representative"* when talking about how Israel is perceived in Switzerland, meaning that he is not particularly political, not wanting to engage in discussions about the state of Israel:

I'm not very representative. (…) Yeah, and also sometimes, people tell me they don't like Israel but to me they are still nice.
(Transcript Doron, p. 18)

---

80 Translated from Swiss German:
"*(U)nd hüt han ich eifach s'Gfühl, sisch [Israel-Bild in der Schweiz] so vo de Medie prägt, das Bild, dass es halt es ungrechts Land isch und es ähm, ja so es 'Justification-Land', wod Lüüt so chli brainwashed sind und kei Grechtigkeit existiert, und 's, ich glaub, ähm, me vermutet d'Israelis wie wenig zue und di meiste wüssed wi nöd, was so Gesellschaft isch, wo im staatliche Diskurs inne äh existiert. Eifach so sehr breit gfächeret isch, so unglaublich vil verschiedeni Schichte git, ähm find me, ich han nöd s'Gfühl, dass es so differenziert agluegt wird, han au nöd s'Gfühl, dass sich d'Lüüt chönd vorstelle, dass, dass es sone Uni git, wien ich gsi bin und dass ich zum Biispiel so Kürs han gha und so Fächer und so Diskurs mir gha hend, ich find, es isch au es sehr selbstkritischs Land, ich find irgendwie d'Schwiiz isch da vil schlimmer, was Tabuisierig aabelangt und, und Sache werded nöd drüber gredt. Ähm ich find, sisch e Gsellschaft, wo du vil meh ja, wo, wo vil fähiger isch, sich selber z'kritisiere als zum Biispil da. Äh, ja, so chli, für das isch mis Gfühl. Ich han würkli s'Gfühl, in Israel, äh, in de Schwiiz oder in Europa hät me s'Gfühl, es wohned eifach nur so irgendwelchi europäischi Jude döte, wo alli grad so schnell so vertriebe händ und äh, und immer äh, als Usred de Holocaust füreholed. Das isch so chli mis Bild. – Was natürlich nöd immer stimmt. Klar, git's die Schichte, wo sich meh demit befassed –*"

Daniel states the following about how he thinks Israel is perceived in Switzerland:

> *It's a good question, I don't know, I don't know really – In Germany* [where the interviewee lived before moving to Switzerland], *I noticed that actually a lot of people had pretty nice images. I can also imagine it's related (to) the Holocaust and then the mutual history. Other European societies, I mean in Italy and in Spain where I spent some time, then I noticed it's a big, big 'no' against Israel. Switzerland I actually don't know, so. I haven't met any negative phenomena but I haven't seen any polls, I guess in the next war, I will have more voices* [information on how Israel is perceived in Switzerland]. *Right now I, I don't really know.*
> (Transcript Daniel, p. 15)

Relating to a completely different, individual aspect of expectation and well-being, Isabella describes her enjoyment of Israel due to its warmer weather, reflecting the existing imaginary of Israel as a warm holiday destination:

> *And also, the weather aspect, I found it so pleasant, just for years – (…) I was really suffering from the winters (here) and I, I'm really someone who is always cold. And for me it was a blessing there, to pretty much have sun and singing birds the whole year [laughs], I really enjoyed it.*
> (Transcript Isabella, p. 10)[81]

Doron talks about climate as well, but applies the use of coldness not to geography and personal well-being but to humans when he says he was a bit afraid people would be "*cold*" in Switzerland (Transcript Doron, p. 2). He then explains that he did enjoy the cold weather when talking about his first impressions of Switzerland, which contributed to his general happiness about being in the country:

> "*I, it was nice, I was really excited. I came in winter, which is my favorite Jahreszeit* [German for season], *season, and yeah, it was great. First of all, the old city, the old buildings, just it is so old, it was so special for me. I really liked it. Somehow, I understand (how) I felt, I felt good. And (it was) so cold, it was also snowy, it was wonderful. I thought 'ok' – I was really happy. (I thought) 'I found my place'. We* [his wife and him] *had lots of difficulties in the first year, really lots of hard times but I always felt ok, I'm glad I came here, uh, yeah. I know I (thought) of the better (aspects) and the way (things are here). And (it's not just about what)*

---

81 Translated from Swiss German:
"*(D)enn au wetter-technisch ischs, han ichs sehr agnähm gfunde, ha jahrelang – (…) Eifach würklich glitte ab dene Winter und bi, bi würkli eifach öper, wo sehr chalt het immer. Und es isch für mich en Säge gsi da eifach irgendwie s ganze Johr Sunne und Vögeli pfiffe, [lacht] han ich sehr gnosse.*"

the place looks like but also the atmosphere. (Here) I felt most days more relaxed somehow. (Transcript Doron, p. 7)

While this is a very positive description of his first impression of Switzerland, Doron talks about Israel always being *"home"* and some difficult times and *"uncertainty"* (Transcript Doron, p. 6) after having moved to Switzerland but then seemingly wants to make sure to also talk about more positive aspects of mobility, emphasizing his happiness about migrating.

Discussing his first impressions of Switzerland in a similar but more detached manner, Alexander says:

Well see, I didn't come with, uh, I didn't come to Switzerland a 'virgin' [laughs]. I've been here a number of times before and, uh, actually, I, I came prepared to (expect) much worse than what I found. So, uh, I was basically surprised for the better just because [laughs] I didn't have any expectation. But I was surprised for the better and I kind of like it. Yeah. (Transcript Alexander, p. 4)

On perceptions of Switzerland in Israel, Hannah argues that especially as a Swiss woman she always has all sympathies and very positive attitudes towards her (Transcript Hannah, p. 21). Switzerland is rarely looked at negatively as Gabriele further illustrates when talking about how Switzerland is perceived in Israel:

In Israel there always is this notion that Switzerland is paradise on earth, yeah. The Garden of Eden. And – that's actually where people think I'm crazy, why um – (…) – Yeah, 'why do you exchange this land of (plenty), or this Garden of Eden with these crazy surroundings here?', right?
(Transcript Gabriele, pp. 8–9)[82]

Gabriele also talks about how when she moved to Israel a few decades earlier there was less information about the country in Swiss media, and the general perception of Israel was much more positive than today with Swiss people mainly connecting Israel with the Kibbutzim and a warm destination to travel to. This rather positive image of Israel in Switzerland in the past is also documented by Jonathan Kreutner (2013), mentioned in chapter 2. Gabriele's main imagination of Israel was that it

---

82 Translated from German:
"*In Israel hat man immer die Vorstellung, dass die Schweiz das Paradies sei auf Erden, ja. Der, der Garten Eden. Und – wo man mich eigentlich für verrückt hält, warum ähm – (…) Ja, warum wechselst du dieses äh, dieses Schlaraffen-, oder diesen Garten Eden mit dieser verrückten Umgebung hier, ja?*"

was poor in comparison to Switzerland and that her standard of living would be much lower after moving there (Transcript Gabriele, p. 8).

Looking at migration to Israel, Dani Kranz (2016, p. 13) describes how moving to Israel through making *Aliyah* can sometimes lead to a clash between an imaginary Israel and lived reality, something often part of migration stories (Benson, 2009). Dani Kranz (2016, p. 13) describes an example of an interviewee: "… who had a vast investment in an imaginary Israel and who suffered from a reality shock once they physically arrived." This seems not to have been the case for the protagonists, who generally did have what they describe as realistic perspectives on the country to which they moved – either Israel or Switzerland – and who make sure to reflect on their differentiated perspective on the two places in the course of their stories. Even Matt, for whom Israel was always the only possible migratory destination, makes sure to explain how he knew living in Israel would be very different from spending his holidays there (Transcript Matt, p. 17). This form of narrative does not leave space for an explicit "reality shock", not even a subtle one, however this does not mean that the protagonists did not encounter difficulties, experience negative emotions, or struggled in some aspects of their daily life due to migration, as described in the next chapter.

5.2 The Daily Struggle

The notion of a "*daily struggle*", or "*everyday struggle*" is a description used by Isabella, as well as Rhea and in various conversations with Israelis and foreigners living in Israel, who talk of a place with a lot of "*pressure*", or, as Matt puts it, "*stress*" or "*fear*". In these narratives, Israel becomes a place that is exhausting, emotionally stirring and in consequence, a place from which someone might need a break or emotional as well as physical distance. Probably due to the conflictual political circumstances in Israel, Switzerland as a comparatively very stable place, did not trigger such strong imagery, even though problems of daily life there were discussed as well. The discussion of struggles and similar topics, however, is not always about internal political tensions, or the potential threat of war with a neighboring country. While part of reality, the meaning of these circumstances should not be overemphasized, as irritation in daily life is usually discussed when talking about more mundane things, such as organizing a visa or interactions during a visit to the supermarket or post office. All these "annoyances" or conflictual interactions then fall under the term "daily struggle".

5.2.1 Taking a break and gaining through distance

As a consequence of the *"daily struggle"*, Israel as a surrounding framework is in some cases presented, as mentioned, as a place from which one needs or might potentially need a break or physical distance. This can, for example, be seen in the following quotation. While originally leaving Israel for a brighter academic future and a better research laboratory, Alexander says that the wish for a better laboratory was actually a pretext for leaving Israel as he felt exhausted:

> *So that was my excuse. So, I applied to places, to universities in the US – that enabled me to do more (research). So it was, it was as an alibi but underneath it, I had all kinds of – I had two things. One was a sense of adventure and it was easy to convey (this) to my wife. And the other one was (that) I pretty much had enough. I had enough of the rightwing and the religious parties and the pressure.*
>
> *Uh, have you ever been to Israel? [I reply that I have but never longer than 3 months at a time]. So, you don't feel the pressure there. So, I can describe to you a day of, I don't know, a, uh, a research assistant or whatever. So, you start your day in your lab, doing your thing, comes lunchtime, you go to the cafeteria and you pick up the newspaper and by the time [laughs], by the time you finish lunch, you're so pissed at everybody [laughs] because of what you read in the newspaper, that (it) is the end of your day.*
>
> *So, yeah, so I, I felt like that. I needed a break and it's not that I didn't like Israel anymore or, um, when we left, we left knowing that (we)'re coming back. You know, like many Israelis. So, I guess we're still looking for a way back.*
> (Transcript Alexander, p. 25)

Matt, describing life in Israel as not only generally more intense but also more stressful in terms of his work life, says:

> *Here (in Israel) there is so much more stress. You run, you run all the time, it's awful. In Switzerland I never finished my (working) day at 9pm. Here, no problem. (…) It can easily happen that I get home from work at 9 or 9:30. It's normal, not something special.*
> (Transcript Matt, p. 11)[83]

Something similar is described by the participants of Dani Kranz's (2016) study on Israelis in Berlin, who talk about an *"Israeli rat race"* of which they only become

---

83 Translated from French:
"Ici (en Israël) il y tellement plus de stress. Tu cours, tu cours tout le temps, c'est horrible. En Suisse j'ai jamais fini ma journée (de travail) à neuf heures. Ici, pas de problème. (…) Ça m'arrive de rentré du boulot à neuf heures ou neuf heures et demie. Ici c'est normal, c'est pas quelque chose d'exceptionnel."

aware and see more clearly when they move abroad and have some physical and emotional distance. Rhea, who might be hyperaware of her framework as a highly politically active person says about moving to Switzerland:

Yeah, for some – it was a break, it came as a break, it was (…) as a break just, just a break. Just a break. Other problems came but on a political base it's a break. (…) you don't feel hunted every day.
(Transcript Rhea, p. 43)

On the aspect of the struggles of everyday life in Israel as well as in Switzerland, where she does not always know "*the rules*", for example of communication or everyday interaction, she says:

You don't feel you need to take care, I mean, people are, you know, basically honest. Nobody's trying to cheat you, basically. And in Israel all the time you think like who is trying to cheat you. Who's trying to check me? Who's trying to do something for me? And, um, here I don't have it. I mean, the prices are low in all Migros [Swiss supermarket chain] stores more or less, I mean sometimes you don't have the products, if it's, um, how do you call that, pom- (…) the one that is open on Sundays. So, they only have the expensive products. But they don't try to cheat you, it's not like the same product (would be extremely overpriced so people feel) robbed. And you do have it in Israel. Like, ok, so they're trying to cheat. And you really need to know it.
But of course, if you are um, a migrant, a stranger, you don't know the rules of everything. Like now, my husband is trying to find a job and we don't know the rules of the game, we don't. And in Israel, you know, you totally know how to deal with that. And here it's like – harder to do it. Also, you know, in the beginning, I had all these problems (with) colleagues. It's not very problematic. But all this communication, which I was you know, Israeli, honest, touching, and they do not touch. They thought I was flirting but I didn't. After that they were friends of mine, most of them are friends of mine and they know, I'm a touchy person. I say, like, 'I am from Israel, it's not just me'. So, these are just minor things. But I do miss the hugging and touching, in Israel –
(Transcript Rhea, pp. 43–44)

Rhea's quotation illustrates a mix of emotions ranging from relief about Switzerland being "*honest*", annoyance about stores cheating in Israel, struggling with not knowing the Swiss "*rules*" of jobhunting, exasperation about complicated interactions of daily life, and missing Israel.

Isabella, who misses Israel as well, still decided to live in Switzerland for now and exemplifies the tensions that can emerge for (some) migrants between "'here' and 'there'" (Boccagni & Baldassar, 2015, p. 74) using the feeling of being *"torn"*. She says:

> *I think, I, I will always be torn between these two worlds. And I just think, from a practical point of view, such a life is easier to live when you're in Switzerland.*
> (Transcript Isabella, p. 9)[84]

She relates life being easier in Switzerland mainly to the difficulty of earning one's living in Israel, where she describes young adults as often having financial support from their parents, something which her Swiss parent could not understand assuming she would be financially independent after graduating from university. She had originally planned to stay in Israel but says about living in Tel Aviv:

> *And Tel Aviv was so shitty, really, sorry. Really, really. It really was (a) fight for survival. Um, which in the end also stops you from being creative, right?*
> (Transcript Isabella, p. 6)[85]

She realizes that personal circumstances might have tainted her view of Tel Aviv, but describes this whole period of her move from another part of Israel to Tel Aviv as at first an adventurous challenge to overcome but then becoming increasingly difficult. Her identity as an artist makes her reflect on the meaning of place for creativity at several points in the interview and while the struggles in Tel Aviv stopped her from being creative, she also says Switzerland is restricting creativity at another point of her narrative.

> *The daily struggle* [she uses this term in a mix of English and German here and later in the interview in English[86]], *I had, had to get really used to it and change. That everything is different, that you need so much energy, need to be pushy, you need to hold your ground every day, you need to fight for everything, being it the supermarket, the post office, it really*

---

84 Translated from Swiss German:
   "Ähm. Ich glaub, ich, ich würd ebe immer zwüsched dene zwei Wälte hin und her grisse si. Und ich glaub eifach praktisch gseh, isch sones Läbe eifacher z'veriibare, wend ide Schwiiz wohnsch."
85 Translated from Swiss German:
   "Und, und Tel Aviv isch arsch härt gsi, also 'Tschuldigung. Würklich, würklich. Es isch würklich dä Überläbeskampf gsi. Ähm, wo halt au dänn schlussändlich au d'Kreativität hämmt, oder."
86 Isabella switched from Swiss German to high German and back and mixing in English words several times throughout the interview, usually speaking high German to make things easier for me as a foreigner but inadvertently switching back to Swiss German, especially when the topic became exciting or difficult. Language switching, code switching, or using terms from other languages is something almost all protagonists did at one point or another during interviews.

was a change. And I think, I sort of, I realized I have the motivation and the go and the energy. I was a bit like a pioneer.
(Transcript Isabella, p. 11)[87]

The image of being a pioneer is an interesting way of positioning oneself, as it presents a self with strong agency and maybe someone who can dissociate from the struggles of "here and there" or from the feeling of being "*torn*". It somewhat leaves one outside of general society and rather connotes someone who migrates on their own terms and paths, and maybe stays as an onlooking stranger or observer, who explores their surroundings with a certain distance. The identity of a pioneer in a new environment is narratively presented as an individual accomplishment in Isabella's story. It is also an image sometimes used by Western lifestyle migrants in India (Korpela, 2009) and could be linked to old imaginaries of the Westerner going to "the Orient" as an adventure (Kabbani, 1986). Other authors discuss "pioneer migrants" as individual migrants not reliant on existing migration movements and groups who move to super-diverse (Vertovec, 2007) places. These "pioneer migrants" are usually highly educated and have a certain amount of cultural and social capital (Wessendorf, 2017), in which case many highly skilled migrants can be classified as such.

When asked later in the interview if she would accept a "dream job" in Israel, Isabella repeats the feeling of finding life exhausting ("*anstrengend*" in German) there, saying she would have to think about it as she is not sure if she could muster the same energy she had for the move in the past again (Transcript Isabella, p. 16), making the pioneer identity a temporary, fleeting notion.

Jacob, who now lives in Switzerland, talks about the competitiveness he experienced while still living in Israel and turns his migration story and related struggles into an asset or capital he brings with him to Switzerland, in a way looking at it from an economic perspective of competitive job markets (Kaufmann, Bergmann, & Joye, 2004; Salazar & Jayaram, 2016):

And I think that it's because the situation there is not that easy, and life is demanding. Always, all the time, every day is a bit of a challenge, intellectually and physically, it is demanding to find solutions all the time, to find your niche. But there, on the other hand you also get a lot of support, I mean, emotionally from family, from friends, um, then it's good.

---

87 Translated from Swiss German:
"*De alltäglichi Struggle, de hani, hani mi, äh, recht müsse dra gwöhne und verändere. Dass alles andersch isch, dass du eifach bruchsch extrem vil Energie, bruchsch Ellböge, du muesch dich behaupte jede Tag du muesch für alles kämpfe, sig das in Supermärt ga, uf Post – ähm das isch scho recht en Umstellig gsi. Und ich glaub aber, ich bin wi, ich han gmerkt, ich han wi gnueg Motivation gha zum das mache und so de Elan und d Energie, ich bi so Pionier gsi es bizli.*"

But financially, and also, I think the opportunities, I mean, the country simply doesn't have as much to offer, I mean you couldn't really survive there, unless, in those known areas [like high-tech]. *And always, always, always having to sell something special. But others have to move abroad to make a living. Simply because the country is small and developed this culture, uh, where many things don't have space, or, yeah, so. I think that the infrastructure and size play a powerful role there. Competition is quite strong, I have to say. So I think that this is, when Israelis go abroad with this competitive way of thinking (it) pays off. (…) It just pays off.*
(Transcript Jacob, pp. 24–25)[88]

As touched upon earlier, Jacob's perspective in this quotation could be explained with the concept of having transnational capital, or more accurately, motility, where migration is not merely seen as physical movement from A to B but as "… movement infused with both self-ascribed and attributed meanings" (Salazar & Jayaram, 2016, p. 1). The concept helps to operationalize the idea of "mobility as capital", similarly to how transnationalism can be looked at from the perspective of cultural competence or cosmopolitanism (Friedman, 2017; Vertovec, 2009, p. 69 f.). Various processes connected to transnationalizing or cosmopolitanizing attitudes and values and additionally leading to numerous competences and attributes, such as emotional competence in the form of the ability to open oneself up to divergent cultural influences among other things, (Koehn & Rosenau, 2002, 2010), can be seen in such narratives. While labor migrants might also gain transnational competences through their mobility (Vertovec, 2009, p. 72), highly skilled migrants usually have more success utilizing and capitalizing on such attributes in contemporary knowledge societies, the way Jacob does above when talking about competitive advantages. Jacob's quotation could moreover be interpreted as him trying to calm

---

88 Translated from German:
"*Und ich glaube, dass weil die Situation dort (in Israel) nicht so leicht ist und das Leben fordert von (einem) wirklich immer die ganze Zeit, jeder Tag ist ein bisschen so eine Herausforderung, intellektuell und auch äh physisch ist es, ist es herausfordernd, Lösungen zu finden die ganze Zeit, sich die Nische zu, zu finden. Aber da, aber auf der anderen Seite (wird man) immer wieder auch unterstützt, also emotional von der Familie, vom Freundeskreis, ähm, dann ist es gut. Aber finanziell und auch ich glaube, die Möglichkeiten, also ist einfach nicht ähm, hat das Land weniger anzubieten, also man könnte da zum Beispiel, könnte dort nicht wirklich überleben. Es sei denn, in den Szenen, die bekannt sind* [wie High-Tech]. *Und (man muss) immer und immer und immer, immer ein äh Kunststück verkaufen können. Aber andere können's da, zum Beispiel -müssen ins Ausland ziehen, damit sie davon eigentlich leben können. Einfach weil das Land klein ist, weil das Land sich eine bestimmte Kultur äh sich angeeignet hat. Das sind ja oft Dinge- nicht äh oder viele Sachen finden einfach keinen Platz oder. Ja, so. Ich glaube, das ist Infrastruktur und einfach Grösse die, die hier eine (Rolle) spielt. (Der) Wettbewerb ist ziemlich gross, muss man sagen. Also ich glaube, dass (für) Israelis, also mit diesem kompetitiven äh Charakter ins Ausland zu gehen, zahlt sich aus. (…) Es zahlt sich einfach aus.*"

himself as he is in a professionally transitional phase, about to start a new job, and might want to affirm that being in Switzerland was the right decision and to illustrate the advantages his "Israeliness" might bring to his local career.

From the perspective of Israel, Margot (Transcript Margot, pp. 37–38) talks about how her "Swissness" is often seen as a professional asset in Israel as it seems to project an image of respectability to her clients. However, she takes a different approach when discussing her place of residence with people or clients in Switzerland. Talking about various struggles connected to Israel, namely the way the country is seen from outside, she sets boundaries in that she talks about how she refuses to do awareness training for foreigners, even though she argues she would be good at it, due to her transnational experiences and educational qualification. She does not want to *"change undifferentiated views into differentiated ones"*. She says she did this sometimes in the past, but, as the experience was upsetting at one time even turning into a fight with a friend, she stopped.[89]

Doron also says that he is tired and sometimes annoyed of getting involved in political discussions about Israel and that it *"happens too often"* and that he is *"pretty much (…) tired of it"* even if there are no personal attacks (Transcript Doron, pp. 12–13). And while he does not let these discussions *"reach"* him emotionally, he also does not want to talk badly about Israel in another country even if he might have some criticism. He says:

> *But this kind of stuff* [things he does not like about Israel] *I can't really say here (…). But when I'm here (in Switzerland) I can't-, somehow, I feel it's-, I can't say this stuff, I don't know, more, more subtly at least. Because anyway, people don't really understand how it goes. It feels to me that people here see mostly the bad side of Israel anyway. Me, I understand how it's more complex.*
> (Transcript Doron, p. 20)

Carlo Strenger (2011), another highly skilled Swiss living in Israel describes how the foundation of Israel is not very different from the foundation of many other states in the world, and that, while it might be tempting to discuss Israel as a "unique case", this is not useful when discussing its standing and the strong reaction it often elicits in Europe and the Arab world. He uses existential psychology to illustrate the strong human wish for meaning and argues that Israel can be seen as a laboratory demonstrating the human desire for absolute systems (German *"Sinnsysteme"*). Due to its history and location, Israel has become a place of projection for various

---

89 Though on a smaller, less personal scale, I had somewhat relatable experiences as a researcher, sometimes being asked "why Israel?" after conference presentations, where people seemingly wanted to make sure I would be "critical enough" in my perspective.

imaginaries, ranging from being the scapegoat for a number of disappointed ideals and utopias (for instance socialist ideals) or the projected site of a clash between the West and Islam. This might explain the many imaginaries and reactions Israel elicits, as is recounted by the protagonists in various ways, something that does not happen as explicitly in response to questions about Switzerland.

From a perspective within Israel, Gabriele says that she had some *"hard times"* in the country, however, one can have *"hard times"* anywhere. Doron, for example, talks about having *"hard times"* after first moving to Switzerland (Transcript Doron, pp. 2–3). When talking about politics, her surroundings, and her occasional reactions to them, Gabriele says:

> *So I had this, occasionally, when being emotional so, yeah, when it was really bad again politically, then (I thought) 'this was it, now I'm leaving!'*
> (Transcript Gabriele, p. 5)[90]

She says that she ended up not leaving as she did not want to tear apart her family but that some of her female Swiss/German acquaintances and friends did leave, taking their children with them. This adds a gendered perspective on migration stories when she says: *"Actually, as soon as you have children, you're stuck"* (original German: *"Eigentlich, sobald man Kinder hat, dann ist man, sitzt man fest."*). Even though for her the decision to move to and stay in Israel was a very conscious one that she does not regret (she emphasizes that she wants to stay where her children are), she does feel foreign periodically (Transcript Gabriele, pp. 5–6). Dani Kranz (2019) extensively explores the vulnerability of migrant women in Israel. Even highly skilled women from the Global North might have difficulty maintaining a career equivalent to the one they had in their country of origin and can be involved in family conflicts related to migration, for example with parents-in-law who expect them to convert in order for future children to be Jewish, which, depending on the case, they did not do.[91]

Still, the struggles and difficulties of the protagonists should not simply be reduced to mainly Israel and sometimes Switzerland as places, as at times it is the decision and experience of migration as a whole which is looked at with ambivalence

---

90 Translated from German:
   "Also ich hatte mal zwischendurch in der, emotionale so, ja, wenn's wirklich politisch wieder ganz schlimm war, dann war das, jetzt reise ich (ab), jetzt hau ich ab!"

91 Conflicts and frustrations arising between (highly skilled) migrant women and their local families is not something that only happens in Israel. Catherine Trundle (2009), for example, describes similar situations for American women married to Italian men in Florence, who struggle with keeping their personal autonomy following migration.

or sadness. This is illustrated not only by Isabella's statement at the very beginning of the thesis, but also by what Alexander said about his children:

(B)ut, uh, I think that every move leaves a scar. Every move leaves a scar and – you can see this in my kids. And we moved a number of times. That's a topic for a different study.
(Transcript Alexander, p. 18)

Despite having a successful career that allows them a transnational life mode, highly skilled migrants can look at their mobility with ambivalence, or in the case of Alexander's quotation above, even sadness. Rhea, in describing a negative experience she had in Switzerland, reflects on her not necessarily being perceived as a migrant, emphasizes her identity as a political activist, and demonstrates awareness of the experiences of other migrants and varying perspectives in her account of a conflictual interaction in Switzerland:

Well, we are now after the ninth of February, you know, with the, the referendum ["against mass immigration"], and, um, the thing is that I'm a highly qualified, high skilled immigrant and I mean, in everyday life I'm passing as European. I mean, I'm not Black, obviously, (…), so I pass not as well, of course, but I can pass as, I don't know, any "other". Uh, a lot of people think I'm Italian, others think I'm French, without me saying it and of course-, but um, I don't have any experience (being) treated as (an) immigrant, you know, on a daily basis. Maybe, maybe one time. I took a picture of one of the referendum posters and we saw this Swiss lady, Swiss old lady, starting to shout at me in Swiss Deutsch' [Swiss German] and I told her like 'I can kein Deutsch' [I don't speak German]. And she started to speak in Hochdeutsch [standard German] so that I (said) 'Ich kann kein Deutsch'. 'I speak English, do you speak English?' and she was like, yeah, 'you immigrants, you come here, you Americans, you come here and you don't know anything about the parties' and I was like 'tshh, go fuck yourself'. Um, so, I mean, I was, as an activist and as a socialist, I was quite surprised (by) the ninth of February results. But I find the immigration policy is very, very kind and very, very generous. I mean, just the idea that we can get (unemployment) money after two years, it's amazing, it's amazing.

And, um, I think, I think Switzerland is really, I mean, as a visiting scholar I'm looking at it and I see it's a very problematic place because (…) you know all this trade, human trade-, free trade, uh, I want to say free traffic but it's not free traffic for persons. But it doesn't affect me. I mean, I don't see anything, uh, I got my visa no problem, it was very easy for me although I'm not married, it was very nice. I was quite surprised (by) the policy of Switzerland, even though we were not married, they did receive me as a family reunion. It's quite rare, and the idea that you can continue the visa and get (unemployment) money that's amazing. And again, I'm not Black and I see all the racism against Black people here, in the end, all kinds of Black, everybody who is not passing as Swiss, I mean, my children are passing as well, I

mean, they are blond, blue eyes, speak Swiss Deutsch so you don't see any problem with that. But I do so see it happen (to) other people like Indian people, sometimes even Italian and, of course, all the refugees are here, they totally are suffering from the – it's not only from the policy, I think the policy is quite ok, but also from the street (and daily interactions). Perspectives. Yeah. That's it.
(Transcript Rhea, p. 11–12)

Analytically breaking down the migration stories of the protagonists into various emotional dimensions shows that there are objectives and decision-makings at the basis of migration choices that come from (or are narrated as coming from) a past place of struggle. Within a biography these "struggles" can either be connected to a specific place or a specific time and lead to the desire to take a break and the hope to achieve more contentment or success in the future through migration. In the course of the biographies, migration then gains significance as an activity that brings contentment, success, or maybe even happiness, however, these positive feelings are not without restriction and can be revised or contradicted in the course of the narratives.

5.2.2 Contested frameworks and political activities

While not the focus of this study, geopolitical structures and conflicts are part of the framework of the study and thus also part of the interview questions and materials collected. As part of this research was conducted in Israel, perhaps, something should be said of the future of the country and the one-state and two-state solution, or bi-communal societies. However, few people I talked to in the field expressed hope for any solution in the near future.

The political situation of Israel and Palestine or the Arab-Israeli conflict were sometimes a topic in interviews and conversations, for example due to the interviewee being politically active or wanting to be politically active in the future, being tired of always having to talk about the Arab-Israeli conflict to (Swiss) acquaintances and having to justify living in Israel, or, simply when talking about lived experiences. For instance, Matt, who lived through his first war in 2014 tells me about the experience and says: "*I had a breakdown after two days*" (original French: "*J'avais un breakdown après deux jours*", Transcript Matt, pp. 17–18).

Another reason the topic came up on a subjective level in the narratives is due to professional circumstances, such as being a journalist or working in tourism. For example, Gabriele, who works in tourism, is strongly influenced by the security situation in Israel and the whole region. During the war in summer 2014, many planned tours were cancelled, which she found so frustrating, she thought about quitting (Transcript Gabriele, pp. 20–21), which is something Matt, who worked in the tourism sector temporarily, did, as he found it too fluctuating and dependent on political circumstances. Gabriele, remembering her frustrations of 2014 and tying them to justifications about living in Israel expected by contacts abroad says:

> *Last [2014] summer it [the tourism sector] collapsed. There were two trips, which I had pretty much already arranged, (which) were cancelled and then I also even didn't want to, yeah, to broach the subject; they also wrote me, yeah, at the moment, yeah, 'you with your wars there!', I mean, there is no conversation, yeah.*
> (Transcript Gabriele, p. 21)[92]

Consequently, in the sense of an ethnographic approach that regards frameworks and surroundings as relevant for the results, the multiple geopolitical and religious conflicts in the Middle East, such as the Arab-Israeli conflict, were an indirect part of this research project, just as much as political events in Switzerland were integrated into the results (although one has to admit that discussions on Swiss politics are rarely as emotionally charged as discussion on Israeli politics and do not require the same level of "justification" and positioning from subjects). Even in Switzerland, Israeli politics were sometimes a topic during fieldwork. During one of my first field research events, a meeting with the Swiss Ambassador to Israel organized by the *Chamber of Commerce Switzerland-Israel*, I took the following fieldnote in my research diary, reflecting how the overall topic can be agitating even in Switzerland and providing a small window on the complexities and the emotional reactions emerging from the issue (Strenger, 2011):

> *I am at the general assembly of the Chamber of Commerce Switzerland-Israel. The Swiss Ambassador to Israel, Dr. Andreas Baum, talks about the bilateral relations and the work of the Swiss embassy, which focuses on political, cultural, and economic aspects. After describing ongoing cultural and economic exchanges he talks about the political aspect. On the political level one of the activities of the embassy is to collaborate with NGOs which advocate the two-state solution. The ambassador also clarifies Switzerland's official position concerning the occupied territories, which is that the occupation is not lawful. Overall Switzerland would like the Middle East peace process to be restarted and supports the Geneva Initiative [93] as a possible accord for a two-state solution and an alternative to violent conflict. While*

---

92 Translated from German:
 "Das Ganze ist dann letzten Sommer zu Fall, letzten Sommer zusammengefallen, wo es dann zwei Reisen, die eigentlich bereits arrangiert waren, wurden dann abgesagt, und dann hatte ich auch lange keine Lust mehr, das überhaupt noch, ja, wieder, zu thematisieren, oder da haben sie mir auch geschrieben, ja, momentan, ja, '(ihr) mit euren Kriegen dort', also wird überhaupt nicht diskutiert, ja."
93 For more information on the Israeli-Palestinian Geneva Initiative to end the conflict see: https://geneva-accord.org, accessed: August 9, 2023.

he says this there is some restlessness and mumbling amongst listeners, nevertheless, when the opportunity arises after the ambassador's presentation, no questions are asked about this official position. However, during the aperitif and networking part of the afternoon, one of the attendees I talk to is very agitated and tells me how disappointed he is about the ambassador talking about "occupied territories". I respond that he is a diplomat, to which my conversational partner becomes annoyed and says: "Diplomat or not, does he even know who he's talking to here?!"[94]

The protagonists themselves try to stay politically involved (for example travelling to Israel to vote, as this is only possible in person; Swiss can participate in elections from abroad) or at least stay informed in both, Switzerland and Israel. Alexander, on staying updated and politically active and looking at Israel from "*outside*", states:

Well, you know, this day and age with the internet and all that, it's really not a problem (to stay informed). (…) (Still) (t)here is, there are all kind of difficulties. First of all – I am aware of the fact that everything looks more extreme from the outside. I've been enough in and out, in all of that. But that's something that is, uh, unpleasant.
(Transcript Alexander, p. 13)

Rhea, the only self-defined activist protagonist says:

[During the last war in 2014] *I needed to do something with myself because it was very hard to see this wide, beautiful Switzerland and having a war and bombs over South Israel and Gaza while I see things (while being) so safe and you know, it was very hard mentally for me. Like you know, all this political, uh, activities is, is for nothing actually, because it lacks any sense but you do feel better. It was hard for me and I did, I went to some demonst-, one demonstration which was against the war which was all Palestinians. I didn't see anything, but first of all, I was afraid and second of all it was not my thing, the political war, (it's) their thing.*
(Transcript Rhea, p. 15)

Here, Rhea frames her own activity as "*for nothing*" during a somewhat melancholic passage, even though being an activist is a large part of her narrative of identity and worldview. She presents activism as merely a strategy for herself to feel better

---

94 Research diary entry from June 25, 2014, edited for clarity.
   Additional information: The hardened attitudes in the Middle East conflict are currently being analyzed by the political scientist Oliver Fink (2021) from a perspective involving emotions. With the help of a quantitative study, he looks at how Palestinians perceive conflict-laden situations in Israel and how emotions (especially of anger and degradation) might influence the potential for violence and in turn how important empathic encounters are for deradicalization.

about the world, yet activism is something she talks about passionately throughout the interview. The multifaceted emotional registers and common emergence of melancholy or notions of "losing heart" in the narratives of activists and volunteers is something several authors discuss. In some cases this is related to feelings of powerlessness in regard to the giant task of achieving social change, while in other cases it has more to do with tensions between retrospective accounts of accomplishment and the original crisis when the state of urgency has passed or moved on elsewhere, as this creates longing for another crisis and the ensuing feelings of accomplishment (Brown & Pickerill, 2009; King, 2005; Sandberg & Andersen, 2020).

Other protagonists, like Hannah and Susanna, say they try to be active and conscious on a small scale in daily life. Susanna, for example, started to learn Arabic. Israelis in Switzerland in turn talk about finding it agreeable to find some physical and in consequence, emotional distance from Israel, as illustrated in the previous section.

5.3 Conclusion and Outlook: Nostalgia, Irritation, and Expectation

In this chapter the often ambivalent and sometimes contradictory feelings about surroundings and places were discussed. Feelings of nostalgia, irritation, and expectation are part of the narratives, including reflections on past, present, and future. Memories and imaginaries shape how the protagonists feel about and engage with their surroundings, in some cases leading to nostalgic narrative sections. In particular, various childhood memories are used to illustrate imaginaries, expectations, or perceived realities of Israel and Switzerland and to give meaning to places. Depending on lived experiences and expectations, Israel and Switzerland can both be perceived as places of nostalgia or hope.

Nevertheless, the surroundings can likewise bring about struggles and complicated or conflictual interactions or annoyances. For instance, Israelis in Switzerland describe "needing a break" from Israel as one of the reasons for moving abroad and discuss how the distance leads to changes of perception and identity, and also personal developments and feelings of accomplishment.

Overall, the examples discussed show how emotions are not merely reactions to surroundings, for example, to activities and interactions, but can also be produced by frameworks such as nation-states, or experiences in specific localities such as cities. Aspects of daily life in Switzerland and Israel, as well as political circumstances and surroundings in the country one has left and/or the country in which one resides, thus have an impact on emotions and experiences reflected upon in migration stories and gain significance in the individual narratives.

The following chapter will look at how the activity of "going abroad" (often in opposition to migrants who "migrate") and sometimes "staying on the move" (often regarding being flexible and mobility as a success or way to self-fulfillment) is connected to various emotions, such as happiness, freedom, or a sense of accomplishment in the protagonists' narratives.

6. Going Abroad and Staying on the Move

The world is rather large and I wanna see many other places.
(Transcript Daniel, p. 4)

When looking at highly skilled migrants, society often sees their mobility as a sign of modern flexibility and success in a globalized world and, on an individual level, as a way to advance careers and self-fulfillment. In this chapter I will discuss what role these notions and related emotions play in the protagonists' interview narratives. Some of the topics discussed here closely relate to the narratives of belonging presented in chapter 4. However, due to their strong meaning for the protagonists, looking at these topics from a somewhat different perspective provides a comprehensive view on the way emotions emerge in narratives on migration. In chapter 4 questions of national identities and flexible citizenship were discussed and narratives of belonging were reflected on through a discussion of self-distinctions, belonging to specific places or groups, and "bubbles" among other things.

Here, in chapter 6, some of these themes recur, as similar topics are discussed from a related but distinct perspective. Among other things, aspects of cosmopolitan identities and related emotions are discussed using narratives of successful migration and staying in motion as a lens. When asking about reasons for moving during the interviews, the answer the researcher receives, among other factors, depends on the current situation the migrant is in. One can imagine that the narratives around reasons and motivations would be different if the person considers their migration "failed" or feels unhappy in their new place of residence, regretting their general decision. This does not seem to be the case with the protagonists, all of them presenting themselves as being generally happy or at least content with their decision to, as they often frame it, "go abroad".

Several questions can be asked here. What sorts of emotions are associated with the narrative of "going abroad"? What differentiates "going abroad" from "migrating"? What role do feelings of accomplishment and self-fulfillment play in migration narratives of highly skilled migrants? What decision-makings are behind migration? What are the motivations behind the decisions? To what kind of transnational or migratory activities do these decisions lead? How is migration narratively justified? In the protagonists' narratives of "going abroad", themes such as cosmopolitan imaginaries and feelings of freedom and achievement seem to play an important role.

While complications or struggles of daily life as highly skilled migrants are also discussed (as illustrated above) within the narratives of "going abroad" and the discussion of migration decisions, positive, often adventurous or liberating meaning is given to places as well as experiences. The migration decisions and related activities are then generally summarized as successful endeavors in the stories. Through this and the discussion of the activity of "going abroad", a successful self with multi-sited or transnational (non-)belonging and distinctiveness from "other migrants" is narrated and presented.

6.1   Not a Migrant

When one (looks at) my geography (it) is strongly influenced by academia. All my decisions were always, were, uh, determined by it. And (being) in Israel, in this case, is almost a coincidence.
(Transcript Simon, p. 16)[95]

Ghassan Hage (2005, p. 470) writes: "[T]he significance of crossing borders is not some objective experience that defines international migration regardless of who is crossing the borders". The subjective meaning of "crossing borders" for highly skilled migrants will be further explored below. As already touched upon in the section on feelings of belonging (chapter 4), the decision to leave one's country of origin or residence in order to "go abroad" is usually an explicit one taken for various reasons, such as needing or wanting a break, love, education, or professional fulfillment. However, it is contradictorily also presented as happening by chance or due to random circumstances. While the general idea or decision to be mobile is clear, the place of destination and specific circumstances of being mobile are not always predefined. Effectively, it might be a narrative method to create distance to a place of origin or past "home" with certain emotions, and to construct a presently successful transnational self with a multi-sited biography through talking about randomness in terms of destination.

Often, a diffuse "going abroad" is the main thread when telling the migration story, without necessarily having a clear destination in mind, especially for skilled migrants who are privileged enough to be part of a global job market or who see themselves as part of a transnational social class, as cosmopolitans, or as belonging to multiple places or nations. Highly skilled migrants consequently might orientate their decision around a mix of factors, such as certain jobs, a sense of adventure (Suter, 2019), imaginaries or ideals of cosmopolitanism (Hannerz, 2002) and the

---

95   Translated from German:
     "Wenn man meine Geographie, die ist, die ist äh, ist stark äh akademisch beeinflusst. Alle meine Entscheidungen waren immer war äh gerichtet davon. Und in Israel, in diesem Fall, ist fast ein Zufall."

desire to explore other countries, a general fear of being stuck, or a wish to avoid personal or professional stagnation (Hage, 2005).

6.1.1 Occurrences and circumstances

Margot tells the story of her initial migration decision and reason for being in Israel and then states concludingly: "*So I was stranded here*" (Transcript Margot, p. 6), narratively reducing her migration to just circumstances in her interview narrative, which seems contradictory to the strong emotions she describes when talking about belonging (chapter 4). However, it can make sense when one considers the fact that highly skilled migrants might not give too much meaning to migration as an activity within their overall biography or wish to distance themselves from other migrants whom they perceive as migrating with a clear strategy and specific aim, and consequently being less open and flexible (or maybe less contemporary). As already illustrated, mainly in chapter 4, contemporary migration narratives disturb several prevalent notions related to the crossing of national borders and the meaning of categories such as citizenship. Russell King (2002, p. 102) writes: "Even the notions of 'home' and 'away' or 'abroad' have become blurred."

Nevertheless, one could also look at expectations and desires of self-fulfillment, cosmopolitan ideals, or the wish to lead a "good *transnational* life" as migration-strategies, which are emerging and constructed through the narratives of highly skilled migrants. This shows some overlapping aspects between the concept of "lifestyle migrants" (Benson & O'Reilly, 2009) and highly skilled migrants.[96] As mentioned, "highly skilled migrants" are a heterogenous group: even in the small sample of protagonists chosen to represent highly skilled migrants in this study, many different, sometimes contradictory emotions, various narratives, subjective notions of migration, and ways of dealing with circumstances become visible.

For example, Doron, whose wife is Swiss and who mainly moved to Switzerland to be with her, not purely out of professional consideration, might see accomplishing "integration" or becoming a "local" as more relevant than other protagonists whose narratives focus more on "going abroad" and presenting a cosmopolitan self. However, Doron, too, says that he "*suddenly*" found himself in Switzerland and then emphasizes that he likes to be there, perhaps as a way to present himself as a "good migrant". Besides, he positions himself as a stranger, who will stay a stranger, meaning that one might try to "integrate", yet can never fully achieve or possibly does not want to fully achieve this imaginary status, leading to a dilemma between

---

[96] There is also some overlapping with the figure of the "cosmopolitan" described by Ulf Hannerz (2002) as will be seen below, however, not all highly skilled migrants fit into the term "cosmopolitan" or "lifestyle migrant".

a supposed ideal of becoming local, never-disappearing feelings of strangeness, and a self-construction as highly skilled migrant, different from "other migrants" through narrations of "going abroad", feelings of detachment or "randomness":

> *Yeah, also, I already said it, I feel comfortable here, I'm glad I, uh, came here. I mean, I never planned it, I, yeah, just met my wife suddenly and I found myself here. It was surprising but I mean, I really feel much more comfortable here than in Israel, like, I feel also in two years, I did a good integration.*
> *The language is the barrier, but the more I speak, the better I speak and (the more) I understand people, the better it feels. And I think it will never be really home, it has to – in the beginning – I think I will always be a stranger here even if I live (here) like fifty years, I will still be a stranger, still have my accent, but, uh, I feel I can get used to living here.*
> (Transcript Doron, p. 25)

Even though, as mentioned, the decision to move is often framed as "*sich so ergeben*" (in German) or "*just happening*" (in English), thus narratively creating feelings of detachment, the migration narrative is also connected to complex memories, physical as well as emotional distance to the country of origin or departure, and accomplishments or hopes for fulfillment in the present, all while including aspects of a flexible transnational identity, as the following quotations by Susanna and Hannah illustrate:

> *(B)ut somehow it just happened. (…) (I don't think I would) go back to Switzerland, but somewhere (else) for a year – in Europe or somewhere in the US or something – um, that's something, I think I would take* [in terms of getting a job offer, for example]. *With, uh, the awareness that it might be, that I would stay there again. But not with a plan.*
> (Transcript Susanna, pp. 33–35)[97]
> *It's, it's a combination* [of reasons]. *I really wanted to go abroad, it did not really matter for me where exactly and then this* [meeting her husband] *was the determining factor why it ended up being Israel after all.*
> (Transcript Hannah, p. 2)[98]

---

97 Translated from German:
   "*Aber 'ne Idee dahinter (...). Aber irgendwie hat sich das halt so ergeben, also. (...). Wenn mir irgendwas angeboten würde ein Jahr-, ein Jahr zurück in die Schweiz glaub' ich nicht, aber irgendwie ein Jahr irgendwo – in Europa oder irgendwo in den USA und so was - ähm das würd' ich glaub' ich schon annehmen. Mit ähm – im Bewusstsein, dass es dann sein könnte, dass ich dann wieder bleibe. Aber nicht mit 'nem Plan.*"

98 Translated from German:

In Alexander's case being in Switzerland is a purely professional decision. But the first migration from Israel to the United States several years before had a more complex basis related to the need of taking a break (an aspect discussed in more detail in section 5.2.1):

> *So, I am not in Switzerland because I wanted to go to Switzerland. I'm in Switzerland because this is the headquarters of* [organization]. *I was representing the company I was working for (before), in this association for many, many years and there was an opportunity there. And it came (with being) in charge with the-, (…), I had my field there. So, I took on the opportunity and left the company and came to work for* [organization]. *So, Switzerland is just – uh – by chance. Could have been in France or in Nigeria, I don't know.*
> Question: *Would you have taken the job if it were in Israel?*
> Alexander: *Oh yeah. For, uh, yeah. With two hands [laughs]! With everything.*
> (Transcript Alexander, p. 2)

Later in the interview, when talking about moving to and looking for future opportunities in Israel or the United States Alexander says:

> *Yeah, to Israel it will be, actually, I don't know, because I didn't really try, But I'm, I'm with an open eye. (…) Um. To the US I think if I really (want to), I most probably can find a job. But, uh, (I'm) not there yet, if it will happen, I don't know. We will see what will happen in the elections* [in Israel, 2015] *in two weeks.*
> (Transcript Alexander, pp. 11–12)

When I open the interview with the prompt of telling me how she came to live in Switzerland, Rhea, connecting narratives of "going abroad" and "needing a break" says:

> *Ok. Um. I always wanted to live abroad, um, that was something that I really wanted, to take some space out of Israel and, uh, this opportunity came and, I mean, me and partner are both academics, so we knew it's gonna (be possible).*[^1]
> (Transcript Rhea, p. 2)

Continuing her story, she says:

[^1]: "*Es, es ist 'ne Kombination. Ich wollte wirklich ins Ausland, es war für mich nicht so kritisch, wo ins Ausland und dann war das* [Treffen des zukünftigen Ehemanns] *der entscheidende Faktor, warum doch nach Israel.*"

> *We just wanted to see, we wanted to live abroad. I would say the reason, yeah. Living (abroad) was strong, on my behalf. Maybe (for) my husband it's, uh, different but – [laughs].*
> (Transcript Rhea, p. 9)

Hence, one can say that: "Migrancy involves a movement in which point of departure and point of arrival are uncertain and mutable" (Grønseth, 2013, p. 11) and add that mutableness or movement is also inherent in narratives about migrancy in general and migration decisions in particular. This means that, as stated earlier, merely looking at geographical mobility is not particularly interesting from an anthropological standpoint (e. g., Hage, 2005). Rather, the migrant self should be explored in its processuality and subjectivity, and the question asked should be about the significance of the movement for the individual.

For highly skilled migrants, the significance of mobility as an activity that influences their narrative of identity and emotions is often more important than the place of origin or destination itself, as reflected in the use of the formulation *"going abroad"* and the multifaceted reasons on which the decision to migrate is based. Within their stories the protagonists sometimes at first frame themselves as being almost randomly in a place but then still try to make sense of their position in the course of telling their further stories. This could either be for the benefit of narrating a fulfilling biography, or mean that, once in a place, feelings of belonging are constructed and maintained through various ways, sometimes within a certain, very specific "bubble", such as academia or another (favorable multinational) environment as discussed above. As mentioned, in their narratives, the protagonists distance themselves from migration as something that is planned and then put into action, the way they perceive lesser skilled or other migrants might do. However, they still have expectations about a positive future connected to migration even if their narrative around migration and hope can seem diffuse.

In this study Matt is an exception to the observation of randomness of destination, as his story is rather a story of making *Aliyah*, where Israel is, and always has been, the only possible destination. However, even he frames the story in a way that is strongly about finding an individual "good life" through mobility. His religiousness, on a spiritual as well as a practical level (he mentions the lack of choice of kosher supermarkets in Switzerland) is one of several aspects, which also include leading a *"more intense"* life (Transcript Matt, pp. 10–11), his marriage and career. Like others, he distances himself from his country of departure, Switzerland, through stories of a more fulfilling life in his new place of residence, Israel, yet parallelly maintains a multi-sited biography connected to several countries, similar to the way other highly skilled or lifestyle migrants might do (Benson & O'Reilly, 2009).

6.1.2 Reasons for migration: love, cosmopolitan imaginaries, transnational ideals

Generally, the emotion of love and maintaining a relationship with a partner plays a crucial role in the reasons and motivation to move related in the narratives. The way the narratives illustrate the need for emotional attachments or belonging to create individual construals of meaning was discussed in chapter 4. Sometimes these factors are more important than job offers or careers, which in some respects contradicts some of the media's predominant discourses around highly skilled migrants as detached individuals constantly flexibly moving across the globe for their careers (Beglinger, 2013/Das Magazin; Bracher/NZZ, 2018; Brönnimann/Tages-Anzeiger, 2013; Kunz/Tachles, 2014; Neue Zürcher Zeitung, 2013; Vögeli/NZZ, 2014). This does not mean that highly skilled migrants themselves do not also reproduce this image of flexibility (and in some cases feelings of detachment from place) in their narratives, for example, when discussing migration as "*just happening*". Concerning relationships as reason for migrating, Doron says, that largely, he moved because of love. He "*met a Swiss girl*" and now here he is (Transcript Doron, p. 1). Simon also partly moved to Israel for his wife, however the main factor was the wish to be at a "*good university*" to pursue his career in academia (Transcript Simon, p. 16), as illustrated in the quotation at the beginning of section 6.1.

Isabella repeats the feeling of finding life "*exhausting*" in Israel several times during her interview and while she would not move back to Israel for a "*dream job*", she would do so for a partner if there were a possibility to go back to Switzerland regularly (Transcript Isabella, p. 26). Gabriele also moved in order to stay with her husband and even though she left Israel again after one year, she then "*made up her mind*" and went back with the plan of staying permanently (Transcript Gabriele, p. 2). So, even if the protagonists mainly defined themselves as "highly skilled migrants who moved for professional reasons", and originally focused their biography on their careers after responding to the call for participants for the study, the stories reveal how the decision to migrate is multifaceted, sometimes contradictory, and often includes love as being one of the guiding factors in the decision to migrate. This was, for instance, also the case with the renowned Israeli neuroscientist Henry Markram, who is originally from South Africa, took a research position at the *Weizmann Institute*, and then stayed and acquired Israeli citizenship after meeting his wife. After several international stations at research institutions, he went to Switzerland as a highly skilled migrant. Until 2015 he led the "Blue

Brain" and then "Human Brain Project",[99] a large-scale scientific research project which aims to map the human brain with the help of supercomputers, making him one of the most famous highly skilled Israeli migrants in Switzerland.

When looking at reasons for migration and the significance migration has for an individual's life, it can be fruitful to look at the relationship between existential and physical mobility (Hage, 2005). The narratives touch on this relationship when, for instance, the emotional meaning of migration within a biography is discussed, or when a successful multi-sited biography is constructed. The physical act of crossing a border and moving from one place to another then can become almost irrelevant for the story, even if the main questions asked are about "migration" and it is defined as such. For example, when asked if he would consider moving back to Israel, Daniel says:

> *I can imagine that life can force you to do actions you do not like. I mean, in the sense of sick parents, in the sense of making use of the parents while the kids (are small). I can imagine many scenarios but, uh, so, of course it's an option. I don't know really what will happen, but I would try to plan my life in such (a way) that I would not have to go there.*
> (Transcript Daniel, p. 7)

At another point his reflections on the topic of circumstances forcing migration trajectories continues:

> *Um, so, Israel is not an option. Because I don't want to go back. Because I already lived there, and I like it, but the world is rather large and I wanna see many other places. And also, my wife shares this passion to move and see some other places, this is why actually we didn't want to stay in* [European city] *and decided to go as far as the German-speaking area. But that means, I can imagine, we will be here also for a specific amount of time until I finish my* [research project] *and she's getting some work done, some experience and then we'll be, there will be another station.*
> (Transcript Daniel, pp. 4–5)

Here, one could ask about the meaning of agency for highly skilled migrants as well as about the notion of "stations" and how many international stations are needed to achieve a "good life" as a highly skilled migrant or cosmopolitan. Is each place simply a transitional place on the way to a fulfilling multi-sited biography based in a desire to see many places? What constitutes "many" places? Further, distance

---

99 The widely discussed project is based at the *École Polythechnique Féderal de Lausanne* and largely funded by the *European Union*. For more information see: https://www.humanbrainproject.eu/en/ and https://people.epfl.ch/henry.markram/?lang=en, accessed: September 5, 2023.

and somewhat uncomfortable emotions are created towards Israel rhetorically (not wanting to go "*there*" but being "*forced*" to), fitting into Daniel's notion of not being a fan of countries, as he expresses early in the interview and continuing his construction of a cosmopolitan self. In other words: "[M]obile people with multiple place affiliations and hybrid or cosmopolitan identities have no wish to fit in to the ideology of one national identity" (King, 2002, p. 102).

Ulf Hannerz (2002, p. 160), when discussing the meaning of "home" in relation to cosmopolitan imaginaries, writes: "Or home is really home, but in a special way; a constant reminder of a pre-cosmopolitan past, a privileged site of nostalgia." As illustrated, for some highly skilled migrants, the plan lies not in moving to one country and settling there but in leading a fulfilling transnational life.

In his narrative Daniel emphasizes an emotional connection to an idea of "being on the move" through talking about his and his wife's "*passion*" to be mobile and them wanting to move away from Switzerland after a few years. Having the ability to move around the globe in such a way is a privilege of which he is aware. Daniel also makes a clear distinction between himself, who enjoys living in different countries and moving around, and "other migrants", who, in his perception, move to stay, or maybe, one could say, without passion:

> *I would say that all in all, I'm not a big fan of the notion of countries. I'm aware that they exist. And I'm lucky enough to have the kind of education that puts you in some multinational status because, if you look around me, in my field, department, people are from Slovakia and from India and from China and Japan and from everywhere. (…) I'm (not looking at) the country I'm living (in), (but) more the, I don't know, I'd say 'actual condition', or 'social condition', if I like the place, if I like the mentality and so on, (that) would be an important question. But (because of this) I cannot say I immigrated to Switzerland. I'm living here now and enjoying and learning the Swiss lifestyle. And I can imagine that in a few years it will be another place with another atmosphere.*
> (Transcript Daniel, p. 6).

The term "migrant" seems to have a mainly negative connotation for mobile, highly skilled individuals who prefer to present themselves as "*relocating*", "*moving*" or "*going abroad*" for education, work, or love (and then in some cases staying on due to "*circumstances*" and things "*happening*"). Perhaps this is because a "migrant" is seen as disrupting, yet not transcending national borders, which does not fit into narratives such as Daniel's, where mobility is a personal adventure, reflecting cosmopolitan imaginaries and transnational ideals. Even though: "Cosmopolitanism in all its variants is part of – not beyond – a global discursive sphere of identity politics that revolve in part around the differentiation between cultural imaginaries of cosmopolitan world openness and anti-cosmopolitan nationalism" (Skovgaard-Smith & Poulfelt, 2018, p. 148).

Linguistically, the rejection of the term "migrant" has of course also something to do with the fact that highly skilled migrants might not stay in a country for very long and thus simply prefer to talk about "*going abroad*" or a "*relocation*" to reflect the limited duration of their stay and potential multiple international moves. Rhea, for instance, says: "*So it's not the same, like, really (being an) immigrant, it's a relocation*" (Transcript Rhea, p. 4). Generally, the duration of the stay is recognized to influence whether migrants use the assimilatory notion of "integration" (staying in a country for an extended period of time and particularly having a spouse from this country can also influence the way migration and integration are perceived) (Scott, 2006), however, Simon, who has lived in Israel for over 30 years would be a notable exception to this rule.

Moreover, a further dimension to the distinction from the term "migrant" can be added when looking at highly skilled migrants as protagonists in knowledge societies in a globalized world, or as characters who represent contemporary ideals of flexibility, multi-sitedness, and cosmopolitanism: "The cosmopolitan may embrace the alien culture, but he does not become committed to it. All the time he knows where the exit is" (Hannerz, 2002, p. 141). Another aspect to consider might be the protagonists' self-perceptions as belonging to a transnational class (Sklair, 2002; Weiss, 2006) making the use of certain terms a way to differentiate themselves from the already mentioned "other migrants", such as labor migrants.

Even Gabriele, who does talk about her integration, does not use the related term "migrant" when talking about herself; she rather puts the issue into an activity, talking about herself as someone who "*emigrated*" or "*migrating being difficult*" (Transcript Gabriele, p. 3 & p. 12). Doron and Jacob, who also mention "integration", both currently plan to stay in Switzerland but stay open to moving somewhere else if an opportunity arises, presenting a flexible migrant self fitting into a globalized world. At the same time, highly skilled migrants, while mobile and partly assuming a transnational identity (which can be easily accessible based on higher education, bilingual abilities, and in some cases bourgeois culture) (Korpela, 2009; Scott, 2006; Sklair, 2002; Vertovec, 2009; Weiss, 2006), are not completely detached from place (Tages-Anzeiger, 2013; Walsh, 2009) as can, for example, be seen in the protagonists' multifaceted discussion of daily struggles, belonging, and emotional memories connected to certain places.

6.2 Feelings of Accomplishment

"There is also a particular sense of achievement in acting as if one were at home wherever one happens to be" (Said, 2000, p. 148). For highly skilled migrants who are privileged enough to move without any or with few constraints to their destination of choice, like the protagonists of this study and other individuals interviewed in the field, the singular narratives, interpretations, and subjective motivations for migration reflect notions of mobility as a way to individualized self-fulfillment on a professional and/or personal level. In some cases, the narratives include a singular sense of belonging or construction of a multi-sited biography, feelings of accomplishment, and the possibility to present an independent, self-determined self, achieved through migration (concurring results are discussed by Maruška Svašek, 2013). This is in accordance with what Russel King (2002, p. 100) calls "migration as consumption and self-discovery", or to the way some lifestyle migrants studied by Michaela Benson and Karen O'Reilly (2009) migrate in order to fulfill their quest for a singular "good life".

Within this study, the national frameworks of Israel and Switzerland can sometimes lead to emotions and parts of the narratives that are unique, or at least framed as unique by the protagonists, while at other times the place itself does not play an important or any role in the migration story. When the country is relevant, Switzerland can, among other things, become a transitory place that is one part of the imaginary of a successful, cosmopolitan self, or a place of stability. Israel can not only become a place from which one needs distance, but also a random choice or a "site of freedom" (Vora, 2011, p. 308), similar to, for example, the way Dubai is such a site for Indian businessmen who either experience Dubai as a "global city" providing economic freedom, or as a nostalgia-infused place of male camaraderie based on its historic significance as a smuggling site (as in this study, such images can be competing as well as overlapping) (Vora, 2011).

The Swiss in Israel and the Israelis in Switzerland who are part of this study construct and narrate their independent and successful self in the present with the help of various conflicting and sometimes negative emotions about the past, present, and future (as illustrated in chapter 5). Some of the more positive specific emotions coming up are feelings of freedom and happiness, though even these are often ambivalent, questioned and reflected upon within the narratives. These emotions can either arise from being and staying "on the move" or from constructing singular forms of (non-)belonging within a place of residence, as was also illustrated in chapter 4 where multi-sited biographies and various narratives of belonging were discussed.

6.2.1 Gendered experiences

For women (skilled as well as unskilled), migration can lead to feelings of accomplishment or achievement in the form of happiness, freedom, independence, or liberation (King, 2002, p. 97). "Mobility and migration do indeed have a specific significance for women: Historically they have been associated with immobility and passivity" (Morokvasic, 2007, p. 69). Especially for Swiss women in Israel, these themes that are emphasized in the narratives and discussions of feelings about gender roles are part of the way migration experiences are described. Isabella, for example, talks about the creative freedom she experienced in Israel and how Switzerland is a place that inhibits her creativity.

> *And then, um, when I had decided to go there* [to Israel], *I knew I wanted to live there for a while (…) and so I looked around professionally and as I was interested in* [arts], *I just, I knew, I didn't want to study this in Switzerland. On the one hand because I had the push, to really leave now, on the other hand because I felt that this is not the right place, because I always felt that, that in the creative fields this country is a bit, kind of, inhibiting (based on) my personal experiences, yeah –*
> (Transcript Isabella, p. 2)[100]

Gabriele, distinguishing her current self from her past self, says:

> *And I also always wanted to work. So, I had a mother who was a homemaker and, uh, I didn't want it like my mother, and this was something that you could materialize here much better than in conservative Switzerland.*
> (Transcript Gabriele, p. 18)[101]

A similar feeling is discussed by Margot as well (Transcript Margot, p. 27 and p. 30). Dani Kranz (2019, p. 8) also has a related quotation from one of her interviewees, a Swiss woman living in Israel:

> Noreen, a Swiss citizen educated in Switzerland, empathized with these problems [of feeling like an outsider and having a stagnating career as a non-Jewish female migrant in Israel], but she had overcome both the language and the professional barriers. She

---

100 Translated from German:
 "Und dann ähm, und als ich mich dann beschlossen habe, dorthin zu gehen, ich wusste, wenn ich dann dort leben möchte eine Zeit lang (…) und da hab' ich mich auch so beruflich umgeschaut und, und ähm, als ich mich eben für [Kunstbereich] interessierte, hab' ich einfach, wusste ich, ich möchte es nicht in der Schweiz ähm lernen, einerseits, weil ich auch den Drang hatte, wirklich mal wegzugehn, andererseits weil ich aber auch gespürt habe, dass, dass das nicht der richtige Ort ist, weil ich es immer so empfand, dass, dass, im kreativen Bereich dieses Land ein bisschen hemmend ist und auch also, ich, also auch meine persönliche Erfahrung auch, ja."

101 Translated from German:
 "Und ich wollte auch immer arbeiten. Also ich hatte eine Mutter, die, die war Hausfrau und äh, ich wollte nicht wie meine Mutter und das konnte man hier auch viel besser verwirklichen als, als in der konservativen Schweiz."

had mastered Hebrew to the extent that she could work – again – in her profession. She had passed all the Israeli exams required from any foreign educated professional in her line of work, and found her work interesting and challenging: 'I am learning about [her specialism] in a different cultural context' indicating that for her, the Israeli professional experience was part of a learning process that she found enriching, and which she directly connected to her reluctance to leave, or return. 'Switzerland is too narrow minded for me' Even before leaving Switzerland to live with her significant other in Israel, she had wanted to leave her native country.

Gabriele (Transcript Gabriele, pp. 2–3) similarly explains how important it was for her to build up her own life not only independently from her Israeli boyfriend and later husband but also from her Swiss background during her first years in Israel. Her activities to achieve this feeling of independence included learning Hebrew, starting a new degree, and converting from Protestantism to Judaism. Should this be considered integration or independence or both? While this could be looked at in terms of "integration" in the narratives of the female protagonists, these themes often take the form of "independence", "freedom", or related emotions. While there might be irritations, especially in the early stages of the migration experience, positive emotions are often part of women's migration narratives when comparing their current place of residence with their country of origin (Maehara, 2013), or their past with their present self.

Due to her wish to live life differently than her mother and her move to Israel where she studied for a second university degree, working in the high-tech sector and being self-employed, Gabriele argues she was able to live her life more freely. She says: "(…) *in Switzerland I would have probably become a depressive housewife*" (Transcript Gabriele, p. 18). She ascribes this experienced freedom to migration through creating a relation between location and emotion and says:

> (…) *(W)ell I'm convinced that with my emigration I had far more opportunities than as a married woman with child, with (…) children, than uh, than it would have been possible in Switzerland.*
> (Transcript Gabriele, p. 19)[102]

Hannah too talks about how different she thinks her biography would have been had she stayed in Switzerland. While her life would be easier in Switzerland, according to her, there would also be more limitations:

---

102 Translated from German:
"(…) (A)lso, also davon bin ich überzeugt, dass ich mit meiner Emigration viel mehr Möglichkeit hatte, als verheiratete Frau mit (…) Kindern, als äh, als es in der Schweiz möglich gewesen wäre."

> *And so I would say, that's why I basically say, I came here a bit naively, but it was obviously another chapter of my life and I completely realize that my life would generally, uh, be easier, if I were to live in Switzerland and not here (in Israel) now.*
> (Transcript Hannah, p. 8)[103]

A little bit later in her story:

> *Bottom line* [uses English term while speaking German], *why I'm here. Or what I – prefer about Israel compared to Switzerland, what-, and what's true today, I don't know if it's still true the day after tomorrow, but it was actually true from the moment I came here, maybe I just couldn't, you know, spell it out then, is that Israel gives me the opportunity to invent myself much more freely than Switzerland would allow it for me personally. That's the – really for me that's the reason to be here and I say this now, because you just asked* [about life changes].
>
> *Yes, it is a time of change (at the moment) and – I'm not sure, how I would've been allowed this, or (would have) allowed this to myself in Switzerland, yes, or no, or maybe, I wouldn't even have arrived at this stage, yeah. (...) I had, I was so, it's such a storybook chronology, the life sequence. So, there is kindergarten, then you're in elementary school, and, and, and, (...), and it's pretty much clear, how you're supposed to live your life and now, simply from the point of view of education and profession. Look, I graduated with a bachelor's degree in* [year] *and now we're in* [year]. *I'm learning, I'm studying for my master's* [at university]. *I completely realize that if I would have stayed in Switzerland, I would have probably done my bachelor's and maybe a few internships, blablabla, would have started my master's and, basically, um – I don't say, it's not that this is bad, but it would have been pretty much predetermined. I think, I would have automatically, and in this sense also voluntarily, found myself in this pattern. And here in Israel it is so much easier to just break out when you want to and, uh, to change your career and everything is pretty much accepted, not just accepted but, there's a bit of chaos.*
> (Transcript Hannah, pp. 14–17)[104]

---

103 Translated from German:
"Und da würd' ich sagen, deshalb sag' ich einfach, ich bin so ein bisschen naiv hierhergekommen, aber es war natürlich einfach ein anderes Kapitel in meinem Leben und äh, und es ist mir völlig klar, dass mein Leben generell äh einfacher wäre, wenn ich jetzt es in der Schweiz verbringen würde als hier."

104 Translated from German:
"Bottom Line, warum ich hier bin. Oder was ich – an Israel besser mag als in der Schweiz, was, und was stimmt heute, ich weiss nicht, ob's übermorgen noch stimmt, aber das stimmt eigentlich. Von dem Moment an, als ich hierhergekommen bin, vielleicht konnt' ich's damals nicht, weisst du, ausformulieren, dass Israel hier mir die Möglichkeit gibt, mich viel freier zu erfinden als es die Schweiz meiner Meinung nach für mich persönlich erlauben könnte. Das ist der, wirklich für mich der Grund, hier zu sein und ich sag das jetzt hier, weil du eben gerade fragst. Ja, es ist Umbruchstimmung und – ich

For Margot, like Hannah, this freedom is not only related to her private life, but also to her professional life, specifically her entrepreneurship. The image of Israel as a place facilitating and rewarding entrepreneurship seems to be part of a general view held by the public (Rütti/NZZ, 2018; Schmid/NZZ, 2018; Segenreich-Horsky/ NZZ, 2015; The Economist, 2010), has been documented by Dan Senor and Saul Singer (2009) in their book on Israel's start-up economy, and is also reflected and reproduced by the protagonists. Margot, for example, thinks it is easier to build up a company in Israel, compared to Switzerland, where people might want more security and are thus more risk averse (Transcript Margot, p. 27 f.). She perceives herself as having gotten *"very lucky"* with her professional life in Israel. As she had already worked in high-tech firms while in Switzerland, her professional transition in Israel was smooth, which was a major part of being content and starting to feel at home in Israel, as it was for other migrant women (Kranz, 2019). She also says that her being Swiss and having worked in Switzerland often is a particular bonus in her professional life as she is seen as *"the key (…) to Europe"* and awarded a preemptive good professional reputation (Transcript Margot, p. 37).

Overall, discussions of freedom in the protagonists' narratives are connected to a specific place: for Swiss women this place can be Israel. While the different stories are joined through common emotions, however, interpretations of self-fulfillment, independence, or freedom manifest in subjective, individual ways, in part perhaps due to different ways of dealing with circumstances and experiences (Kranz, 2019, p. 12).

Contrasting these notions of Israel as a place providing more freedom, Jacob talks about the advantages of living in Switzerland, reflecting upon and creating images of Switzerland as a "special place or case" (Steinberg, 2015), which raises the question of whether the narrated feelings of freedom lie in the significance of the activity of migration or in a specific place in connection with individual experiences and biographies, which limits or changes the emotions individuals experience and discuss in their migration narratives:

> bin mir nicht sicher, wie ich mir das in der Schweiz erlauben könnte, ja oder nein, oder vielleicht wär' ich ja gar nicht zu diesem Punkt gekommen, ja. (…) Ich hatte, ich war so, es ist so ein Bilderbuchablauf, der Lebensablauf. Also (da ist der) Kindergarten, dann gehst du zur Grundschule und und und, und, und es ist einfach so ziemlich klar, wie du dein Leben zu leben hast. Und jetzt rein ausbildungstechnisch und beruflich, schau, ich hab' [Jahr] meinen Bachelor abgeschlossen, wir sind [Jahr]. Ich lerne, ich studier' in meinem Master [an Universität]. Ich, es ist mir völlig klar, wär' ich in der Schweiz geblieben, hätt' ich wahrscheinlich Bachelor (gemacht), vielleicht ein Jahr irgendwie Praktika, blablabla, wär' zum Master und, einfach, ähm – ich sag das nicht, es ist überhaupt nicht, dass es schlecht ist, aber es wär' einfach ziemlich vorgegeben gewesen. Ich glaub', ich hätte mich automatisch und dem Sinne auch freiwillig in diesem Raster gefunden. Und hier in Israel ist es viel einfacher auszubrechen, wenn du es möchtest und äh Quereinstiege und alles ist ziemlich so akzeptiert, nicht nur akzeptiert, sondern so geht's ein bisschen zu und her."

I think it's a country (that) allows people to really live like they actually want to. There are so many liberties, (...) there are, of course, many restrictions as well, which are natural, uh, right. I don't know, but actually there is this certain 'path of life' and there is – society here demands of everyone to, um, align yourself to it. But I think, that, (while) that's everywhere, maybe here it's a bit more pronounced, because it's a bit different from (other places). (...) (A)nd, uh, a bit stricter. There are things that seem strange, (...) but fundamentally the country and life here, you can really-, you can find many-, (you) can find your own niche here. I think there is a calm, which one doesn't have (somewhere else). Also, everyone has their privacy, um, and there are just less problems here, which (can) make life difficult. And yeah. So. That's about it.
(Transcript Jacob, pp. 9–10)[105]

6.2.2 Reflections on happiness

Happiness, contentment, self-fulfillment, and related emotions, interpretations, and reflections on such feelings as well as the relationship between happiness and specific time periods, places, or national frameworks are part of the narratives in various ways. Doron, for example, reflects on general happiness and contradictions in his story when he says:

Somehow, I feel people in Israel are happier and it doesn't make any sense. Because quality of life is so much better here, everything is so much better. But somehow people here, I feel, they don't appreciate it. (...) Of course, there are different people, and some are different, but in general, that's my feeling.
(Transcript Doron, p. 23)

Jacob describes the destination of Switzerland as a place one can *"make it to"*, narratively making it a place of achievement and relates it to memories of happiness

---

105 Translated from German:
"*Ich glaube, es ist zuerst einmal ein Land, dass es den Menschen ermöglicht, wirklich so zu leben, wie sie es eigentlich wollen. Also es gibt hier sehr viele Freiheiten, oder es gibt natürlich auch sehr viele Einschränkungen, die sind natürlich. (...) Ich weiss nicht so, aber eigentlich, ja so einen bestimmten Lebensweg und (...) die Gesellschaft hier fordert von allen irgendwie ein bisschen, ähm, (sich) nach dem auszurichten. Ähm, aber ich glaube, das ist äh, das ist überall so. Vielleicht ist es hier ein bisschen ausgeprägter, weil es ein bisschen anders ist, als viele andere (Gesellschaften). Ein bisschen strenger, (da) gibt's Dinge, die (einem) ein bisschen komisch vorkommen, (...) aber grundsätzlich (sind) das Land und das Leben hier, man kann hier wirklich seine Nische finden, glaube ich. Es gibt hier eine Ruhe, die man sonst nicht hat, also jeder hat auch seine Privatsphäre, äh, und es gibt hier einfach weniger Probleme, die, die das Leben erschweren. Und ja. Also. Das ist ungefähr, so (meine Meinung zur Schweiz).*"

when asked how his family, friends, and surroundings reacted to the news of his moving:

> *They found it funny that one (…), (that) someone did manage to make it back to Switzerland, well, or came here, because they – it was a great time here for us as a family, and they were happy, of course, so only positive reactions, yeah, and they said: 'Now stay there'. Yeah. [laughs].*
> (Transcript Jacob, p. 20)[106]

Here, Switzerland gains meaning as a specific place connected to positive imaginaries or happy memories and nostalgia, and moving there is described as an "accomplishment" or "achievement", related to the desire of "staying there" in the future. The destination as a desirable location and the related positive connotations are reflected in the quotations, thus giving it a positive "geography of meaning" (Benson, 2009), rooted in nostalgia about past happy times as a family. Desires and imaginaries of a future self are, of course, also part of the narratives of unskilled migrants, however, their experienced "reality checks" and possibilities often limit their personal transnational or migratory aspirations and require adjustments and "downsizing" (Boccagni, 2017) different from the adjustments highly skilled migrants who were part of this study have had to make in order to fulfill their aspirations.

As mentioned in section 6.1, the place of destination does not always carry a much meaning and is sometimes put into the background of migration narratives. For example, Dani Kranz's (2016) results show that of the Israelis in Germany, about 30% say they moved abroad out of a general sense of adventure and it can be assumed that many of the Israelis in Switzerland would say something similar. It is also a motivation related by other skilled Western migrants (Benson & O'Reilly, 2009). Ghassan Hage (2005) does not discuss a sense of adventure but, using another perspective, discusses how migrants often verbalize a "fear of being stuck" when talking about the significance of migration in their biography, which, in the case of the narratives used in this study, might be turned around as it is often expressed as a "wish for staying on the move".

Rhea mainly thinks about questions of happiness while talking about her children and the current political circumstances in Israel, which is something Margot does in a similar manner. Rhea's deliberation on happiness in the context of a question about

---

106 Translated from German:
"*Die haben's lustig gefunden, (…) dass (es) irgendjemand doch wieder zurück in die Schweiz geschafft hat, also oder gekommen ist. Weil sie, war es eine schöne Zeit für uns als Familie hier und die haben sich gefreut natürlich. Also, immer nur positiv reagiert und gesagt ja, und jetzt bleib dort. Ja. [lacht].*"

the tensions between her Israeli-Jewish identity and her hopes for her children's future is a long passage presented almost in its entirety because it illustrates well how ambivalent feelings and complexities inherent within the decision to migrate can be part of migration narratives, even for highly skilled migrants who move voluntarily and on privileged trajectories. Further, it demonstrates how the contrast between Israel and Switzerland as frameworks can play a central role in the emotional reflections of some of the protagonists:

> *Because, I mean, the complexity of* [national and individual] *identity for me (–) it's not something you can separate. Obviously, I'm a complex person (…), like every other person, not only me, but, um, it's like people say: 'Israel…' – and I say it – 'Israel should have a very strong army'. Yeah, I think so. I think it's very important. But I just don't want my children to be in it. (…) Because I think if, uh, something happens, they might die. But I don't want mine (to die). How can you say this? I mean, it's an unsolved paradox, which is always relevant. Now, when we're caught in huge criticism about Israeli politics, I will say, 'I want Israel to have a strong army', but I don't want to go to stupid, um, stupid ego- and stupidity(-driven) wars. But I'm not the Prime Minister. So, this (is) unsolved, I totally understand why people go religious. And you have this unsolved paradox. Because you know, and I pray as well, for the sake of my (family members) who are in the army and the sake of the families who are under attack (…), but I also pray for (the people in) Gaza. (…).*
>
> *The question is where the children will be happier. It's a question (we discuss) quite often, (with my) family, my friends here, Jewish-Israeli friends here. (…) What makes someone happier? (In) Israel, they are very happy. With the sun, with the friends, (…), with the family, they are very, very happy, much – happier than here. Which is also a question, right? What is happiness, what is 'happier', and what if they (would) only know Israel – (…). But, um, and I think it's, I mean they can be happy, they are happy here as well, in the stranger –, in this path, in this dimension of being a stranger. But they won't be strangers, the children. It's us. And I prefer (an) unhappy life lived, like, with a child, than a happy dead child. Um. I think. But you know, most children don't die in Israel. (…) But this threat is, like, killing the mother. [laughs and sighs].*
>
> *So, I don't know. I'm sorry. I still don't know. I just don't want to-, I mean, I just don't want another war. And (there's) gonna be another war, another war, (…). I mean, when there were the elections and I went home to Israel, I mean, if he wasn't elected, if Bibi* [Netanyahu] *wasn't elected, I (would be) so much happier. On a very basic term. I would have hope. Which I don't have now. (–) And I think, we are not gonna move back as long as he (is in power). Yeah. Um. But you know, I could go to Israel and help the other parties, but I don't. So. I'm sorry. Hard question.*

(Transcript Rhea, pp. 38–39)

Hannah, when asked about the future and potentially moving to another country soon, reflects on being happy in more abstract, individual terms, without including political circumstances, presenting a flexible present and future self:

> *Hmm – No, I just think, um – we're good – here. I think we would be good somewhere, well, how should I say, maybe somewhere else, but I just think, well that it's mainly about, that one should be a bit grateful for it, and for oneself, but, I also think, always, always, always question if it's right. Not from a place of burden just, a, just like, is this working for me? Is it ok? Do I have to change something, in any areas of life? – That's important, I think, in order to be as happy as possible.*
> (Transcript Hannah, p. 38)[107]

As these examples illustrate, questions about the future, in particular, can lead to reflections on happiness and its connection to locality, mobility, and surroundings. In such discussions migration has served a more or less satisfactory personal purpose, even if it is and/or was connected to difficulties and caused by past "struggles".

6.3 Conclusion and Outlook: Going Abroad and Staying on the Move

In this chapter the various ways migration is looked at within the narrative of a successful multi-sited biography were discussed. The protagonists discuss their mobility as the activity of "going abroad" and through differentiating themselves from "other migrants". Through this, the significance of migration often becomes an ongoing event with a certain dimension of randomness, which happened in the course of a life but was not something specifically planned. The reasons for migrating are multifaceted, even for highly skilled migrants who predominantly moved to another country due to professional reasons. Besides professional advancement, love, as well as the wish to lead a cosmopolitan or transnational life, are put forward as main motivations.

Once migration took place and is retrospectively discussed and reflected upon, feelings of achievement, accomplishment, freedom, and contentment or happiness are associated with the event and the impact it had on one's biography. Narrating

---

107 Translated from German:
 "*Mmh – Nein, ich glaube einfach ähm - man, es geht uns gut, hier. Ich glaube, es würde uns auch gut gehen, also, wie soll ich sagen, vielleicht auch irgendwo anders. Aber ich glaub', also es geht einfach darum, dass man auch ein bisschen dankbar ist dafür und sich aber, ich denke auch, immer, immer, immer hinterfragt, ob es stimmt, ob's richtig ist. Nicht von einem so bedrückenden Ort so, einfach so, stimmt's für mich, ist es ok, muss ich irgendwas ähm anpassen in allen Lebensbereichen und – das denk' ich, ist wichtig, damit man doch so glücklich wie möglich sein kann.*"

migration stories creates various forms of feelings. However, these feelings can be ambivalent, conflictual, and everchanging. As discussed in chapter 4, singular or subjective forms of (non-)belonging are created by the protagonists. In this chapter the discussion focused on how the activity of "going abroad" is put into effect and seen as leading to various positive emotions and experiences, such as freedom (especially for Swiss women in Israel) and a successful, content, flexible, and in some cases, cosmopolitan self.

Edward Said (2000, pp. 147–149) writes that: "Exiles cross borders, break barriers of thought and experience" and that there can be freedom and originality in conscious independence or detachment from notions of "home" and national belongings. While there is a self-evident and crucial difference between exiles, who are banished or forced to leave a place and (highly skilled) migrants, who leave a place voluntarily (Said, 2000, pp. 143–144), some of the protagonists' narratives reflect such aspects of freedom, originality, and accomplishment provoked through the activity of crossing borders and give meaning to these concepts in the course of interview narratives about "going abroad".

In the next, final, chapter I will summarize the results and their significance and provide an outlook for future research in the field of highly skilled migration and emotions.

7. Conclusion: Migration and Emotion

It's all about emotion.
(Expert interview, Prof. Dr. David Horn, Tel Aviv, July 7, 2018)

As asked earlier, the main question guiding this study was: What role do emotions play in migration stories? In this final chapter I will reflect concludingly on the superordinate theme of migration, summarize the main results of the study, and conclude the initial discussion on the meaning of emotions in migration research and the choice of Israel and Switzerland as research fields. Finally, I will provide an outlook on potential future research topics for anthropological migration and emotion research.

The focus of the study was on a small group of highly skilled migrants from Switzerland in Israel and highly skilled migrants from Israel in Switzerland. I contextually touched on the general topic of highly skilled migration in the current local and global framework and the complexities of the definition of "highly skilled/highly qualified migrant". As the literature shows, who is seen as "highly skilled/highly qualified" has a lot to do with place and time, as well as with policies and the economic situation of a state. It relates strongly to who is wanted or needed and who is not (Cranston, 2017; Kõu, Van Wissen, Van Dijk & Bailey, 2015; Mahroum, 2001; Parsons, Rojon, Rose & Samanani, 2020; Sandoz, 2019).

The results of the study were achieved through contextualization and triangulation of various forms of data (interview transcripts, conversation notes, fieldnotes, and newspaper articles) to ensure multiple perspectives on the topic. I centered on twelve exemplary protagonists with homogenous biographies in detail, trailing emotions in their migration narratives, in order to understand the significance of migration within singular multi-sited biographies in specific localities. Migrating in these and similar stories is a decision justified by various aspirations and framed emotionally as a unique narrative of belonging; nostalgia, irritation, expectation; and going abroad. Through the emotional dimensions in their singular migration stories, the protagonists are able to construct an independent and successful self in a globalized world and give meaning to their migration experiences.

As illustrated, the protagonists have sometimes very different, even divergent ways of dealing with circumstances and telling their stories. The results accordingly reflect the heterogeneity of the group "highly skilled migrants" and the difficulty of bringing them under one umbrella, or into one concluding definition (Benson & O'Reilly, 2009; Götzö & Sontag, 2015; Scott, 2006). Several authors suggest a focus on specific localities (Götzö & Sontag, 2015; Scott, 2006). In the case of this study, the two countries of origin and destination of Israel and Switzerland were chosen as such specific localities, and the focus was put on the narratives and biographies of selected actors. Still, there are remarkable differences in the way the significance of migration within a biography is narrated by the protagonists.

These complex results are quite common when looking at "high skilled migration" and biographies (see for example: Dani Kranz, 2019). In the protagonists' stories, this partly could have to do with the singular way emotions and memories are used to frame and share migration stories and also with aspects of surroundings, subjectivities, and individual circumstances. Overall, this issue, unsurprisingly, also has to do with the fact that "highly skilled" is a very broad denominator, which is why some authors (e. g.: Sam Scott, 2006) suggest working with typologies and dividing highly skilled migrants into various subgroups to be studied. Depending on the focus of a study, this can be fruitful and should already be considered in the sampling stage.

In this study, the self-definition as highly skilled was accepted as such and used as a common denominator for participants. The self-perception and self-definition as "highly skilled migrants" of the different protagonists led to ambivalent, contradictory, and widely divergent perspectives on migration experiences and narratives of identity. Using the denominator "highly skilled migrant" additionally seems to reflect certain views on the world, such as class distinctions, sometimes reproducing and, at other times, questioning or transcending the division of the world into nation-states. This means that the category of "highly skilled migrant" is challenging, making migrating mundane while simultaneously reproducing aspects of belonging for migrants based on land, territory, or nationality (Vora, 2008).

However, even though the presented stories come from a small homogenous group of protagonists and are merely few particular examples representing high skilled migration, there are similarities in emotions and recurring themes. First, migrating in these and similar stories is not a purely economic necessity or professional decision, but a multifaceted decision based on various combinations of experiences and emotions about the past, present, and future. There is rarely a critical and single reason when looking at skilled and highly skilled migrants' motivations for moving. Decisions to move are demonstrably explained and reflected upon with emotions and a wish to lead a "good life" through individualized self-fulfillment, which includes going abroad for various reasons, at least temporarily (for example, as a break from one's country of origin or as a freeing adventure on the way to professional fulfillment or a "better" self). Yet, there are also some contradictions, ambivalences, and dichotomies in how this uniquely "good life" as a highly skilled migrant manifests and what it consists of. For instance, there are tensions and contradictions between described feelings of belonging to a place and a wish to raise one's children in safety or achieving a professional aim.

For the highly skilled migrants, the motivations for moving are multifaceted and, although professional fulfillment and a lucrative job might be important factors, biographical features and various emotions still play an essential role in the decision-making process as well as the recounting of experiences. While migration should not be essentialized and automatically seen as *the* defining event in an individual's life or seen as something extraordinary in a historical perspective (there always has been some form of migration and mobility throughout human existence), it is still often perceived as exceptional or at least worth studying in a world divided into nation-states yet connected through globalization and transnational activities.

Part of this is that "[W]e assume that the world consists of states or separate societies, but we never allow ourselves to consider the kind of theoretical prerequisites on which such a world is based" (Højrup, 2003, p. 3). Imaginaries of a world divided into states, sedentariness as being the norm and being on the move as being the exception, as well as of highly skilled migrants as moving around the globe without having to engage with local frameworks, are deeply ingrained in our general understanding of topics of belonging, identity, and subjectivity, and cases like the ones presented help us question these notions and move away from thinking in containers such as integrated-unintegrated, migrant or migrant-non-migrant (and maybe also Israeli-or-Swiss).

Overall, one can say that highly skilled migrants want to realize themselves and their individualized biographies or create a "good life" on their own, personal terms. In their narratives of identity, national attachments play a subordinated role for feelings of belonging, but attachments to places do serve as contrasting backdrops in discussions of the topic of belonging and associated feelings – either as self-presentation of being a global citizen or cosmopolitan belonging to a transnational class and living in a certain professional "bubble" with no need for nationalities; or as individual longing for a place of home that no longer exists as one has been gone for too long or moved too many times, making the country of origin a strange place upon return.

While privileged in their freedom of movement and decision-making, the skilled and highly skilled migrants encountered in this study are not as rational or detached from personal experiences, frameworks, and localities as might be assumed at first glance and should not merely be understood as "privileged migrants" who do not encounter struggles and conflicts related to their mobility. As the expert interviewee Professor David Horn said poignantly during our interview on highly skilled migrants, their decision to move, and their choice of country of residence: "*It's all about emotion.*"

In the above chapters on specific emotions it was illustrated how analytically complex, fluid, and diffuse themes run through the study. The difficulty of defining "emotion" as well as "highly skilled migrant" soaks into the results as a connecting and sometimes confusing factor. Feelings of belonging can be narrated not only as biographies of non-belonging or multi-sitedness, but also as attachment to a specific locality, landscape, "home", or "bubble". Past, present, and future selves are used to reflect upon subjective feelings of nostalgia, irritation, and expectation, specifically through creating imaginaries of Israel and Switzerland as places of departure and destination, through recounting struggles or annoyances emerging out of interactions, as well as with notions of hope connected to the future. When discussing, or justifying migration, this is mainly done through a narrative of "going abroad", where a successful, happy, content, and, in some cases mobile and flexible, self in the present is created with the help of various conflicting and sometimes negative emotions from the past and future, such as anxiety, as well as with a distinction from "other" migrants or locals.

7.1 Emotional Dimensions in Migration Narratives

As already stated, the intersection between migration and emotion is important enough to warrant more research (Boccagni & Baldassar, 2015; Skrbiš, 2008). This is due to the historically prevalent focus on economic push and pull factors, brain drain and brain gain, and related approaches in migration research, as well as the focus on labor migration and questions of borders and integration. While there has been extensive research using other perspectives on the topic in recent years, there still is room for more data when looking at the link between emotion and migration in specific cases or places and in connection with high skilled migration. Using this approach allows for a focus that goes beyond merely looking at mobility and the action of migration itself (Hage, 2005; Walsh, 2012, p. 57) as it instead includes the significance of emotional ties to people, surroundings, and temporality in migration narratives (Skrbiš, 2008).

The previous chapters have shown that emotions have a peculiar, inherent temporal aspect in that a tracing of emotions within narratives means that one only has the singular narrative in a specific moment in time to work with – past and future events are interpreted with present emotions by the storytellers.[108] However, I argue that a qualitative analysis of emotions in migration stories is a sound and gainful approach to uncover how migration experiences are recounted, framed, and given meaning. In other words, it is an approach that enables us to learn more about the

---

108 This of course is not only the case with emotions but could be said about all biographical narratives and interview transcripts. Individual stories always also reflect the time and place in which they are produced and narrated and are influenced by the listener or interviewer.

significance of migration within complex narratives consisting of various elements. The importance of emotions for individual construals of the self, positions, and perceptions within migration narratives makes them an interesting theme. Hence, a tentative theory developed out of the data at hand and connecting emotions and migration could be the following: Emotions, as they involve both, meaning and feeling (Leavitt, 1996, p. 515, see pp. 40–41 in this thesis), help uncover tensions and contradictions in migration narratives. Emotions can not only be used to reference experiences of "'here' and 'there'" (Boccagni & Baldassar, 2015, p. 74) but also point to various (perceived) dichotomies; for instance, Israel–Switzerland, Swissness–Israeliness, reality–imaginary, integration–migration, native–stranger, migrant–non-migrant, migrating–going abroad, nationalism–cosmopolitanism, local–global, unskilled–skilled, mobility–stagnation, or intent–randomness.

In summary, through an analysis of emotions in biographies and narratives, it is possible to understand how subjects position themselves locally and in wider societal and political patterns of a globalized world (Walsh, 2012, p. 57). How emotions influence wider social processes can, of course, not be analyzed with a study like the one presented, but one can assume that they do in one way or the other, as individuals do not exist in a vacuum and are not only influenced by their surroundings, but, in turn, have an influence on them.

7.2 Comments on Frameworks and Surroundings

"The truth of a myth transcends the facts it recounts. The truth is to be found in what it tells about the world and in what it tells about the culture that considers it a valid argument about the world" (Azaryahu, 2007, p. 16). In 1909 Arnold van Gennep wrote that in the civilized regions of the future there would be no need for passports, that borders might be visibly marked by cornerstones or posts but will de facto only exist on maps. This prediction has not come true globally. While the free movement of people is, for example, possible within the European Union, passports still carry a strong weight, at least symbolically (Pitt-Rivers, 1984, pp. 44–48).

Citizenships and borders play a crucial role in migrants' mobilities and many borders are still strongly surveilled. It can sometimes seem to skilled and highly skilled migrants from the West that they live in a borderless, or at least passport-less world, as modern economies and knowledge societies need them and compete for them. Maybe one could even say that the character of the highly skilled migrant is a human manifestation of transnational processes or contemporary economies in a globalized world. However, while part of a privileged group of migrants due to their qualifications, skills, social belonging, status or class, their migration stories can still lead to complicated, contradictory feelings of belonging and attachment, and their migratory experiences are worth further exploring. Understanding more about various forms of migration and its significance for individuals is crucial for a better understanding of a world, in which over 270 million people are on the move.

The two small nation-states of Israel and Switzerland both have a unique history in their respective geographic region, interesting structures, and internal and external conflicts. In this study they served as specific cases for frameworks and surroundings, but the study could have been made looking at highly qualified migrants moving from and/or to other states. While some of the results are very specific to either Israel or Switzerland, as both are somewhat "special cases", other results might have been similar and transferable. Some of the specificities seem to lie in Israel not only being a place one might "need a break" from, but also a place in which one can be free and happy; and in Switzerland not only being a place that provides one with a knapsack of advantages and privileges[109] such as a good education, security, and stability, but also restrictions with regard to adaptable, individual self-fulfillment.

7.3 Outlook and Future Research

As mentioned before, the theme of emotions emerged out of the data and was not decided upon in advance. I attempted to demonstrate that more anthropological research with a focus on migration and emotions could be useful.

Perhaps using a somewhat different approach could yield additional interesting results. For example, a classic ethnography where one could observe interactions as they happen before interviewing subjects would be an option. For future studies it may be interesting to include only "super-skilled" informants in executive positions (Sklair, 2002), which would provide the opportunity to use economic anthropology and superdiversity (Vertovec, 2010) as a lens as well as a focus on one single type of highly skilled migrant. Another possibility includes focusing on one specific feeling amongst migration stories, such as the feeling of freedom achieved through migration, which came up in this study. Focusing on non-Jewish Israelis abroad, or more specifically Muslim or Christian Israelis, could also be an interesting approach, however the numbers might be very small. They were not part of the sample as one might have to use other networks, for instance, church communities in order to

---

[109] The notion of privileges in regard to race as something one carries in an invisible knapsack was coined by Peggy McIntosh (1989), and "*casually carrying Swissness*" with herself is used as an image by Hannah during her interview. Original German: "*(...) und ich es* [die positive Züge der Schweiz] *deshalb einfach so locker auf mir trage (...)*" (Transcript Hannah, p. 5).

find contacts. Another approach would be to directly compare the experiences of highly skilled Swiss in different regions.

No matter what group of skilled or highly skilled migrants is studied, the topic always provides a way to observe and discuss construals of meaning, the self, and narratives of identity in a contemporary globalized world. Or put more simply, this form of research teaches us about the significance of migratory experiences through stories.

Overall, emotions, as well as migration, provide interesting fields for anthropologists, as they are everchanging and reflect the processuality and complexity of the human condition and the world. Providing further knowledge about the topic with a "cosmopolitan appreciation of a human singularity" (Grønseth, 2013, p. 15) can hopefully expand academic dialogues on human conditions shared across borders, without denying differences and individualities.

Emotions play a role for a sense of belonging to nation-states and places, but individuals can belong to more than one state and transnationalism has to be considered for future policies, as Steven Vertovec (2009) discusses. Linda Basch, Nina Glick Schiller, and Cristina Szanton Blanc (1994) demonstrated how individuals can identify with several places at once in their foundational work over 25 years ago, challenging notions and expectations of integration that still seem prevalent today, especially in political discourses around nation, border, and "home".

Migration and multi-sited biographies are common and not always exceptional. Adding to knowledge on different forms of migration and mobility helps to "de-problematize" – or maybe even "de-exoticize" – the topic and to understand migration without making it into a problem that needs solving. In this study, migration as an activity was simply understood as moving from one country to another. Further, from an anthropological standpoint, it can be seen as "a window to a diverse life" (O'Reilly, 2016): one window, though, not the only one. Albeit often interesting and sometimes conspicuous in the sense of representing a break, rupture, or change and leading to internal conflicts and contradictions in some biographies of highly skilled migrants, migration is also a very mundane and common activity. This means that the meaning of migration within a biography should not be overemphasized either. Focusing on emotions – a universal human experience – could be one way of de-problematizing the activity of "migration".

Migration studies have the tendency to start from a perspective in which migration is the most important event in a person's life, which is empirically not always easy to prove. "It is a mistake to think that if people move across national borders, such a movement will necessarily be the most significant and defining element in their lives. … Indeed, there are many people who do not experience their international movement either as a form of cultural dislocation or as migration" (Hage, 2005, p. 469). Especially highly skilled and privileged migrants who already have moved several times might not necessarily see migration across state borders as something exceptional or very different to moving within a country.

This discussion is necessary as traditional migration research often looks at the movement of people across state borders as a "structural and ordinal problem" on a global scale, which, in turn, is then seen as leading to various kinds of conflicts (Nuscheler, 2005, p. 275). This discourse on migration is correspondingly picked up by the media, politics, and parts of the general public where migration's complexity is then reduced to a simple but urgent problem or even crisis – in the past years mainly in terms of debates about refugees and a fear of undeserving "economic migrants", differentiating who "deserves" to migrate and who does not. Rather than seeing migration as something exceptional, it might be worthwhile to focus future migration research on aspects of policy and democracy, maybe as a way of discussing potential future forms of citizenship, nation, community, and participation.

References

Abu-Lughod, L. (1996). Writing against culture. In R. G. Fox (Ed.), *Recapturing anthropology: working in the present* (pp. 466–479). Santa Fe: School of American Research Press.

Appadurai, A. (1995). The production of locality. In R. Fardon (Ed.), *Counterworks: managing the diversity of knowledge* (pp. 204–225). London: Routledge.

Appadurai, A. (1997). *Modernity at large: cultural dimensions of globalization*. Minneapolis: University of Minnesota Press.

Aratnam, G. J. (2012). *Hochqualifizierte mit Migrationshintergrund: Studie zu möglichen Diskriminierungen auf dem Schweizer Arbeitsmarkt*. Basel: Edition Gesowip.

Augé, M. (1992). *Non-lieux. Introduction á une anthropologie de la surmodernité*. Paris: Seui.

Azaryahu, M. (2007). *Tel Aviv, mythography of a city*. Syracuse, NY: Syracuse University Press.

Barbalet, J. (1996). Social emotions: confidence, trust and loyalty. *International Journal of Sociology and Social Policy, 16*(9/10), 75–96.

Barnard, A. (2000). *History and theory in anthropology*. Cambridge: Cambridge University Press.

Basch, L.; Glick Schiller N. & Szanton Blanc, C. (1994). *Nations unbound: transnational projects, postcolonial predicaments, and deterritorialized nation-states*. Langhorne: Gordon and Breach.

Basch, L.; Glick Schiller, N. & Szanton Blanc, C. (1995). From immigrant to transmigrant: theorizing transnational migration. *Anthropology Quarterly, 1*, 43–60.

Beatty, A. (2014). Anthropology and emotion (Malinowski Memorial Lecture, 2013). *Journal of the Royal Anthropological Institute, 20*, 545–563.

Beck, U. & Grande, E. (2010). Jenseits des methodologischen Nationalismus. In U. Beck, N. Braun & A. Nassehi (Ed.), *Zeitschrift für Sozialwissenschaftliche Forschung und Praxis (Themenheft Variationen der Zweiten Moderne)*, 3(4/61), 187–216.

Bekemans, L. (2002). Culture vs. globalisation in Europe: actual tension or possible dialogue? In L. Anckaert, D. Cassimon & H. Opdebeeck (Eds.), *Building Towers. Perspectives on Globalisation* (pp. 191–211). Leuven: Peters.

Ben-Sasson, H. H. (Ed.). (2007). *Geschichte des jüdischen Volkes. Von den Anfängen bis zur Gegenwart* (5. Aufl.). München: C. H. Beck.

Benson, M. (2009). A desire for difference: British lifestyle migration to Southwest France. In M. Benson & K. O'Reilly (Eds.), *Lifestyle migration. Expectations, aspirations and experiences* (pp. 121–136). Farnham: Ashgate.

Benson, M. & O'Reilly, K. (2009). *Lifestyle migration. Expectations, aspirations and experiences*. Farnham: Ashgate.

Bertelsmann Stiftung, Migration Policy Institute (Eds.). (2010). *Talent, competitiveness and migration. The Transatlantic Council on Migration*. Gütersloh: Verlag Bertelsmann Stiftung.

Bloemraad, I. (2004). Who claims dual citizenship? The limits of postnationalism, the possibilities of transnationalism, and the persistence of traditional citizenship. *International Migration Review, 38*(2), 389–426.

Boccagni, P. (2017). Aspirations and the subjective future of migration: comparing views and desires of the "time ahead" through the narratives of immigrant domestic workers. *Comparative Migration Studies, 5*(4), 1–18. https://doi.org/10.1186/s40878-016-0047-6

Boccagni, P. & Baldassar, L. (2015). Emotions on the move: mapping the emergent field of emotion and migration. *Emotion, Space and Society, 16*(2015), 73–80.

Bommes, M. (2002). Migration, Raum und Netzwerke. Über den Bedarf einer gesellschaftstheoretischen Einbettung der transnationalen Migrationsforschung. In J. Oltmer (Ed.), *Migrationsforschung und Interkulturelle Studien: Zehn Jahre IMIS. Schriften des Instituts für Migrationsforschung und Interkulturelle Studien (Vol. 11)*, 91–105.

Bossert, S. (2009). *Hummus und Chuchichäschtli. Empirische Sozialforschung zur Auswanderung von Schweizer Jüdinnen und Juden nach Israel*. [Lizenziatsarbeit im Fach Allgemeine Geschichte des Mittelalters und der Neuzeit]. Universität Basel.

Bossert, S. (2014). Alija von Schweizer Jüdinnen und Juden nach Israel. In J. Picard & D. Gerson (Eds.). *Schweizer Judentum im Wandel. Religion und Gemeinschaft zwischen Integration, Selbstbehauptung und Abgrenzung* (pp. 307–335). Zürich: Chronos Verlag.

Boucher, A. & Cerna, L. (2014). Current policy trends in skilled immigration policy. *International Migration, 52*(3), 21–25.

Brah, A. (1996). *Cartographies of diaspora. Contesting identities*. New York: Routledge.

Brettell, C. B. (2013). Anthropology of migration. In I. Ness (Ed.), *The Encyclopedia of Global Human Migration*. Retrieved from https://onlinelibrary.wiley.com/doi/abs/10.1002/9781444351071.wbeghm031, accessed August 11, 2023.

Brettell, C. B. & Hollifield, J. F. (2015). *Migration theory. Talking across disciplines*. New York: Routledge.

Brown, G. & Pickerill, J. (2009). Space for emotion in the spaces of activism. *Emotion, Space and Society, 2*(1), 24–35.

Bundesamt für Statistik, BFS (2019a). *Auslandschweizer/innen – Mehrfachbüger/innen*. Retrieved from: https://www.bfs.admin.ch/bfs/de/home/statistiken/bevoelkerung/migration-integration/auslandschweizer.assetdetail.12247841.html, accessed August 11, 2023.

Bundesamt für Statistik, BFS. (2019b). *Bevölkerung*. Retrieved from https://www.bfs.admin.ch/bfs/de/home/statistiken/bevoelkerung.html, accessed August 11, 2023.

Bundesamt für Statistik, BFS. (2020a). *Ständige und nichtständige Wohnbevölkerung nach detaillierter Staatsangehörigkeit*. Retrieved from https://www.bfs.admin.ch/bfs/de/home/statistiken/bevoelkerung/migration-integration/auslaendische-bevoelkerung.assetdetail.13707208.html, accessed August 11, 2023.

Bundesamt für Statistik, BFS. (2020b). *Bevölkerungsstand und -Struktur. Indikatoren: Schweizer im Ausland. Im Ausland niedergelassene Schweizer nach Wohnsitzstaat*. Retrieved from https://www.bfs.admin.ch/bfs/de/home/statistiken/bevoelkerung/migration-integration/auslandschweizer.html (Länderinformationen/Information on countries) and https://viz.bfs.admin.ch/assets/01/ga-01.05.09.01/ga-d-01.05.09.01.html (Karte/Map), accessed August 11, 2023.

Bunke, S. (2006). *Heimweh. Studien zur Kultur- und Literaturgeschichte einer tödlichen Krankheit*. Freiburg im Breisgau: Rombach-Wissenschaften.

Burton, E. K. (2015). An assimilating majority? Israeli marriage law and identity in the Jewish state. *Journal of Jewish Identities, 8*(1), 73–94.

Camenisch, A. & Müller, S. (2017). From (e)migration to mobile lifestyles: ethnographic and conceptual reflections about mobilities and migration. *New Diversities, 19*(3), 43–57.

Cappai, G. (2013). *Fra realtà locale e processi globali. Emigrazione, associazionismo ed identità nelle società multiculturali. Considerazioni teoriche, empiriche e metodologiche*. Halle/Saale: Hallescher Verlag.

Casey, E. S. (1987). *Remembering: a phenomenological study*. Bloomington: Indiana University Press.

Cattacin, S. & Chimienti, M. (2009). Lokale Politik der Eingliederung der Migrationsbevölkerung in der Schweiz-Zwischen Pragmatismus und Populismus. In F. Gesemann & R. Roth (Hg.), *Lokale Integrationspolitik in der Einwanderungsgesellschaft* (pp. 655–671). Wiesbaden: VS Verlag.

Central Bureau of Statistics Israel (2019). *Population of Israel*. Retrieved from https://www.cbs.gov.il/en/mediarelease/Pages/2019/Population-of-Israel-on-the-Eve-of-2020.aspx, accessed August 11, 2023.

Central Bureau of Statistics Israel (2020). *Population by religion and population group*. Retrieved from https://www.cbs.gov.il/en/subjects/Pages/Population-by-Religion-and-Population-Group.aspx, accessed August 11, 2023.

Charmaz, K. (2000). Grounded theory methodology: objectivist and constructivist qualitative methods. In N. K. Denzin & Y. S. Lincoln (Eds.), *Handbook of qualitative research* (2nd ed.) (pp. 509–535). Thousand Oaks, CA: Sage.

Charmaz, K. (2006). *Constructing grounded theory: a practical guide through qualitative analysis*. London: Sage.

Cohen, N. & Kranz, D. (2014). State-assisted highly skilled return programmes, national identity and the risk(s) of homecoming: Israel and Germany compared. *Journal of Ethnic and Migration Studies, 41*(5), 795-812. https://doi.org/10.1080/1369183X.2014.948392

Coleman, S. (2007). *Locating the field: space, place and context in anthropology*. Oxford: Berg Publishers.

Collett, E. & Zuleeg, F. (2010). Soft, scarce and super skills: sourcing the next generation of migrant workers in Europe. In Bertelsmann Stiftung, Migration Policy Institute (Ed.), *Talent, competitiveness and migration. The Transatlantic Council on Migration* (pp. 337–361). Gütersloh: Verlag Bertelsmann Stiftung.

Connor, J. (2007). *The sociology of loyalty*. New York, NY: Springer Science + Business Media.

Cranston, S. (2017). Expatriate as a 'good' migrant: thinking through skilled international migrant categories. *Populations, Space and Place, 23*(2058), 1–12. https://doi.org/10.1002/psp.2058

Cranston, S.; Schapendonk, J. & Spaan, E. (2018). New directions in exploring the migration industries: introduction to special issue. *Journal of Ethnic and Migration Studies, 44*(4), 543–557.

Csedö, K. (2008). Negotiating skills in the global city: Hungarian and Romanian professionals and graduates in London. *Journal of Ethnic and Migration Studies, 34*(5), 803–823.

D'Amato, G. (2008). Historische und soziologische Übersicht über die Migration in der Schweiz. *Schweizerisches Jahrbuch für Entwicklungspolitik (Migration und Entwicklung: Eine Zweckallianz), 27*(02), 177–195.

Das, V. & Poole, D. (Eds.). (2004). *Anthropology in the margins of the state*. Santa Fe: School of American Research Press.

Davidson, J., Bondi, L. & Smith, M. (2007). *Emotional geographies*. New York: Routledge.

Dee Haas, H. & Czaika, M. (2013). The globalization of migration. Has the world really become more migratory? *International Migration Review, 48*(2), 283–323.

DellaPergola, S. (2011). When scholarship disturbs narrative. Ian Lustick on Israel's migration balance [comment]. *Israel Studies Review, 26*(2), 1–27.

Diner, D. (2017, December 8). *Wissensarsenale der jüdischen Moderne – Zum Abschluss der Enzyklopädie jüdischer Geschichte und Kultur* [lecture]. Abschiedsfest/Farewell Event Prof. Dr. Jacques Picard, Universität Basel, Basel, Switzerland.

Eichhorst, W. (2011). Arbeitswelt und Lebenswelt im Globalisierungszeitalter. In T. Mayer, R. Meyer, et al. (Hg.), *Globalisierung im Fokus von Politik, Wirtschaft, Gesellschaft. Eine Bestandsaufnahme* (pp. 225–236). Wiesbaden: VS Verlag.

Eidgenössisches Departement für auswärtige Angelegenheiten, EDA. (2020). *Auslandschweizerinnen und Auslandschweizer*. Retrieved from https://www.eda.admin.ch/eda/de/home/leben-im-ausland/die-fuenfte-schweiz.html, accessed August 11, 2023.

Epstein, B. (2016, March 18). Master mit Erfolgsgarantie. *tachles 11*(16), pp. 14–15.

Erez, T. (2013). Mission not accomplished: negotiating power relations and vulnerability among Messianic Jews in Israel. In F. Markowitz (Ed.), *Ethnographic encounters in Israel. Poetics and ethics of fieldwork* (pp. 40–58). Bloomington: Indiana University Press.

Eriksen, T. H. (1992). In limbo: notes on the culture of airports [lecture]. *EASA Meeting Prague*. Retrieved from https://www.hyllanderiksen.net/articles, accessed August 11, 2023.

Favell, A. (2003). Games without frontiers? Questioning the transnational social power of migrants in Europe. *European Journal of Sociology, 44*(3), 397–427.

Fialkova, L. & Yelenevskaya, M. (2007). *Ex-Soviets in Israel. From personal narratives to a group portrait*. Detroit Michigan: Wayne State University Press.

Fialkova, L. & Yelenevskaya, M. (2013). *In search of the self: reconciling the past and the presence in immigrants' experience*. Tartu: ELM Scholarly Press.

Fink, O. (2021). Emotionen als Schlüssel im Nahost-Konflikt [article about ongoing research project at the University of Basel on emotions and emotion regulation in intractable conflicts, text written by S. Kirchmayr]. *UNI NOVA 01*(2021). Retrieved from https://www.unibas.ch/de/Aktuell/Uni-Nova/Uni-Nova-137/Uni-Nova-137-Emotionen-als-Schluessel-im-Nahost-Konflikt.html?pk_campaign=UN_20210518_Schlafmohn, accessed August 11, 2023.

Fleischman, Y., Willen, S., Davidovitch, N. & Mor, Z. (2015). Migration as a social determinant of health for irregular migrants: Israel as case study. *Social Science and Medicine, 147*, 89–97.

Flick, U. (2011). *Qualitative Sozialforschung: Eine Einführung* (4. Aufl.). Reinbek: Rowohlt Taschenbuch Verlag.

Friedman, J. (2004). Champagne liberals and "classes dangereuses". Class, identity and cultural production in the contemporary global systems. *Journal des anthropologues, 96–97*, 151–176. Retrieved from https://journals.openedition.org/jda/1817, accessed August 11, 2023.

Friedman, J. (2017). The global citizenship agenda and the generation of cosmopolitan capital in British higher education. *British Journal of Sociology of Education, 39*(4), 436–450. Retrieved from https://www.tandfonline.com/doi/abs/10.1080/01425692.2017.1366296, accessed August 11, 2023.

Geertz, C. (1964). Tihingan: a Balinese village. *Journal of the Humanities and Social Sciences of Southeast Asia, 120*(1), 1–33. Retrieved from https://brill.com/view/journals/bki/120/1/article-p1_1.xml, accessed August 11, 2023.

Glaser, B. G. & Strauss, A. (2008). *The discovery of grounded theory: strategies for qualitative research* (3rd ed.). New Brunswick: Aldine Transaction.

Glick Schiller, N. & Çağlar, A. (2009). Towards a comparative theory of locality in migration studies: migrant incorporation and city scale. *Journal of Ethnic and Migration Studies, 35*(2), 177–202.

Gold, S. J. (2018). Israeli infotech migrants in Silicon Valley. *RSF: The Russell Sage Foundation Journal of the Social Sciences, 4*(1), 130–48. https://doi.org/10.7758/rsf.2018.4.1.08

Gonzáles-Hidalgo, M. & Zografos, C. (2019). Emotions, power, and environmental conflict: expanding the 'emotional turn' in political ecology. *Progress in Human Geography, 44*(2), 235–255.

González, A. M. (2017). In search of a sociological explanation for the emotional turn. *Sociologia, Problemas e Práticas, 85*(2017), 27–45.

Götz, I.; Lehnert, K.; Lemberger, B. & Sondelmayer S. (Eds.). (2010). *Mobilität und Mobilisierung: Arbeit im sozioökonomischen, politischen und kulturellen Wandel*. Frankfurt a. M.: Campus Verlag.

Götzö, M. (2014). Theoriebildung nach Grounded Theory. In C. Bischoff, W. Leimgruber et al. (Hg.), *Methoden der Kulturanthropologie* (pp. 444–458). Bern: Haupt Verlag UTB.

Götzö, M. & Sontag, K. (2015). The pursuit of happiness? Migration von Hochqualifizierten. *Schweizerisches Archiv für Volkskunde, 111*, 41–62.

Gray, B. (2008). Putting emotion and reflexivity to work in researching migration. *Sociology, 42*, 935–952.

Gromova, A. (2013). *Generation "Kosher Light". Urbane Räume und Praxen junger russischsprachiger Juden in Berlin*. Bielefeld: transcript Verlag.

Grønseth, A. S. (2013). *Being human, being migrant. Senses of self and well-being*. New York: Berghahn Books.

Gross, D. M. (2011). High-skill migration to Canada and Switzerland: Retention, attraction and competition with the United States through policy. *Metropolis: British Columbia Working Paper Series, 11*(3). Retrieved from https://policycommons.net/artifacts/1206832/high-skill-migration-to-canada-and-switzerland/1759941/, accessed September 5, 2023.

Gutkowski, S. (2019). Love, war and secular 'reasonableness' among hilonim in Israel-Palestine. In M. Scheer, N. Fadil & B. Schepelern Johansen (Eds.), *Secular bodies, affects and emotions. European configurations* (pp. 123–140). London: Bloomsbury.

Hacohen, D. (2002). Mass immigration and the demographic revolution in Israel. In E. Karsh (Ed.), *Israel: The first hundred years (Volume III: Israeli society and politics since 1948)* (pp. 177–190). London: Frank Cass Publishers.

Hage, G. (2005). A not so multi-sited ethnography of a not so imagined community. *Anthropological Theory, 5*(4), 463–475.

Hage, G. & Papadopoulos, D. (2004). Migration, hope and the making of subjectivity in transnational capitalism. Ghassan Hage in conversation with Dimitris Papadopoulos. *International Journal for Critical Psychology, 12*, 95–117.

Handelskammer Schweiz-Israel/Chamber of Commerce Switzerland-Israel (2018). *Economic data*. Retrieved from https://www.swissisrael.ch/services, accessed September 5, 2023.

Hannerz, U. (2002). Kosmopoliten und Sesshafte in der Weltkultur. In P. U. Merz-Benz & G. Wagner (Hg.), *Der Fremde als sozialer Typus* (pp. 139–161). Konstanz: UVK Verlagsgesellschaft.

Harkin, M. E. (2003). Feeling and thinking in memory and forgetting: Toward an ethnohistory of the emotions. *Ethnohistory, 59*(2), 261–284. Retrieved from https://read.dukeupress.edu/ethnohistory/article/50/2/261/8418/Feeling-and-Thinking-in-Memory-and-Forgetting, accessed August 11, 2023.

Harpaz, Y. (2019). *Citizenship 2.0: dual nationality as a global asset*. Princeton: Princeton University Press.

Harvey, D. (1989). *The condition of postmodernity*. Cambridge, MA: Blackwell.

Harvey, D. (2005). *A brief history of neoliberalism*. Oxford: Oxford University Press.

Haumann, H. (Ed.) (1997). *The first Zionist Congress in 1897 – causes, significance, topicality*. Basel: Karger.

Helbling, M. & Kriesi, H. (2014). Why citizens prefer high- over low-skilled immigrants. Labor market competition, welfare state and deservingness. *European Sociological Review, 30*(5), 595–614.

Hercog, M. & Sandoz, L. (2018a). Highly skilled or highly wanted migrants? Conceptualizations, policy designs and implementations of high-skilled migration policies [editorial]. *Migration Letters, 15*(4), special issue.

Hercog, M. & Sandoz, L. (2018b). Selecting the highly skilled: Norms and practices of the Swiss admission system for non-EU immigrants. *Migration Letters, 15*(4), 503–515.

Hercog, M. & Tejada, G. (2014). Incorporation of skilled migrants in a host country: insights from the study of skilled Indians in Switzerland. *IMDS Working Paper Series, 58*(60), 1–17.

Hess, S.; Kasparek, B.; Kron, S.; Rodatz, M.; Schwertl, M. & Sontowski, S. (Eds.). (2016). *Der lange Sommer der Migration. Grenzregime III*. Berlin: Verlag Assoziation A.

Hettling, M.; König, M.; Schaffner, M.; Suter, A. & Tanner, J. (1998). *Eine kleine Geschichte der Schweiz. Der Bundesstaat und seine Traditionen*. Frankfurt am Main: Edition Suhrkamp.

Hilgert, D. (2013). Third junior scholars conference in German-Jewish history: Germans and Americans in Israel – Israelis in Germany and the United States (Conference Report). *Bulletin of the German Historical Institute, Washington DC.*, 109–114.

Ho, E. L.-E. (2009). Constituting citizenship through the emotions: Singaporean transmigrants in London. *Annals of the Association of American Geographers, 99*(4), 788–804.

Hochschild, A. (1979). Emotion work, feeling rules, and social structure. *American Journal of Sociology, 85*(3), 551–575.

Højrup, T. (2003). *State, culture and life-modes. The foundations of life-mode analysis*. Burlington: Ashgate Publishing.

Illouz, E. (2007). *Cold intimacies. The making of emotional capitalism*. Cambridge, UK: Polity.

Illouz, E. (2015). *Israel*. Berlin: Suhrkamp Verlag.

Inda, J. X. & Rosaldo, R. (2008). Tracking global flows. In J. X. Inda & R. Rosaldo (Eds.), *The Anthropology of Globalization. A reader* (2nd ed.) (pp. 3–46). Malden, MA: Blackwell Publishing Ltd.

International Organization for Migration, IOM. (2019a). *World Migration Report*. Retrieved from https://publications.iom.int/system/files/pdf/wmr_2020.pdf, accessed August 11, 2023.

International Organization for Migration, IOM. (2019b). *Glossary on Migration (2019 Edition)*. Retrieved from https://publications.iom.int/system/files/pdf/iml_34_glossary.pdf, accessed August 11, 2023.

Jagannath, A. (2014). Discourse of awareness: development, social movements and the practices of freedom in Nepal. *The Journal of the Association for Nepal and Himalayan Studies, 24*(1), 144–145.

Jaspers, K. (1996). *Heimweh und Verbrechen* [Original 1909]. München: Belleville.

Joppke, C. & Rosenhek, Z. (2001). *Ethnic-priority immigration in Israel and Germany: resilience versus demise*. Florence: European University Institute Working Papers in Political and Social Sciences. Retrieved from https://ccis.ucsd.edu/_files/wp45.pdf, accessed August 11, 2023.

Kabbani, R. (1986). *Europe's myths of Orient. Devise and Rule*. London: MacMillan Press.

Kalir, B. (2006). *Christian aliens in the Jewish state. Undocumented migrants from Latin America striving for practical national belonging in Israel* [dissertation at the University of Amsterdam]. Retrieved from https://dare.uva.nl/search?identifier=22143b09-3676-4e8f-bf51-00d3f7c2cf82, accessed September 5, 2023.

Kalir, B. (2015). The Jewish state of anxiety: between moral obligation and fearism in the treatment of African asylum seekers in Israel. *Journal of Ethnic and Migration Studies, 41*(4), 580–598.

Kamil, O. (2008). *Arabische Juden in Israel. Geschichte und Ideologie von Ben Gurion bis Ovadia Yosef.* Würzburg: Ergon Verlag.

Kaufmann, V.; Bergman, M. M. & Joye, D. (2004). Motility: mobility as capital. *ijurr (International Journal of Urban and Regional Research), 28*(4), 754–756.

Kearney, M. (1995). The local and the global. The anthropology of globalization and transnationalism. *Annual Review of Anthropology, 24,* 547–565.

Kemp, A. (2004). Labour migration and racialization: labour market mechanisms and labour migration control policies in Israel. *Social Identities: Journal for the Study of Race, Nation and Culture, 10*(2), 267–292. https://doi.org/10.1080/1350463042000227380

King, R. (2002). Towards a new map of European migration. *International Journal of Population Geography, 8,* 89–106.

King, D. (2005). Sustaining activism through emotional reflexivity. In H. Flam & D. King (Eds.), *Emotions and Social Movements* (pp. 150–169). New York, NW: Routledge.

Kleinginna, P. R. Jr. & Kleinginna, A. M. (1981). A categorized list of emotion definitions, with suggestions for a consensual definition. *Motivation and Emotion, 5*(4), 345–379.

Koehn, P. & Rosenau, J. (2002). Transnational competence in an emergent epoch. *International Studies Perspectives, 3*(2), 105–127.

Koehn, P. & Rosenau, J. (2010). *Transnational competence. Empowering professional curricula for horizon-rising challenges.* New York: Routledge.

Kohler Riessman, C. (1993). *Narrative analysis.* Newbury Park: Sage Publications.

Korpela, M. (2009). When a trip to adulthood becomes a lifestyle: Western lifestyle migrants in Varansi, India. In M. Benson & K. O'Reilly (Eds.), *Lifestyle migration. Expectations, aspirations and experiences* (pp. 15–30). Farnham: Ashgate.

Koser, K. & Salt, J. (1997). The geography of highly skilled international migration. *International Journal of Population Geography, 3*(4), 285–303.

Kõu, A. & Bailey, A. (2014). Movement is a constant feature in my life – contextualising migration processes of highly skilled Indians. *Geoforum, 52,* 113–122.

Kõu, A.; Van Wissen, L.; Van Dijk, J. & Bailey, A. (2015). A life course approach to high-skilled migration: lived experiences of Indians in the Netherlands. *Journal of Ethnic and Migration Studies, 41*(10), 1–20.

Kranz, D. (2016). Forget Israel – the future is in Berlin! Local Jews, Russian immigrants, and Israeli Jews in Berlin and across Germany. *Shofar: An Interdisciplinary Journal of Jewish Studies, 34*(4), 5–28.

Kranz, D. (2019). The global north goes to the global north minus? Intersections of the integration of highly skilled, non-Jewish female partner and spousal migrants from the global north in Israel. *International migration 2019*, 1–16. https://doi.org/10.1111/imig.12574

Kreutner, J. (2013). *Die Schweiz und Israel: Auf dem Weg zu einem differenzierten historischen Bewusstsein*. Zürich: Chronos Verlag.

Leavitt, J. (1996). Meaning and feeling in the anthropology of emotions. *American Ethnologist*, 23(3), 514–539. https://doi.org/10.1525/ae.1996.23.3.02a00040

Leivestad, H. H. (2016). Motility. In Salazar, N. & Jayaram, K. (Eds.), *Keywords of mobility. Critical engagements* (pp. 133–151). New York: Berghahn Books.

Levitt, P. (2003a). Transnational ties and incorporation: the cases of Dominicans in the United States. In D. Gutierrez (Ed.), *The Columbia History of Latinos in the United States since 1960* (pp. 229–258). New York: Columbia University Press.

Levitt, P. (2003b). "You know, Abraham was really the first immigrant": religion and transnational migration. *International Migration Review*, 37(3), 847–873.

Levitt, P. (2012). What's wrong with migration scholarship? A critique and a way forward. *Identities: Global Studies in Culture and Power*, 19(4), 493–495. https://doi.org/10.1080/1070289X.2012.676255

Liebig, T.; Kohls, S. & Krause, K. (2012). The labour market integration of immigrants and their children in Switzerland. *OECD Social, Employment and Migration Working Paper, Nr. 128*. Retrieved from http://www.oecd.org/switzerland/49654710.pdf, accessed August 11, 2023.

Lipshitz, G. (1998). *Country on the move: migration to and within Israel, 1948–1995*. Dordrecht: Kluwer Academic Publishers.

Lopez Rodriguez, M. (2010). Migration and a quest for 'normalcy'. Polish migrant mothers and the capitalization of meritocratic opportunities in the UK. *Social Identities*, 16(3), 339–358.

Lowell, B. L. & Findley, A. (2001). Migration of highly skilled persons from developing countries: Impact and policy [synthesis report]. *International Migration Papers. International Labour Organisation Paper (ILO)*, 44, 5–35.

Luft, S. (2011). Globalisierung, Migration und Arbeitsmärkte. In T. Mayer, R. Meyer, et al. (Hg.), *Globalisierung im Fokus von Politik, Wirtschaft, Gesellschaft. Eine Bestandsaufnahme* (pp. 281–302). Wiesbaden: VS Verlag.

McIntosh, P. (1989). White privilege: unpacking the invisible knapsack. *Peace and Freedom*, 7/8. Retrieved from https://psychology.umbc.edu/files/2016/10/White-Privilege_McIntosh-1989.pdf, accessed August 11, 2023.

Maehara, N. (2013). Well-being and the implication of embodied memory: from the diary of a migrant woman. In A. S. Grønseth (Ed.), *Being human, being migrant* (pp. 93–115). New York: Berghahn Books.

Mahroum, S. (2001). Europe and the immigration of highly skilled labor. *International Migration. International Organization for Migration* (IOM), 39(5), 27–43.

Marcu, S. (2011). Emotions on the move: belonging, sense of place and feelings identities among young Romanian immigrants in Spain. *Journal of Youth Studies, 15*(29), 207–223. https://doi.org/10.1080/13676261.2011.630996

Massmünster, M. (2014). Sich selbst in den Text schreiben. In C. Bischoff, W. Leimgruber et al. (Eds.), *Methoden der Kulturanthropologie* (pp. 522–538). Bern: Haupt Verlag UTB.

Matei, S. C. (2014). Globalization – an anthropological approach. *Procedia – Social and Behavioral Sciences, 149,* 542–546.

Mitchell, R. (1993). *Secrecy and fieldwork.* Newbury Park, CA: Sage.

Mohanty, C. T. (2013). Transnational feminist crossings: on neoliberalism and radical critique. *Signs, 38*(4), 967–991. Retrieved from https://www.jstor.org/stable/10.1086/669576?seq=1#metadata_info_tab_contents, accessed August 11, 2023.

Morokvasic, M. (2007). Migration, gender, empowerment. In I. Lenz, C. Ulrich and B. Fersch (Eds.), *Gender orders unbound: globalisation, restructuring and reciprocity* (pp. 69–97). Opladen: Barbara Budrich.

Müller, M. (2013). Migration und Religion in der Schweiz: Historischer und gesellschaftlicher Kontext. In M. Müller (Ed.), *Migration und Religion: Junge hinduistische und muslimische Männer in der Schweiz* (pp. 25–55). Wiesbaden: VS Verlag.

Nedelcu, M. (2012). Migrants' new transnational habitus: rethinking migration through a cosmopolitan lens in the digital age. *Journal of Ethnic and Migration Studies, 38*(9), 1339–1356.

Niedenthal, P. M. & Ric, F. (2017). *Psychology of emotion* (2nd ed.). New York: Psychology Press.

Nuscheler, F. (2005). Migration als Konfliktquelle und internationales Ordnungsproblem. In P. Imbusch & R. Zoll (Eds.), *Friedens- und Konfliktforschung* (3rd ed.) (pp. 275–285). Wiesbaden: VS Verlag für Sozialwissenschaften.

O'Reilly, K. (2016, September 13): *Commentary by Karen O'Reilly* [Conference panel discssion]. SIEF Working Group "Migration and Mobility" Meeting. Current approaches to migration and mobility in ethnology, folklore and anthropology. University of Basel, Basel, Switzerland.

Ong, A. (1996). Anthropology, China and modernities: the geopolitics of cultural knowledge. In H. L. Moor (Ed.), *The future of anthropological knowledge* [The uses of knowledge: global and local relations: A.S.A. Decennial Conference Series] (pp. 60–92). London: Routledge.

Ong, A. (1999). *Flexible citizenship: the cultural logics of transnationality.* Durham: Duke University Press.

Organisation for Economic Co-operation and Development, OECD. (1995). *The measurement of scientific and technological activities. Manual on the measurement of human resources devoted to S&T* ("Canberra Manual"). Luxemburg: OECD Publications.

Organisation for Economic Co-operation and Development, OECD. (2017). *Will migration help increase the educational level of the European labour force by 2030?* Retrieved from https://www.oecd.org/els/mig/migration-data-brief-2.pdf, accessed August 11, 2023.

Organisation for Economic Co-operation and Development, OECD. (2018a). *Country statistical profile Switzerland 2018/4*. Retrieved from https://www.oecd-ilibrary.org/economics/country-statistical-profile-switzerland-2018-4_csp-che-table-2018-4-en, accessed August 11, 2023.

Organisation for Economic Co-operation and Development, OECD. (2018b). *Country statistical profile Israel 2018/4*. Retrieved from https://www.oecd-ilibrary.org/economics/country-statistical-profile-israel-2018-4_csp-isr-table-2018-4-en, accessed August 11, 2023.

Organisation for Economic Co-operation and Development, OECD. (2019). The new immigrants Global trends in migration towards OECD countries between 2000/01 and 2015/16. *Migration Data Brief*. Retrieved from https://www.oecd.org/migration/mig/Migration-data-brief-4-EN.pdf, accessed August 11, 2023.

Organisation for Economic Co-operation and Development, OECD. (2020). *Gross domestic spending on R&D (indicator/investment in R&D)*. Retrieved from https://data.oecd.org/rd/gross-domestic-spending-on-r-d.htm, accessed August 11, 2023.

Oz-Salzberger, F. *Israelis in Berlin*. Frankfurt a. M.: Suhrkamp Verlag.

Parsons, C.; Rojon, S.; Rose, L. & Samanani, F. (2020). High skilled migration through the lens of policy. *Migration Studies, 8*(3), 279–306. https://doi.org/10.1093/migration/mny037

Picard, J. (1997). *Die Schweiz und die Juden 1933–1945. Schweizerischer Antisemitismus, jüdische Abwehr und internationale Migrations- und Flüchtlingspolitik* (3. Aufl.). Zürich: Chronos Verlag.

Picard, J. (2014). Biografie und biografische Methoden. In C. Bischoff, K. Oehme-Jüngling, W. Leimgruber (Eds.), *Methoden der Kulturanthropologie* (pp. 177–194). Bern: Haupt Verlag UTB.

Pine, F. (2014). Migration as hope: space, time, and imagining the future. *Current Anthropology, 55*(S9), 95–104.

Pitt-Rivers, J. (1984). La revanche du rituel dans l'Europe contemporaine. Dans: *École pratique des hautes études, section des sciences religieuses. Annuaire. Tome 93, 1984–1985* [almanach] (pp. 41–60). Retrieved from https://www.persee.fr/doc/ephe_0000–0002_1984_num_97_93_16143, accessed August 11, 2023.

Plamper, J. (2012). *Geschichte und Gefühl. Grundlagen der Emotionsgeschichte*. München: Siedler Verlag. English translation: Plamper, J. (2015). *The history of Emotions. An introduction*. Oxford: OUP Oxford.

Portes, A.; Guarnizo, L. & Landolt, P. (1999). The study of transnationalism: pitfalls and promises of an emergent research field. *Ethnic and Racial Studies, 22*(2), 217–237.

Pries, L. (2008). *Die Transnationalisierung der sozialen Welt. Sozialräume jenseits von Nationalgesellschaften*. Frankfurt a. M: Suhrkamp Verlag.

Pries, L. & Westerholt, K. (2013). Internationale Migration und die Herausforderung von Braindrain und Braingain. In H. U. Brinkmann & H. H. Uslucan (Hg.), *Dabeisein und Dazugehören* (pp. 47–66). Wiesbaden: Springer Fachmedien.

Rabinowitz, D. (1997). *Overlooking Nazareth: the ethnography of exclusion in Galilee*. Cambridge: Cambridge University Press.

Randeria, S. (Ed.). (2016). *Border Crossings. Grenzverschiebungen und Grenzüberschreitungen in einer globalisierten Welt*. Zürich: vdf Hochschulverlag.

Randeria, S. & Eckert, H. (Ed.). (2009). *Vom Imperialismus zum Empire. Nicht-westliche Perspektiven auf Globalisierung*. Frankfurt a. M.: Suhrkamp Verlag.

Razin, A. (2018). *Israel's immigration story: winners and losers* (NBER Working Paper No. 24283). Cambridge, MA: National Bureau of Economic Research. Retrieved from https://www.nber.org/system/files/working_papers/w24283/w24283.pdf, accessed August 11, 2023.

Sabar, G. (2010). Israel and the 'Holy Land': the religio-political discourse of rights among African migrant labourers and African asylum seekers, 1990–2008. *African Diaspora, 3*(1), 42–75.

Said, E. (1995). *Orientalism* (25th ed.). London: Penguin Books.

Said, E. (2000). *Reflections on exile and other essays*. Cambridge, MA: Harvard University Press.

Salazar, N. & Jayaram, K. (Eds.). (2016). *Keywords of mobility. Critical engagements*. New York: Berghahn Books.

Sandberg, M. & Andersen, D. J. (2020). Precarious citizenship and melancholic longing: on the value of volunteering after the refugee arrivals to Europe 2015. *Nordic Journal of Migration Research, 10*(4), 41–56. https://doi.org/10.33134/njmr.357

Sandoz, L. (2019). *Mobilities of the highly skilled towards Switzerland. The role of intermediaries in defining "wanted immigrants"*. Cham: Springer Nature.

Sassen, S. (1996). *Losing control? Sovereignty in an age of globalization*. New York: Columbia University Press.

Sassen, S. (2010). The state and globalization. *Interventions: International Journal of Postcolonial Studies, 5*(2), 241–248. https://doi.org/10.1080/1369801031000112978

Schäfer, S. & Henn, S. (2018). The evolution of entrepreneurial ecosystems and the critical role of migrants. A phase-model based on a study of IT startups in the greater Tel Aviv area. *Cambridge Journal of Regions, Economy and Society, 11*(2), 317–333. https://doi.org/10.1093/cjres/rsy013

Scott, S. (2006). The social morphology of skilled migration: The case of the British middle class in Paris. *Journal of Ethnic and Migration Studies, 32*(7), 1105–1129.

Segev, T. (2001). *Elvis in Jerusalem. Post-Zionism and the Americanization of Israel*. New York: Metropolitan Books.

Senor, D. & Singer, S. (2009). *Start-up nation: the story of Israel's economic miracle*. New York: Twelve.

Shokeid, M. (1988). *Children of circumstances: Israeli emigrants in New York*. Ithaca: Cornell University Press.

Shuval, J. (2006). *Immigrants on the threshold*. New Brunswick NJ: Transaction Publishers.

Sibold, N. (2020). Hora in Brugg. Jugendbünde, Aufbruchstimmung und Generationenkonflikte in der Nachkriegszeit. In J. Picard & A. Bhend (Hg.), *Jüdischer Kulturraum Aargau* (pp. 419–423). Baden: Hier und Jetzt Verlag.

Simonova, O. (2019). Emotional culture as sociological concept: on emotional turn in understanding of modern society. *Culture e Studi del Sociale, 4*(2), 147–160.

Sklair, L. (2002). The transnational capitalist class and global politics. Deconstructing the corporate-state connection. *International Political Science Review, 23*(2), 159–174.

Skoggard, I. & Waterston, A. (2015). Introduction: toward an anthropology of affect and evocative ethnography. *Anthropology of Consciousness, 26*(2), 109–120.

Skovgaard-Smith, I. & Poulfelt, F. (2017). Imagining 'non-nationality': cosmopolitanism as a source of identity and belonging. *Human Relations 71*(2), 129–154. https://doi.org/10.1177/0018726717714042

Skrbiš, Z. (2008). Transnational families: theorising migration, emotions and belonging. *Journal of Intercultural Studies, 29*(3), 321–246.

Smith, M. P. & Favell, A. (2006). *The human face of global mobility: international highly skilled migration in Europe, North America, and the Asia-Pacific*. New Brunswick, NJ: Transaction.

Sontag, K. (2018a). *Mobile entrepreneurs. An ethnographic study of the migration of the highly skilled*. Leverkusen: Verlag Barbara Budrich.

Sontag, K. (2018b). Highly skilled asylum seekers: Case studies of refugee students at a Swiss university. *Migration Letters, 15*(4), 533–544.

Steinberg, J. (2015). *Why Switzerland?* (3rd Ed.). Cambridge: Cambridge University Press.

Strauss, A. & Corbin, J. (Eds.). (1997). *Grounded theory in practice*. Thousand Oaks: Sage Publications.

Strenger, C. (2011). *Israel. Einführung in ein schwieriges Land*. Berlin: Jüdischer Verlag im Suhrkamp Verlag.

Suter, B. (2017, June 29). Skilled migration to (global) cities in Northern Europe, China and Sub-Saharan Africa: exploring privilege and processes of incorporation [conference presentation]. 14th IMISCOE Annual Conference, Rotterdam, Netherlands. https://www.imiscoe.org/images/conference-2017/imiscoe-rotterdam-2017-program-booklet.pdf, accessed August 11, 2023.

Suter, B. (2019). Migration as adventure. Swedish corporate migrant families' experiences of liminality in Shanghai. *Transitions: Journal of Transient Migration, 3*(1), pp. 45–48.

Svašek, M. (2005). The politics of chosen trauma. Expellee memories, emotions and identities. In K. Milton & M. Svašek (Eds.), *Mixed emotions: anthropological studies of feeling* (pp. 195–214). Oxford: Berg.

Svašek, M. (2006). Postsocialist ownership: emotions, power and morality in a Czech village. In M. Svašek (Ed.), *Postsocialism: politics and emotions in Central and Eastern Europe* (pp. 95–114). Oxford: Berghahn Books.

Svašek, M. (2008). Who cares? Families and feelings in movement. *Journal of Intercultural Studies, 29*(3), 213–230.

Svašek, M. (2010). On the move: emotions and human mobility. *Journal of Ethnic and Migration Studies, 36*(6), 865–880. https://doi.org/10.1080/13691831003643322

Svašek, M. (2013). Narrating mobile belonging. A Dutch story of subjectivity in transformation. In A. S. Grønseth (Ed.): *Being human, being migrant* (pp. 68–92). New York: Berghahn Books.

Svašek, M. & Skrbiš, Z. (2007). Passions and powers: emotions and globalisation. *Identities: Global Studies in Culture and Power, 14*(4), 367–383.

Swiss Forum for Migration and Population Studies, SFM. (2010). *Die Fünfte Schweiz: Auswanderung und Auslandschweizergemeinschaft*. Neuchâtel: Swiss Forum for Migration and Population Studies (Author).

Swiss Info. (2016, 20. Juni). Die Auslandschweizer wurden als Musterpatrioten präsentiert (Interview mit Rudolf Wyder, ehemaliger Direktor der Auslandschweizer Organisation. ASO). *Swiss Info*. Retrieved from: https://www.swissinfo.ch/ger/100-jahre-aso-_-die-auslandschweizer-wurden-als-musterpatrioten-praesentiert/42210326, accessed August 11, 2023.

Tani, M.; Guo, F. & Hugo, G. (2010). New developments in Australia's skilled migration flows. *Asian and Pacific Migration Journal, 19*(1), 1–3.

Tachles. Das jüdische Wochenmagazin. (2014, May 23). Forschungszusammenarbeit Schweiz-Israel. Enge Vernetzung. *tachles* 21(14), p. 15.

Tonkin, E. (2006). Being there: emotion and imagination in anthropologists' encounters. In K. Milton & M. Svašek (Eds.), *Mixed emotions. Anthropological studies of feeling* (pp. 50–70). Oxford: Berg Publishers.

Trundle, C. (2009). Romance tourists, foreign wives or retirement migrants? Cross-cultural marriage in Florence, Italy. In M. Benson & K. O'Reilly (Eds.), *Lifestyle migration. Expectations, aspirations and experiences* (pp. 51–68). Farnham: Ashgate.

Urry, J. (1999a). Globalization and citizenship. *Journal of World-Systems Research, V*(2), 311–324.

Urry, J. (1999b). *Sociology beyond societies. Mobilities for the twenty-first century*. London: Routledge.

Urry, J. (2007). *Mobilities*. Cambridge: Polity Press.

Vertovec, S. (2007). Superdiversity and its implications. *Ethnic and Racial Studies, 30*, 1024–1054.

Vertovec, S. (2009). *Transnationalism*. New York: Routledge.

Vertovec, S. (Ed.). (2010). *Anthropology of migration and multiculturalism. New directions*. New York: Routledge.

Vora, N. (2008). Producing diasporas and globalization. Indian middle-class migrants in Dubai. *Anthropological Quarterly 81*(2), 377–406.

Vora, N. (2011). From golden frontier to global city: shifting forms of belonging, "freedom", and governance among Indian businessmen in Dubai. *American Anthropologist, 113*(2), 306–318.

Vora, N. (2013). *Impossible citizens. Dubai's Indian diaspora*. Durham: Duke University Press.

Walsh, K. (2009). Geographies of the heart in transnational spaces: love and the intimate lives of British migrants in Dubai. *Mobilities, 4*(3), 427–445. https://doi.org/10.1080/17450100903195656

Walsh, K. (2012). Emotion and migration: British transnationals in Dubai. *Environment and Planning D: Society & Space, 30*(1), 43–59.

Weiss, R. S. (1994). *Learning from strangers. The art and method of qualitative interview studies*. New York: The Free Press.

Weiss, A. (2006). Vergleichende Forschung zu hochqualifizierten Migrantinnen und Migranten. Lässt sich eine Klassenlage mittels qualitativer Interviews rekonstruieren? *Forum: Qualitative Sozialforschung, 7*(3). Retrieved from http://nbn-resolving.de/urn:nbn:de:0114-fqs060326, accessed August 11, 2023.

Welz, G. (2009). "Sighting/siting globalization." Gegenstandskonstruktion und Feldbegriff einer ethnographischen Globalisierungsforschung. In S. Windmüller, B. Binder, T. Hengartner (Eds.), *Kultur-Forschung. Zum Profil einer volkskundlichen Kulturwissenschaft* (pp. 195–210). Münster: LIT-Verlag.

Wessendorf, S. (2017). Pioneer migrants and their social relations in super-diverse London. *Ethnic and Racial Studies, 42*(1), 17–34.

Willen, S. (Ed.). (2007). *Transnational migration to Israel in global comparative context*. Lanham MD: Lexington Books.

Williams, A.M. & Baláž, V. (2005). What human capital, which migrants? Returned skilled migration to Slovakia from the UK. *International Migration Review, 39*(2), 439- 468.

Wimmer, A. & Glick Schiller N. (2002). Methodological nationalism and beyond: nation-state building, migration and the social sciences. *Global Networks, 2*(4), 301–334.

Yonah, Y. (2007). Reclaiming diaspora: the Israeli state, migration, and ethnonationalism in the global era. *Diaspora: A Journal of Transnational Studies, 16*(1/2), 190–228.

Yuval-Davis, N. (2006). Belonging and the politics of belonging. *Patterns of Prejudice, 40*(3), 197–214.

Zaletel, P. (2006). Competing for the highly skilled migrants: implications for the EU common approach on temporary economic migration. *European Law Journal, 12*(5), 613–635.

Sources

List of Main Protagonists

Long, biographical interviews cited in the text took place with the following individuals:

Israelis in Switzerland	Swiss in Israel
Alexander: Male, 50s International organization Private sector	**Simon:** Male, 60s Academia
Rhea: Female, 30s Academia	**Hannah:** Female, 20s Art sector Self-employed
Jacob: Male, 30s Pharmaceutical industry Media Education	**Margot:** Female, 30s High-Tech Self-employed
Daniel: Male, 20s Academia	**Susanna:** Female, 40s IT/Library science
Doron: Male, 30s Health sector	**Matt:** Male, 30s Education Tourism
Isabella: Female, 30s Art sector Education	**Gabriele:** Female, 50s Tourism Self-employed High-tech

Additional Sources

List of selected events, partners for short interviews and relevant field conversations
Various events organized by the *Chamber of Commerce Switzerland-Israel* were visited. Mentioned in the text are:
- "General Assembly of the *Chamber of Commerce Switzerland-Israel*"
  Zurich, June 25, 2014
- "Dr. Andreas Baum, Botschafter der Schweiz in Israel"
  Zurich, June 25, 2014

- "Israeli Entrepreneurs in Switzerland: Anat and Dov Bar-Gera"
  Zurich, September 11, 2014
- "Christian Bindella, Gast der Handelskammer Schweiz"
  Zurich, October 29, 2015

Other events and organizations contacted and visited:
- Book presentation by Jonathan Kreutner (Book: *Die Schweiz und Israel: Auf dem Weg zu einem differenzierten historischen Bewusstsein*) at the *Israelitische Cultusgemeinde Zürich*
  Zurich, July 2, 2014
- Lecture by and discussion with Carlo Strenger at the *Haus der Religionen-Dialog der Kulturen*
  Bern, October 11, 2015
- Events at *Migwan* (liberal Jewish congregation in Basel, attended by some of the Israelis living in Basel)
  https://www.migwan.ch, accessed August 10, 2023

- Meeting with people of the *Facebook* Group "Israelis in Zurich"
  2015
- Meeting with members of the *Swiss Club in Israel*
  http://swissil.com/was-war-los-.html, accessed September 5, 2023
  2015
- Event organized by the *Swiss Embassy in Israel*, Tel Aviv
  https://www.eda.admin.ch/telaviv, accessed August 10, 2023
  2015

Research Diary/Fieldnotes
Written from 2013–2018

Expert Interview
Professor Dr. David Horn, *School of Physics and Astronomy, Tel Aviv University*
  Tel Aviv, July 7, 2018

Newspaper Articles

Aiolfi, S. (2015, February 12). Ein weltweiter "Krieg um Talente". *Neue Zürcher Zeitung*, p. 35.
Alexander, N. (2014, October 20). Sometimes, emigrating from Israel is enriching. *Haaretz*. Retrieved from https://www.haaretz.com, accessed: August 11, 2023.
Alexander, N. (2015, April 5). Out of exile: Meet the Israeli ex-pats who are heading home again. *Haaretz*. Retrieved from https://www.haaretz.com accessed: August 11, 2023.
Beglinger, M. (2013, September 9–13). Alle wollen hierher. *Das Magazin/Tages-Anzeiger*, pp. 25–33.
Bollag, P. (2014, November 24). Misstöne in Basel. *Jüdische Allgemeine*. Retrieved from https://www.juedische-allgemeine.de, accessed: August 11, 2023.
Bracher, K. (2018, September 9). Die Schweizer sind super langweilig und so sauber ist es hier auch nicht. *Neue Zürcher Zeitung am Sonntag*, pp. 15–19.
Brönniman, C. (2013, May 22). Zuwanderung wird auf lange Sicht zur Hypothek. *Tages-Anzeiger*, p. 3.
Dachs, G. & Mertins, S. (2014, October 19). In Berlin kostet der Pudding viel weniger. *Neue Zürcher Zeitung am Sonntag*, p. 7.
Debelle, Y. (2015, May 11). Sang- und klanglos ausgewiesen. *Beobachter*. Retrieved from https://www.beobachter.ch, accessed: August 11, 2023.
Feldges, D. (2015, October 22). Talentspäher jagen Hochqualifizierte. *Neue Zürcher Zeitung*, p. 33.
Haaretz. (2014, October 19). Meet the Israeli emigre who sparked the Berlin pudding protest. *Haaretz*. Retrieved from https://www.haaretz.com, accessed: August 11, 2023.
Kunz, N. (2013, March 22). Zwischen hier und dort. Israelische und jüdische Expats in der schweiz. *tachles*, pp. 8–9.
Münch, P. (2013, October 12/13). Berlin, wir fahren nach Berlin. *Süddeutsche Zeitung*, Nr. 236, p. 1.
Neue Zürcher Zeitung (2013, December 7). Die Folgen der früheren Zuwanderungspolitik. *Neue Zürcher Zeitung*, pp. 28–29.
Neue Zürcher Zeitung. (2016, October 13). Herr Doktor, bitte gehen Sie. *Neue Zürcher Zeitung*, p. 19.
Neue Zürcher Zeitung. (2018, June 23). "Wir ändern uns jeden Tag" [Interview mit Siemens-Konzernchef Joe Kaeser]. *Neue Zürcher Zeitung*, p. 29.
Peretz, L. (2016, August 9). A heartfelt plea to all Israelis who have moved to Berlin. *Haaretz*. Retrieved from https://www.haaretz.com, accessed: August 11, 2023.
Pfister, A. (2015, February 5). War of talents. *Tages-Anzeiger*, p. 21.
Rist, M. (2013, October 4). Migranten mit besserem Rucksack. *Neue Zürcher Zeitung*, p. 34.
Rütti, N. (2018, February 22). Geteiltes Startup-Land Israel. *Neue Zürcher Zeitung*. Retrieved from https://www.nzz.ch
Salloum, R. (2014, October 11). Hype um israelischen Facebookpost. Auf ins Pudding-Paradies. *Spiegel Online*. Retrieved from http://www.spiegel.de, accessed: August 11, 2023.

Schmid, U. (2017, December 27). "Daueraufenthalter" in der eigenen Stadt. *Neue Zürcher Zeitung*, p. 6.

Schmid, U. (2018, March 9). Die sittsamen Verbrecher im "Silicon Wadi". *Neue Zürcher Zeitung*, p. 9.

Segenreich-Horsky, D. (2015, April 11). Integration heisst das Zauberwort für Israel. *Neue Zürcher Zeitung*, p. 30.

Shumsky, D. (2013, December 10). Diaspora is part of the Zionist vision. *Haaretz*. Retrieved from https://www.haaretz.com, accessed: August 11, 2023.

Tages-Anzeiger. (2013, May 13). Ausländische Fachkräfte werden in Zürich sesshaft. *Tages-Anzeiger*. Retrieved from https://www.tagesanzeiger.ch, accessed: August 11, 2023.

taz (2014, December 19). "Als wären wir Kriminelle". *taz*. Retrieved from https://taz.de, accessed: August 11, 2023.

The Economist. (2010, December 29). Beyond the start-up nation. *The Economist*. Retrieved from https://www.economist.com, accessed: August 11, 2023.

The Economist. (2013, October 12). The gated globe [special report on world economy]. *The Economist*, pp. 3–20.

The Economist. (2014, October 11). Next year in Berlin. *The Economist*. Retrieved from https://www.economist.com, accessed: August 11, 2023.

Uni, A. (2013, June 29). Faszination und Unbehagen [über junge Israelis in Berlin]. *Neue Zürcher Zeitung, Nr. 148*, p. 9.

Vögeli, D. (2014, March 6). Hochqualifizierte sind sozial schlecht integriert. *Neue Zürcher Zeitung*, p. 19.

Zeller, R. (2014, February 10). "Ja" zur Masseneinwanderungsinitiative. *Neue Zürcher Zeitung*. Retrieved from http://www.nzz.ch, accessed: August 11, 2023.

Zwischenzeilen Magazin. (2013a, August 13). Brain-Drain: Neu Spitzengehalt für Spitzenforscher in Israel. *Zwischenzeilen Magazin*. Retrieved from https://israelzwischenzeilen.com, accessed: August 11, 2023.

Zwischenzeilen Magazin. (2013b, October, 22). Angst vor Brain Drain: Israel diskutiert Abwanderung von Wissenschaftlern. *Zwischenzeilen Magazin*. Retrieved from https://israelzwischenzeilen.com, accessed: August 11, 2023.

Zwischenzeilen Magazin. (2018, October 17). Brain Drain: Auch Israel verliert Akademiker. *Zwischenzeilen Magazin*. Retrieved from https://israelzwischenzeilen.com, accessed: August 11, 2023.

Appendices

Appendix A: Information on Broader Research Project

This thesis was conceived as part of a broader qualitative research project on the migration of highly qualified people funded by the *Swiss National Science Foundation* and running from 2015–2018. The title of the project was: "Narratives of Identity, Multi-sited Biographies, and Transnational Life-Modes of Highly Qualified Migrants. Two Case Studies".

Case Study A (Swiss in Israel and Israelis in Switzerland), Hélène Mona Oberlé: **"It's all about emotions". Narratives of highly skilled migrants: A study of Swiss in Israel and Israelis in Switzerland**

Case Study B (Swiss in the Senegambia region and Senegambians in Switzerland), Khadeeja Haddy Sarr: **Straddling between two worlds: The phenomena experienced by skilled migrants from Senegambia and Switzerland**

(see next page for a summary of Case Study B)

Summary Case Study B/Senegambia and Switzerland

The phenomenological design of this doctoral study explores how skilled migrants from Senegambia and Switzerland ascribe meaning to their experiences through a lived phenomenon. Investigating descriptions of daily encounters uncovers the deeper meaning of what it means to be a skilled migrant. The thesis will explore chains of webs of entanglement such as relations, networks, inclusion, exclusion, acceptance, access, and rights.

This study favors a phenomenological approach that seeks to penetrate the deeper existential dimensions of being a skilled migrant. In this sense, the core of this study explores *what* phenomenon the skilled migrant experiences, *how* he or she experiences it, and *why* he or she experiences it. Identifying a phenomenon becomes relevant in an era where globalization continues to take place in various forms. In this thesis, globalization is understood as a description of movements, integration, the interaction of people, knowledge, and exchange. It compels migrants to engage in processes and everyday interactions that confront them with unknown, unfamiliar spaces animated by new and equally strange, encounters in their daily social interactions. As such, it is crucial to unearth the paradoxes occasioned by processes of globalization through various reflections.

The analytical framework in this study comes in two dimensions. First, the thesis will explore the lives of skilled migrants within structures: social, cultural, political, and economic differences in Senegambia and Switzerland. These structures bring attention to *surroundings* (people and their daily situations) and *institutional frameworks* (policies and legislations), in which opportunities or restrictions influence the lives of skilled migrants, i. e. the right to vote or visa requirements. Second, the thesis will use transnationalism as an analytical lens. Employing a transnational lens reveals how salient interactions between migrants and both host societies and institutions shape various experiences. For this reason, I contend that migrant experiences are inextricable from encounters they have with both people and policies. In other words, migrant experiences are constituted through confrontations with social processes, such as values and norms across their social fields, which also sheds light on their migrant agency.

This study uses an interdisciplinary approach entailing the use of anthropological, sociological, and psychological migration theories to analyze narratives from 20 skilled migrants. Findings reveal that skilled migrants experience the phenomenon of being *strangers* whilst encountering strange experiences, strangeness. Overall, the study attempts to contribute to a broader theoretical understanding of the world views of skilled migrants as *strangers* beyond national boundaries and borders. This study initiates a debate to migration scholarships on intricacies of global migration and the continual need for research on (skilled) migration. The attempt is to contribute to further migration research by building a bridge between the

Global North and South to advance the debate on phenomenological experiences of skilled migrant straddling between two worlds.

Appendix B: Call for Participants

<u>SEEKING ISRAELIS LIVING AND WORKING IN SWITZERLAND
TO PARTICIPATE IN AN ANTHROPOLOGICAL RESEARCH STUDY</u>
Narratives of Identity, Multi-Sited Biography, and Transnational Life-Experiences of Highly
Qualified Migrants: Israel and Switzerland

Dear Sir or Madam,

I am currently looking for interviewees for my PhD project titled "Narratives of Identity, Multi-Sited Biography, and Transnational Life-Experiences of Highly Qualified Migrants". The study will examine phenomena of globalization and transnationalization amongst highly skilled Israeli migrants residing in Europe and highly skilled Swiss living in Israel. The aim of this study is to analyze and further understand transnational biographies, life experiences and decision-making processes of highly qualified migrants through their own narratives. The project is being carried out at the Institute of Cultural Anthropology and European Ethnology at the University of Basel and the Department of Sociology and Anthropology at Tel Aviv University. Participation will consist in filling out a short questionnaire and taking part in a qualitative interview that usually lasts between 60–90 minutes (but can last longer, depending on your availability).

Following criteria have to be met by the participants:

- Bachelor's degree or higher
- Israeli citizenship or Israeli-Swiss dual citizenship
- Professional within any field or self-employed

Should you be interested in participating and receiving further information on the study please contact the principal investigator:

Hélène Mona Oberlé, M.A.
    PhD Candidate
    Institute of Cultural Anthropology and European Ethnology
    Rheinsprung 9/11
    CH-4051 Basel
    Tel:
    E-Mail:

Thank you and kind regards,
    Hélène Oberlé

Appendix C: Qualitative Interview Guide

Central issue/Stimulus	Content check/Ask if not mentioned (adapt formulation)	Specific questions (end of interview if not possible earlier)	Upkeeping questions
Biographical approach 1. A move to another country always has a story or even several stories. Could you tell me something about that history?	• Journey • First experience/ impression in country • Reasons for country • Expectations towards country • Ties to "Jewish Community" in CH/ties to CH-Community in IL • Ties to "home country" • Language and cultural habits, norm, values • Migrant? Sense of belonging/Self-description • Settling in (socially, professionally, personally) • Acceptance/rejection • Transnational marriage and children Human agency (social)	• If you had the opportunity to settle "back home", would you do it? Or would you want to stay? To go somewhere else? What is keeping you from settling "back home"?	• Could you please specify? • Could you please tell me more? • And then? What do you see as challenges and advantages in the host society/home country?
Professional skills and outcomes 2.a) Could you describe your work and workspace/place and your professional activities?	• Education • Language skills • Professional skills • Expectation (career) • Equal opportunity-different decision/country • Future career plans Family issues in career planning		• Describe a typical day at work • Could you imagine an alternative profession?
Business approach, corporate cultures 2.b) Please describe some of your transnational activities	• Business investments (home, host, others) • Human agency (economic) • Remittances, investments and the like Business/professional relationships at "home"		• Could you further describe it? • Could you give examples? • Why is that so important to you? What motivates you to invest/not invest?

Ethnographical approach/Impact of surroundings 3. How do you experience the ethno-national issues/national frameworks and do they have some impacts on your personal and professional life?	• Migration policies in Switzerland and in Israel • Brain gain/drain • Israeli/Zionist and Arab/Palestinian relations • Cultural Images of "Europe" and "Middle/Near East" • Religious/secularist life styles Human agency (political)		• Would you define yourself as religious/secular? • Are you politically involved in one country or the other? How did you experience the summer of 2014? Where were you?
Conclusion/Finalization (Questions on perspectives and personal identity policies) 4. How do you evaluate the future?	• Private/professional • National/global Economic/environmental	Where do you see yourself 10 years from now?	Is there anything else you would like to add?

Appendix D: Informed Consent Form

This study requires that all individuals participating give their consent in writing. Please read the following and sign if you confirm your participation.

I freely and voluntarily consent to participate in the research project entitled "Narratives of Identity, Multi-Sited Biography, and Transnational Life-Modes of Highly Qualified Migrants: Two Case Studies" at the Institute of Cultural Anthropology and European Ethnology at the University of Basel. I am participating in the case study on Israel and Switzerland with Hélène Oberlé as principal investigator.

The broad goal of this research project is to explore the formation and perception of my cultural identity and (professional) biography in the context of a globalized world. I have been asked to complete a questionnaire and to participate in a qualitative biographic interview.

I understand that if at any time during the session I feel unable or unwilling to continue, I am free to stop answering without negative consequences. That is, my participation in this study is completely voluntary, and I may withdraw from this study at any time.

I understand that the qualitative biographical interview needs to be recorded and transcribed for purposes of data analysis. I have been told that records and transcripts will be handled with utmost care and will be stored in a secure manner. Confidentiality will be upheld as possible. However, I understand that excerpts of my interview and descriptions of my (professional) biography might be used in the publication of the final results.

I wish to protect my identity and want all information and data about myself to be anonymized in the final publication of the results and any possible further publications on the project:

               ( ) Yes   ( ) No

I have been given the opportunity to ask questions regarding the procedure, and my questions have been answered to my satisfaction. I have been informed that if I have any further questions about this project I should contact Hélène Oberlé (—@unibas.ch). If I have any comments or concerns about the study or the procedures, I can also contact the project supervisor Prof. Dr. Jacques Picard

(—@unibas.ch). I have read and understood the above and consent to participate in the study. My signature is not a waiver for legal rights.

_____ _____
Participant   Place, Date

I have explained and defined in detail the research procedure to the participant.

_____ _____
Principal Investigator   Place, Date

Appendix E: Basic Questionnaire

This questionnaire is part of the research project entitled "Narratives of Identity, Multi-Sited Biography, and Transnational Life-Modes of Highly Qualified Migrants: Israel and Switzerland". It will provide the principal investigator with general information about the participant and ensure the systematic preparation of the planned biographic interview. All data will be handled with utmost care and securely stored. Interview-/Case-Nr.:

Please answer the following questions about yourself.

Personal details

How old are you?

What is your Gender? ( ) Male ( ) Female ( ) non-binary

Nationality and Country of Residence

What is your nationality/are your nationalities?

What is your country of origin?

What is your main country of residence?

How many years have you been living in your current country of residence?

Do you have another country of residence? (if yes, please name the country/countries)

In which one of the above countries do you participate politically?

_____

Is everything the way you expected it to be in your current country of residence? Please elaborate.

_____
_____

For the next several questions, please choose a number from 0–10 and write it next to each statement to indicate how much you agree with that statement.

0	1	2	3	4	5	6	7	8	9	10
Not at all										Extremely

1. _____ I like living in my current country of residence
2. _____ Living in m current country of residence is how I expected it to be beforehand

Languages

What language is your mother tongue?
_____

What other languages are you fluent in?
_____

Marital Status and Family

What is your relationship status?(E.g. married, single, cohabitating, divorced, etc.)
_____

If you are married/in a relationship: What is the country of origin and nationality of your spouse/partner?
_____

Do you have children?   ( ) Yes   ( ) No
If yes
How many children do you have?   _____

How old are your children?

_____

What is the nationality of your children?

_____

Education, Career and Profession

What is your field of education?

_____

What is your highest level of education?

_____

What is your current profession?

_____

Where do you work? (E.g. company xy, self-employed in xy field, etc.)

_____

Is everything the way you expected it to be in your current work situation? Please elaborate.

_____
_____
_____

For the next several questions, please choose a number from 0–10 and write it next to each statement to indicate how much you agree with that statement.

0	1	2	3	4	5	6	7	8	9	10
Not at all										Extremely

1. _____ I like my current job
2. _____ My current professional life is the way I planned it to be